1895

The New Where to Watch Birds

Other books by John Gooders

Where to Watch Birds in Europe
How to Watch Birds
Wildlife Paradises
The Bird-Watcher's Book
The Second Bird-Watcher's Book
The Third Bird-Watcher's Book
A Day in the Country
Collins Bird Guide (with Stuart Keith)
Birds – A Survey of the Bird Families of The World
Wildlife Photography (with Eric Hosking)
Birds of the World (9 vols, Editor)
The Encyclopedia of Birds (7 vols, Editor)
The Bird Seeker's Guide
Finding Birds Around the World (with Peter Alden)
Collins British Birds
Birds That Came Back
Kingfisher Field Guide to British Birds

The New
Where to Watch Birds

John Gooders

 ANDRE DEUTSCH

First published 1986 by
André Deutsch Limited
105 Great Russell Street London WC1

Second impression 1987

Phototypeset by Falcon Graphic Art Ltd
Wallington, Surrey
Printed in Great Britain by
Ebenezer Baylis & Son, Worcester

ISBN 0 233 97731 7

Contents

Preface

In his introduction to the first edition of this book way, way back in 1967, Roger Tory Peterson said, 'The more people travel about to see birds the more they become a recreational resource to be reckoned with and to be preserved.' Well, it has happened. That very first edition picked out the best places to watch birds in Britain. Many of them reappear in this largely rewritten, and indeed reconstructed, edition. Meanwhile, however, a quite staggering number of formerly unprotected sites have become nature reserves. Perhaps, in some small way, *Where to Watch Birds* has been instrumental in the process.

Certainly there has been a bird-watching boom, even perhaps a birding revolution. In the 1960s one could walk for miles along lonely estuary shores with only the birds for company. With wild cries they would flee before one, sharpening the skills of identification. Today many birds are identified at close range from reserve hides. In the 1960s hides were few and far between and were decidedly uncomfortable places in which to spend much time. Today there are not only a great many, but they are also huge, multi-storeyed constructions, often on stilts, occasionally glass-fronted and even, in some special spots, armed with comfortable chairs and carpets. Of course, they were needed. Otherwise the huge band of birders that exists today would drive the birds away from their favoured haunts by their very presence. Birds have had to face another problem – bird-watchers! It is in many ways sad that in order to cope with this problem we have had to be regimented and controlled. We have had to accept that areas should be closed on certain days, that the number of people that can visit should be limited, that permits must often be obtained in advance and actually paid for. Where will it all end? The army of bird-watchers continues to grow at an extraordinary rate. Will we eventually see a complete stadium of hides encircling a particularly popular marsh? Will reserve permits have seat numbers printed on them? Perhaps there will even be programmes on sale along with the souvenirs. Far-fetched? Of course!?

During my research for this book I revisited Radipole Lake in Weymouth for the first time in many years. There was a reserve centre, nicely constructed paths, walkways with screens, glass-fronted hides, special access for the disabled, tap rails for the blind, and extraordinary little metal posts with buttons that invited pressing. Irresistible! I pressed one and an anonymous voice informed me that I was at a good spot to see gulls. I looked up and sure enough there they were. I was told which were which, what they were doing and even treated to a chorus of mixed gull cries. The real gulls took no notice at all. Where will it all end?

Friends tell me that the Isles of Scilly support an October population of over 2000 birders, most of whom are not long-haired and dirty and do not sleep rough. At first, way, way back when St Agnes had a bird observatory, the islanders tolerated the odd trespassing bird-watcher. As the numbers grew a real problem developed with bulb fields being trampled, gates and fences being damaged, etc. There were even notices saying 'Bird-watchers keep out'. Today the twitching army is so large that it has spawned a small ornitho-tourist industry and extended the Scilly season by a month or more. Bird-watchers are once more welcome on the islands.

As with so many other sports (birding is really more a sport than a study), birding has developed its own language. 'Twitcher' is a prime example, but 'dudes', 'sibes', 'gripped' and so on all have definite meanings. It is a language that has developed with the birding boom.

The original edition of *Where to Watch Birds* was checked over by the RSPB and many references to 'rare' birds were deleted as a result. Species such as the Bearded Tit were eliminated from several places along with virtually every reference to birds of prey away from reserves. Today even the staff of the Society have produced guide books that detail exactly where to go to see such birds. The Nature Conservancy Council, once so secretive about its reserves, is now encouraging visitors by producing leaflets and organizing displays and nature trails complete with hides at appropriate spots. Even poverty-stricken local naturalists' trusts are getting better organized and are finding the money to open their reserves to a wider audience. The changing attitudes of all these conservation bodies can be seen as a response to the bird-watching boom.

The *New Where to Watch Birds* gives the same details of habitat, birds, seasons and access and has the same aim – to put the watcher in contact with the birds in the easiest possible and most direct way. It is, however, arranged differently. Instead of using the old county system that caused me no end of headaches in searching out obscure sewage works in virtually bird-free zones, this book is based on larger regions. Birders are even more mobile than they were and take little or no notice of county boundaries.

The individual places, too, have been changed by grouping neighbouring sites together into larger units. This has the advantage of economy of space by avoiding repetition and enables more details of birds and habitats to be given. It also has the effect of reducing the number of entries from over 500 to less than half that number, though there are still approximately the same number of individual birding spots. Individual sites within a larger area can still be found by using the index.

Sites vary in size from a whole estuary like the Ribble to a single island such as Handa. Each is treated in a uniform, easy to follow way. A description of the area together with its main attractions is followed by a seasonal summary of the birds that regularly occur in order of importance, or in systematic order, or both. Access details describe the route from the nearest large town or major road. At the beginning of each entry the appropriate Ordnance Survey (OS) 1:50,000 series map number is given. These maps are an indispensable birding aid and by showing public rights of way have made birding considerably easier than it was in 1967.

The addresses of major national bodies are given in the Appendix at the rear of the book. Despite my pleas, the addresses of local societies still change too rapidly to be included. Those wishing to join can obtain the appropriate address from a local library or via their local RSPB members' group. Group addresses may be obtained from RSPB headquarters at The Lodge, Sandy, Bedfordshire.

Finally I must thank all of those who have helped in the preparation of this new book. To all of my birding friends whose brains were continually picked, I apologise. It's over now and we can get back to birding without checking obscure access points.

Above all, however, I must thank all of those who contributed to the original *Where to Watch* plus all those nice people who have, over the years, taken the trouble to write to me about changes to established spots and with details of new ones. Without their help this book would be far less useful.

John Gooders
Ashburnham, East Sussex
31 October 1985

Very few abbreviations are used and most are then readily understandable. For the sake of completeness the most regular are given here:

CT	Conservation Trust
LNR	Local Nature Reserve
NNR	National Nature Reserve
NP	National Park
NT	National Trust
NT	Naturalists' Trust (prefixed by name of Trust)
NTS	National Trust for Scotland
RSNC	Royal Society for Nature Conservation
RSPB	Royal Society for the Protection of Birds
SOC	Scottish Ornithologists' Club
SWT	Scottish Wildlife Trust
TNC	Trust for Nature Conservation

*** Each entry is 'star-rated' from one to five for quality or quantity of birding. All the places are good, but some are better than others.

Code for the Bird-Watcher*

1 General The welfare of the bird and its nest should be your first consideration. Do not let your own pleasure or curiosity interfere with this.

2 Nests During the breeding season listen intently for warning notes and be sure you do not stray in the vicinity of a nest long enough for the eggs or young to be chilled. Be careful in choosing a place to watch or eat, or you may be keeping a bird from its nest. If you watch nests do so from a distance with binoculars; if you visit nests be careful to replace herbage and foliage around them.

3 Breeding Colonies Do not walk over shingle or places where ground-nesting birds breed in colonies. You cannot be sure that you will not endanger eggs or young, not only by treading on them, but by frightening chicks and exposing eggs so that they become easy prey to predators.

4 Fires Heath fires are easily started and have disastrous effects on the bird population and their nests, so be careful with those matches and cigarette ends.

5 Dogs If you take a dog with you, always keep it to heel or on a lead; an undisciplined dog can create havoc in the breeding season.

6 Litter Bird-watchers are increasing, so too is litter all over the countryside. Please help in the anti-litter campaign and see that your birding haunts are kept tidy.

7 Security! Do not advertise the breeding haunts of rare species. Egg collectors are always seeking information and many a rarity has been betrayed to them in this way. If you find a rare species breeding, inform the RSPB and let it remain a secret.

8 Courtesy Always get the permission of the land owner or occupier before entering on private property. Please keep to the paths in woodland or farmland during the nesting season and also ensure that gates are properly closed behind you.

9 Finally At all times make as little noise and disturbance as you can. You'll see more birds and frighten them much less.

*Reproduced with kind permission of the Royal Society for the Protection of Birds.

East Anglia

Essex, Norfolk, Suffolk

1 Ouse Mouth
2 Hunstanton and Snettisham
3 Holme and Titchwell
4 Scolt Head and Burnham Overy
5 Wells and Holkham
6 Cley and Blakeney
7 The Broads
8 The Yare Valley
9 Breydon Water
10 The Brecks
11 Covehithe
12 Walberswick
13 Minsmere
14 Havergate
15 Deben Estuary
16 Stour and Orwell Estuaries
17 Walton-on-the-Naze
18 Abberton Reservoir
19 Blackwater Estuary and Fingringhoe Wick
20 Bradwell and Dengie
21 Hanningfield Reservoir
22 Southend
23 East Tilbury

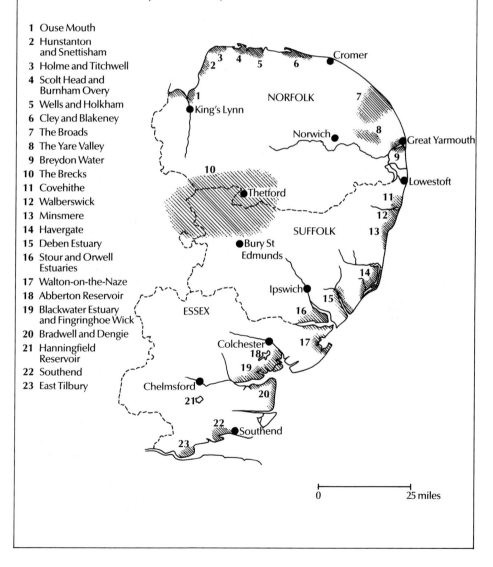

Abberton Reservoir*** OS168

One of the very best bird-watching reservoirs in the country and ranked number one by many watchers. It was perhaps inevitable that constructing such a water only 7km (4m) from the bird-rich Essex coast would produce something out of the ordinary, but as it was filled during 1940 the war-time bird-watchers could hardly have guessed at what was to come. Some 13 wildfowl species are regular with an average total of 7500 birds. These include up to 5000 Mallard, 1000 Teal, 5000 Wigeon, 250 Gadwall and Pintail, 500 Shoveler, 1000 Pochard, 2500 Tufted Duck and 500 Goldeneye. There are also Shelduck, Smew and a flock of up to 150 Bewick's Swans that commute between here and the Old Hall Marshes at Tollesbury.

In season there are grebes, the occasional diver, a variety of passage waders including Ruff, Wood Sandpiper, Little Stint and a host of terns, including substantial flocks of Black Tern in both spring and autumn. Red-crested Pochard still appear in autumn, but in smaller numbers than previously.

Winter Great Crested Grebe, Little Grebe, Bewick's Swan, Canada Goose, Shelduck, Teal, Wigeon, Gadwall, Pintail, Shoveler, Pochard, Tufted Duck, Goldeneye, Smew
Spring Garganey, Black Tern, Whimbrel
Autumn Red-crested Pochard, Ruff, Wood Sandpiper, Green Sandpiper, Little Stint, Greenshank, Black Tern, Common Tern

Large areas of the reservoir can be seen from public roads. Leave Colchester southwards on the B1026. After 9km (5½m), an iron gate on the left gives views over a large area. A further 1km (½m) south is the main bird-watching causeway. At the northern end of this is a public hide overlooking a shallow bay with artificial islands. Continue southwards and after 1½km (1m) the B1026 turns sharply left. At this point an unclassified road leads northwards signposted Layer Breton. In 1km (½m) this leads to another causeway across the stretch with natural banks.

Blackwater, Bradwell and Fingringhoe Wick*** OS168

The Blackwater is by any standards a significant bird-watching area and is of interest at every season. Large muddy bays attract many waders and wildfowl, especially in winter, including important numbers of Brent (nearly 5000) and Grey Plover (over 500). Most of the common waders are present at this season, including over 10,000 Dunlin. Autumn passage brings large flocks of Redshank (nearly 3000) and Curlew as well as the scarcer passage species especially to the RSPB reserve at Old Hall and Tollesbury Wick. At this time many species roost at high tide at Heybridge gravel pit near Maldon.

Old Hall marshes were acquired by the RSPB in 1984 and are in process of the Society's forward-looking policy of habitat improvement.

As this policy takes effect the reserve is developing into one of the prime sites in south-east England.

On the south shore Bradwell Bird Observatory caters for the ringing enthusiast as well as offering a good starting point for exploring the mouth of the estuary. Dengie Flats to the south are a noted wader roost with Knot, while Sales Point to the north offers views of the interesting late winter build-up of divers and grebes, including a regular flock of Slavonian that are also found off Tollesbury where Bewick's Swans winter.

To the north The Essex Naturalists' Trust (NT) reserve at Fingringhoe Wick offers shoreline waders along the Crouch Estuary as well as a first-rate collection of passage waders on adjacent old gravel pits. A small wood (abundant Nightingale) is also included and the Trust have a fine interpretive centre here together with hides and an effective 'scrape'.

Winter	Red-throated Diver, Slavonian Grebe, Great Crested Grebe, Bewick's Swan, Brent Goose, Shelduck, Pintail, Wigeon, Red-breasted Merganser, Hen Harrier, Grey Plover, Dunlin, Curlew, Turnstone, Knot, Short-eared Owl, Twite, Snow Bunting
Summer	Shelduck, Redshank, Ringed Plover, Oystercatcher, Common Tern, Yellow Wagtail, Nightingale, Grasshopper Warbler
Autumn	Hen Harrier, Sparrowhawk, Grey Plover, Whimbrel, Black-tailed Godwit, Curlew Sandpiper, Little Stint, Wood Sandpiper, Green Sandpiper, Sanderling, Wheatear, Whinchat, Siskin, Snow Bunting

Bradwell Leave Maldon on the B1018 toward Burnham-on-Crouch and follow signs to Southminster to join the B1021. Turn left toward Bradwell and

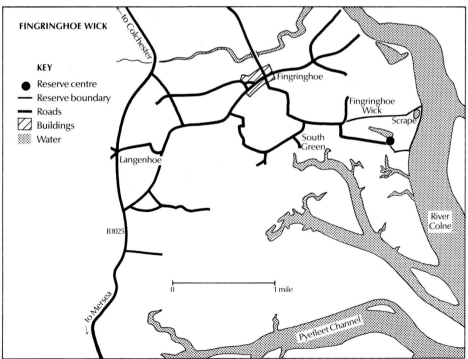

then right to Bradwell-on-Sea. Turn right and drive 2km (1¼m) to car park by Eastlands Farm. Walk 1km (½m) to St Peter's-on-the-Wall (Saxon) and nearby Observatory hut.

Fingringhoe From Colchester take the B1025 southwards and turn left after 4km (2½m) on to minor roads following signs to South Green. Turn left off this road to the reserve car park and centre. A nature trail leads to stategically sited hides. The reserve is open daily except Monday, but is reserved for members only on Sunday.

Tollesbury Leave the A12 at Kelvedon eastwards on the B1023 to Tollesbury. Pass through village, bearing right and parking at end of public road. Take the farm road on the left and then footpath to seawall. For Old Hall Marshes leave Tollesbury northwards – there is only one road of any substance – and watch for track on right in 2km (1¼m). Follow this to seawall and continue to Great Cob. Continue round seawall along south side of Salcott Channel, eventually taking footpath on left to return to car. The RSPB reserve at Old Hall will be open to the public when hides and habitat construction work has been completed. Contact the RSPB for details. OS Ref: TQ958122.

The Brecks***   OS144

The Brecks cover a huge area centred on Thetford and extend over three counties. Wild sandy wastes once frequented by no more than a few sheep, are now areas of productive farming and forestry. Over half the total is now coniferous forest of varying age, and the few compara- tively large areas of open heath that remain are mostly protected by nature reserves.

The Brecks are good for birds, and the traditional species are still found, though often in changed habitats. Stone-curlew now breed on agricultural land as well as heath, while the other speciality, the Crossbill, has benefited from the planting of maturing conifers.

Among the best remaining heaths, East Wretham belongs to the Norfolk NT and includes the two important meres of Langmere and Ringmere. The Trust also owns Thetford and Weeting Heaths, which are National Nature Reserves and there is a further NNR at Cavenham Heath, access to which is partly restricted. The RSPB's reserves at Horn and Weather Heaths are totally restricted.

The mere at Livermere Park holds an interesting variety of wildfowl, and the heathland meres often hold Bewick's Swan and Goosander.

Winter Bewick's Swan, Goosander, Shoveler, Hen Harrier, Brambling, Siskin
Summer Gadwall, Shoveler, Canada Goose, Ringed Plover, Snipe, Redshank, Curlew, Stone-curlew, Long-eared Owl, Nightjar, Woodlark, Willow Tit, Wheatear, Whinchat, Redstart, Nightingale, Grasshopper Warbler, Goldcrest, Red-backed Shrike, Siskin, Hawfinch, Redpoll, Crossbill

East Wretham Leave Thetford northwards on the A11 and fork left after 2km (1¼m). Stop near Ringmere and explore, especially the old pines to the west. This area is as good as any in Breckland and produces most of the species that attract visitors. Permits (not Tuesdays) from the Warden, East Wretham Heath Nature Reserve, Thetford, Norfolk IP24 1RU enclosing stamped addressed envelope. *Tel:* Great Hockham (095 382) 339. Report to Warden at 10 a.m. or 2 p.m. at TL 914886.

Livermere Leave the A143 5km (3m) north of Bury and 1km (½m) north of Great Barton northwards to Great Livermere. Take the lane to the church. There is generally no objection to bird-watchers walking along the main track to the mere, provided they keep to the footpath.

River Lark and Cavenham Heath Leave Bury northwards on the A1101 to Icklingham. Past the village and ¼ mile past the junction with the B1112 turn left on a track to Temple Bridge. General access along River Lark and over heath.

Brandon Sawmill Leave Brandon northwards on the A1065. In the fork on the northern side of the level crossing is an old pine wood and sawmill.

Weeting Heath Continue north from Brandon, taking the left-hand fork and turn left at Weeting towards Hockwold. The reserve lies on the left-hand side of the road and there is a caravan in summer where permits can be obtained from the Warden. Norfolk NT with hides. A Stone-curlew spot.

Breydon Water***   OS134

Breydon Water is the estuary of the Rivers Waveney, Yare and Bure, and lies immediately inland from Great Yarmouth on the boundary between Norfolk and Suffolk. It is a huge area 5km (3m) by 2km (1¼m), and is the haunt of good numbers of waders, wildfowl, and other species. Brent, White-fronts and Pink-feet are more or less regular and Bean Geese, from the marshes at Buckenham, and Bewick's Swans are erratic visitors. Small birds always include Twite and Snow Bunting, and Lapland Bunting are often present. It is a poor winter that does not produce good numbers of Short-eared Owls, and Hen and Marsh Harriers are reasonably regular; also, in appropriate winters, Rough-legged Buzzards may be present. At this time of the year the marshes are lonely places and the well-wrapped-up bird-watcher may walk for miles with no one but birds for company. For some reason, Breydon has never really caught the bird-watching imagination, probably over-shadowed by the other delights of East Anglia.

A wide variety of waders are present in autumn; Black Terns are noted on both passages and Spoonbill and Avocet can be seen most years.

Winter Marsh Harrier, Hen Harrier, Merlin, Peregrine, Short-eared Owl, Wigeon, Shelduck, Pintail, Shoveler, Scaup, Goldeneye, Brent Goose, White-fronted Goose, Pink-footed Goose, Bewick's Swan, Knot, Grey Plover, Snow Bunting, Twite, Lapland Bunting

Spring Spoonbill, Whimbrel, Spotted Redshank, godwits, Ruff, Avocet, Black Tern

Autumn Whimbrel, Spotted Redshank, godwits, Ruff, Green Sandpiper, Wood Sandpiper, Curlew Sandpiper, Grey Plover, Marsh Harrier, Short-eared Owl

Southern Shore Cross the River Yare by the Haven Bridge and immediately turn right along the river bank. Walk along the southern shore for 5km (3m) to Burgh Castle. Alternatively start the other end, turning right past Burgh Castle Church, for more countrified surroundings. This is a good long walk, but farm tracks provide a number of 'escapes' along the way. Leave Yarmouth westward on the A47 to Stracey Arms and take a left to Halvergate. At a T-junction in 2km (1¼m) turn left and proceed towards Manor House and park. A footpath leads around Manor House and out across the marshes to The Fleet and seawall. Follow the seawall southwards (right) to Berney Arms Mill and strike inland along a track back to Manor House. With estuary, fleets and damp grazing this is a good area for a variety of birds and a decent-length walk of about 9km (5½m). This shore can also be worked from Great Yarmouth by crossing the River Bure by Vauxhall Bridge and following the river wall as it bears right next to Vauxhall Station.

The Broads****   OS134

The Broads are a series of freshwater lakes and marshes created over the centuries by extensive peat digging, which lie in the valleys of the Norfolk rivers that eventually drain into Breydon Water and thus into the sea at Yarmouth. They are partly reclaimed and overgrown with reeds, but still form a truly huge expanse of wetland. Most of them lie alongside rather than on the rivers, and several of them show banks that have been left uncut, and give rise to a series of islands in the open water.

Thousands of people charter motor-boats and spend their holidays cruising the miles of inter-connected waterways. Yet the area remains very difficult to 'work' and in many cases access by water is far easier than by land. Out-of-season boats are cheap to hire, the birds are generally undisturbed and a splendid bird-watching holiday can be enjoyed in either spring or autumn. There are maps available which clearly show which broads are accessible by boat. They include, incidentally, Hickling and Horsey, probably the best for birds at all seasons.

The Broads have had a chequered history. It was here that the Bittern and Marsh Harrier returned to re-establish themselves after periods of absence at the turn of the century. It was in the Broads that the Bearded Tit made its last successful stand and from whence it spread first to the Suffolk coast and then across England and Wales. Greylag Geese have become re-established and can be seen at several broads, while winter sees a considerable influx of duck. Common Terns breed and passage periods bring waders to Hickling, one of the best inland sites in the country for these birds.

Winter Cormorant, Bewick's Swan, Whooper Swan, Greylag Goose, Canada Goose, Egyptian Goose, Teal, Wigeon, Gadwall, Shoveler, Pochard, Tufted Duck, Goldeneye, Hen Harrier, Marsh Harrier, Short-eared Owl

Spring Black Tern, waders

Summer Bittern, Canada Goose, Greylag Goose, Garganey, Marsh Harrier, Water Rail, Common Tern, Bearded Tit, Sedge Warbler, Reed Warbler, Grasshopper Warbler, Savi's Warbler, Cetti's Warbler

Autumn Black Tern, Greenshank, Wood Sandpiper, Redshank, Spotted Redshank, Black-tailed Godwit, Short-eared Owl

16

Bure Marshes NNR Lies in the Bure Valley between Acle and Hoveton and covers over 412ha (1018a) of broad, reed marsh, fen and woodland. Declared in 1958 and owned partly by the Norfolk Naturalists' Trust, the reserve includes Ranworth and Cockshoot Broads, Woodbastwick Fen, and Hoveton Little Broad. Among a major assortment of birds is a flock of feral Greylags numbering 400, and feral flocks of Canada and Egyptian Geese. Bearded Tit and Bittern are outstanding among an interesting collection of breeding species. Some areas can be seen from surrounding roads and tracks, and from a nature trail at Hoveton Great Broad. This starts at the north bank of the River Bure, just upstream of the entrance to Salhouse Broad, near Wroxham, and is accessible only by boat, which may be moored free of charge. A leaflet and guide are available. Permits can be obtained from the Nature Conservancy Council, Regional Office for East Anglia, 60 Bracondale, Norwich, Norfolk NRI 2BE. *Tel*: (0603) 20558. Watchers intent on Broadland specialities would be better advised to look elsewhere.

Hickling Broad One of the largest broads, it lies north of Potter Heigham, 5km (3m) from the sea. It was declared an NNR in 1958 but has been a reserve, owned largely by the Norfolk NT, since 1945. The present reserve covers 481ha (1204a) of open water, reed marsh and fen and is an outstanding bird area at all seasons. Spring and autumn bring a host of passage waders and Black Terns are regular. Breeding birds are quite outstanding with Marsh Harrier, Bearded Tit and Bittern all present. The reserve is open every day during the summer months (April to October) except Tuesdays. The 'Water Trail' is a half-day excursion by boat visiting a number of different hides *en route*. There is also a half-day excursion by foot that visits fewer hides; this is a cheaper trip. Bookings and details are available from the Warden, Stubb Road, Hickling, Norwich NR12 OBW. *Tel:* (069 261) 276. Unsold permits of the day's quota may be obtained from the Warden between 09.00 and 09.30 each day. The Warden's house is reached by taking Stubb Road from the Greyhound Inn in the village and then the third turning to the right at a small crossroads. Parts of the reserve may be seen from roads and public footpaths. Hickling lies east of the A149 north of Yarmouth.

Horsey Mere The property of the National Trust and one of the most famous of East Anglian bird resorts. The Mere covers 48ha (120a) and is surrounded by extensive reed beds. Its position, 3km (2m) from the sea, has added to its attractions. Winter brings large numbers of wildfowl, including occasional herds of Bewick's Swans, and Hen and Marsh Harriers are noted. Waders pass through, but in neither the number nor the variety of the Hickling wader grounds. Bearded Tit, Water Rail, Bittern and Short-eared Owl breed. Marsh Harriers are regularly noted and sometimes stay to breed. Autumn brings a return passage of waders and terns, and a variety of passerines. Most of Horsey is difficult to view, but there is a footpath around the north-eastern fringe starting at the Windmill 1km (½m) south of Horsey village. Leave the A149 2km (1¼m) north of Rollesby eastwards on the B1152 to Martham. Continue via B1159 to Horsey. **Note**: Horsey Hall is not open to the public — even bird-watchers.

Cley and Blakeney***** OS132/133

Outside ornithological circles Cley-next-the-Sea, to give it its full and proper name, is unknown. Nearby Blakeney is a yachting haunt and much better known as a result. Together these two flint-built villages occupy a unique place in ornithological history and are as popular today as they have ever been. Indeed, the sheer number of binoculars and telescopes amost any day of the year has to be seen to be believed.

Over the past 150 years, nearly 300 distinct species have been recorded within the parish boundaries, including a remarkable list of rarities and vagrants. Cley, together with adjacent Salthouse, lies at the eastern end of the long stretch of marshes and tidal saltings that guard the North Norfolk coast and provide the most extensive area of fresh marsh on the whole coastline. Yet this alone does not account for the remarkable attraction that the area has for birds. It is perhaps its geographical position, at the point where the Norfolk coast begins to run directly east to west, that is the dominant factor. Whatever the causes, lagoons, hides and the East Bank at Cley are the best places in England to see passage waders – and to meet well-known bird-watchers. Nancy's café in the village serves as an unoffical 'hotline' for information.

The main bird-watching areas lie between the villages of Cley and Salthouse and between the sea and the A149. The large shingle beach protects a series of lagoons, the best of which are those known as Arnold's Marsh, lying immediately east of the East Bank. This compara-tively small area is owned by the National Trust and administered by the Norfolk NT which owns the Cley Marshes proper on the other side of the East Bank. The open coastal lagoons give way to a series of reed-fringed pools with reed beds and carefully created 'scrapes' with well-sited hides. Indeed, the quantity of duck here at certain seasons can be compared with anywhere in East Anglia. Wigeon and Teal are numbered in their thousands and even pools beside the main road are overlooked by well-constructed hides where birds can be seen at close and even photogenic ranges.

Behind the beach west of the Cley Coastguard Station, lie several areas of sueda bushes providing cover to incoming migrants. This is a good spot for small warblers and chats such as Bluethroats. The area of elder, brambles and osiers at Walsey Hills on the Salthouse boundary is now a fully established watch-point with a warden and information centre, and rare or interesting birds can still be seen by the careful observer. Indeed, Cley's specialities are unusual birds, migrants and vagrants of all shapes and sizes as well as an interesting collection of breeding marsh birds. Skuas, shearwaters, Gannets and other seabirds are daily in autumn, and the beach itself holds Shore Lark, and wintering flocks of Snow Buntings from October onwards. The lagoons are the haunt of waders throughout the year and Avocet, Black-tailed Godwit and Ruff usually manage to breed.

The reeds and open pools, however, provide Cley's attractions during the breeding season with Bearded Tits numerous, while Marsh Harriers quarter the reed beds and are established here again in some numbers after quite a lengthy absence. Sedge and Reed Warblers are abundant, and it is worth keeping an ear open for the explosive Cetti's and reeling Savi's Warblers that have colonized the marshes of eastern England in recent years. Bitterns may be heard booming and may even be seen on occasion, and Water Rails are virtually commonplace.

Lying immediately north of the coastal A149, Blakeney consists of four distinct habitats: The Point, the Harbour north of the main channel; the beach as far as Cley; and the saltings immediately north of Blakeney village. The National Trust maintains the dunes and shingle system of the Point as a bird sanctuary. Roughly 2km (1¼m) square, the point is extensively used by the public, yet still holds 1000 pairs of Common Terns. It is also ideally situated to receive passerine migrants and large falls occur most autumns.

Blakeney Harbour itself is the haunt of numerous waders, especially during autumn and winter. Brent Geese reach a peack of several thousand in January–February, divers and scarce grebes turn up, and the Osprey is almost a regular autumn visitor.

Winter	Brent Goose, Greylag Goose, Wigeon, Teal, Pintail, Shoveler, Hen Harrier, Knot, Black-tailed Godwit, Bar-tailed Godwit, Glaucous Gull, Shore Lark, Bearded Tit, Snow Bunting, Twite
Spring	Fulmar, Spoonbill, Garganey, Common Tern, Sandwich Tern, Little Tern, Black Tern, Bar-tailed Godwit, Whimbrel
Summer	Bittern, Marsh Harrier, Water Rail, Ruff, Black-tailed Godwit, Common Tern, Little Tern, Savi's Warbler, Cetti's Warbler, Bearded Tit
Autumn	Gannet, Eider, Wood Sandpiper, Green Sandpiper, Curlew Sandpiper, Little Stint, Knot, Bar-tailed Godwit, Whimbrel, Spotted Redshank, Greenshank, Arctic Skua, Little Gull, Short-eared Owl, Shore Lark, Bluethroat, Barred Warbler, Snow Bunting, Lapland Bunting

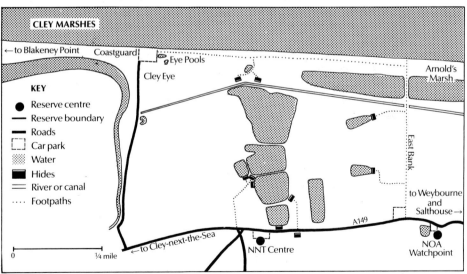

East Bank Leave Cley eastwards and watch for car park on left (north side of the A149) after 2km (1¼m). The 'Bank' runs to the sea. Most watchers continue left (west) to Cley Harbour with its coastguard lookout.

Coastguards Leave Cley eastwards and watch for first turning left (north) signposted Cley Beach. There is a car park at the end. Walk west to Blakeney Point (a long, hard slog) or east to the East Bank.

Cley Marshes Reserve Owned by the Norfolk NT, Cathedral Close, Norwich NR1 4DF, from whom permits can be obtained. Unsold permits may be available on the day from the well-marked visitors' centre at the eastern end of the village overlooking the marshes. There is a public hide here.

Weybourne Lies at the eastern extremity of the marshes and a roughish road leads to the beach and car park. A walk westwards produces waders, while eastwards there are crumbling cliffs with Fulmar.

Blakeney Point May be reached by regular boat service from Morston Quay, well signposted in the village. There is a tea house at the Point and carefully marked paths through the ternery in summer. A few pairs of Arctic Terns nest among the Common most years.

Covehithe***

OS156

To the north of Minsmere, Walberswick and the Blyth, and totally over-shadowed by them, lies Covehithe with its old ruined church and fast-eroding cliffs. Yet, while the sea erodes the cliffs, the current builds up the beaches to enclose a series of lagoons backed by reed beds. To the north man has excavated gravel and created a series of flooded pits within a few yards of the beach.

There are three broads – Benacre, Covehithe and Easton – all within easy walking distance. Benacre, which is an NNR, has a larger area of mud near the shore and is usually best for passage waders. But all three have areas of open water backed by large reed beds that are regularly visited by Marsh Harriers from the reserves further south. Great Crested Grebes and diving duck, scarce elsewhere along this coast, are regularly present and passage terns stop-over to rest and bathe. Gulls are always a feature and Mediterranean and Glaucous are seen with some frequency.

Further north the gravel pits of Benacre Ness (almost the easternmost point of Britain) are too deep for many waders, but unusual migrants do turn up along the edges. The areas of bushes and scrub are sometimes full of small birds, while Wheatears and other birds of open ground flit over the rabbit-cropped turf.

The cliffs at Covehithe itself supported a good Sand Martin colony until their recent decline and are an excellent vantage point for sea-watching, on what is not, to be fair, a particularly good seabird coast. The odd skua, diver, Fulmar or Kittiwake is the best that can be expected. This is wild bird-watching with good walking, frequently without too many people. Indeed only other bird-watchers and sea-anglers are encountered outside summer weekends.

Winter Great Crested Grebe, Little Grebe, Tufted Duck, Pochard, Glaucous Gull, Mediterranean Gull, Snow Bunting

Spring Ringed Plover, Redshank, Sandwich Tern, Common Tern, Wheatear

Autumn Divers, waders, terns, Arctic Skua, warblers, chats, thrushes

Benacre Leave the A12 at Wrentham eastwards on a minor road signposted Covehithe. Follow road past the church – worthy of a stop for excellent flint-work – to the sea. Park near the end and, at your own risk, walk along the cliff tops northwards to Benacre Broad and on to Benacre

Pits. The broad is now an NNR and there is a public hide on the south side, a short walk from the shore. Alternatively walk southwards to Covehithe and Easton Broads. Leave Southwold on the A1095 and fork right (northwards) in Reydon. Keep right at next fork and stop at bridge overlooking the reed beds at the back of Easton Broad.

Easton Take sandwiches and walk northwards out of Southwold along the beach passing Easton, Covehithe and Benacre Broads *en route* to Benacre Pits and Ness. Continue to Kessingland and hope for a bus back along the A12 towards Blythburgh and Southwold. With careful time-tabling, buses may be used from Blythburgh to Southwold and Kessingland to Blythburgh making a grand day's birding.

Deben Estuary*   OS169

A long, but narrow, estuary that stretches inland from the coast some 4km (2½m) north of Felixstowe to Woodbridge. The Deben is especially narrow in the lower reaches and birds tend, therefore, to spread out along the entire shoreline and are less impressive than the concentrations on, for instance, the Stour to the south. For this reason the Deben is often neglected.

Winter Teal, Wigeon, Shelduck, Turnstone, Redshank, Curlew
Spring Turnstone, Black-tailed Godwit
Autumn Waders

Ramsholt Leave the A12 at the Woodbridge by-pass and follow signposts towards the town. At Melton, 2km (1¼m) to the north, turn eastwards over the river and take the right-hand fork on to the B1083. Continue for 7km (4¼m) and turn right by Shottisham Hall 1km (½m) past Shottisham. After 3km (2m) turn right for Ramsholt Quay.

Waldringfield Leave the A12 at Martlesham opposite the Red Lion. Some 4km (2½m) south of Woodbridge turn eastwards into a maze of tiny lanes and follow signposts to Waldringfield. A footpath along the edge of the estuary to the north gives extensive views over the best part of the saltings after 1km (½m). This right of way may be disguised by 'locals' and particularly new 'locals'.

Kirton Signposted Newbourn-Hemley from Waldringfield, and Kirton from the A1093 to Felixstowe. A signpost points eastwards in the village to Park Lane. Follow this until the metalled surface ends. Turn right along the footpath to the shore.

East Tilbury*   OS178

Though just across the River Thames from the better known Cliffe Marshes of Kent, the Tilbury area has been radically improved by the creation of gravel pits inside the seawall. As a result it is now regularly watched, and to the winter duck and waders that frequent the Mucking Flats can be added a goodly assortment of waders and terns on the pits, plus the occasional Peregrine.

Winter Shelduck, Wigeon, Pintail, Grey Plover, Dunlin, Redshank
Passage Waders, terns, gulls

Leave the A13 east of Gray's Thurrock 2km (1¼m) after it crosses the A128 southwards on unclassified roads to East Tilbury. Park in the lay-by (OS Ref: 684776) and walk down the right of way past the gravel machinery to the pit which is on the left and thence on to the seawall. Continue southwards to Coalhouse Fort Yard and then back through the village past or via The Ship public house.

Hanningfield Reservoir** OS168

Constructed in 1954 and usually overshadowed by nearby Abberton Reservoir, Hanningfield has its local devotees and frequently attracts a good variety of birds. Winter wildfowl are numerous and regularly include Gadwall and Shelduck (both breed), as well as Shoveler, Goldeneye, Goosander and large flocks of Tufted Duck and Mallard. In autumn Little Grebes build up to a maximum of 100 and both Black-necked and Slavonian are regular. Terns and gulls are often interesting and passage waders include the usual freshwater species. Ruddy Duck are becoming regular here.

Winter Shelduck, Teal, Wigeon, Shoveler, Gadwall, Pintail, Pochard, Tufted Duck, Goldeneye, Goosander, Ruddy Duck
Summer Great Crested Grebe, Shelduck, Gadwall
Autumn Little Grebe, Slavonian Grebe, Black-necked Grebe, Garganey, Little Ringed Plover, Common Sandpiper, Spotted Redshank, Greenshank, Ruff, Little Stint, Black Tern, Common Tern

Leave Chelmsford southwards on the A130 and turn left after 10km (6¼m) signposted West Hanningfield. Turn left in the village and view from the dam in 200m (220yd). Continue southwards and watch for a well-used unofficial lay-by on the right with access through a hedge to splashy shallows and interesting wood. Continue taking right-hand turns for further viewpoints.

Havergate**** OS169

Famed as the original site of recolonization by the Avocet after the Second World War. Lying some 4km (2½m) south of Orford and reached only by boat, Havergate is an island in the River Ore and is surrounded by artificial embankments originally constructed to protect summer grazing. Wartime neglect facilitated its conversion into an area of semi-saline lagoons rich in food and offering Avocets (and other birds) an ideal breeding ground. The RSPB were quick (and bold) to acquire the island soon after and have, over the years, improved the habitat and actively managed the birds they wished to encourage. Now a large colony of Avocets, together with a few gulls, terns and Short-eared Owls, breed in seclusion. Once the chicks have hatched safely the water level is lowered to provide as much feeding as possible just as Arctic waders are returning from further north. The result is frequently one of the best collections of waders along this already rich coastline. All can be watched in comfort from the hides that overlook each lagoon. In winter the water level is raised to form a retreat for numerous wildfowl, including some quite reasonable concentrations of duck, though its importance for these birds has declined in recent years.

Orford itself is a pleasant little yachting village with its own Gedgrave Marshes along the landward side of the Ore. These are worthy of exploration and from the seawall opposite Havergate, Avocets and Short-eared Owls may be seen. The former also gather throughout the season, particularly in spring and autumn, along Butley Creek.

To the north the grazing marshes along the Alde become rather splashy in winter and attract a fair variety of wildfowl. Avocets once bred, but the site was drained and the birds now do no more than fly over on their way to and from feeding grounds on the Alde Estuary. To the south is the tiny village of Shingle Street at the mouth of the Orwell where gulls and skuas may be an attraction in autumn.

Winter	Wigeon, Pintail, Teal, Shoveler, Short-eared Owl, Hen Harrier
Spring	Garganey, Spotted Redshank, Common Tern, Sandwich Tern
Summer	Avocet, Oystercatcher, Common Tern, Little Tern, Short-eared Owl
Autumn	Avocet, Spotted Redshank, Greenshank, Wood Sandpiper, Green Sandpiper, Little Stint, Curlew Sandpiper, Ruff, Curlew

Take the A1152 northwards out of Woodbridge and cut through on the B1048 to Orford.

Havergate Island May be visited on several days each week during the summer by permit available in advance from the Warden. Contact RSPB for details. Cost includes boat journey to and from the island. Take packed lunch and refreshments.

Gedgrave Marshes Are accessible by taking the seawall (river bank) southwards from Orford Quay and walking 4km (2½m) to Butley Creek passing Havergate along the way. Alternatively a minor road passes Orford Castle and continues to Butley Creek; several tracks lead eastwards to the river bank.

Marshes north of Orford Can be explored by leaving Orford northwards on the B1084 and taking a series of minor roads to the north via Sudbourne.

Holme and Titchwell****   OS132

Holme is ideally situated geographically to receive migrants, a fact which is enhanced by a small plantation of pines and scrub on the immediate landward side of the coastal dunes. Being the only cover for a mile or more the wood attracts all manner of small birds. The more usual passerine migrants are often plentiful, particularly in autumn.

Holme Dunes is a reserve of the Norfolk NT and covers 160ha (400a) of dunes, foreshore and fresh marsh. At its centre is the excellent but small Broad Water with its breeding Bearded Tits. Muddy edges regularly attract a wide variety of waders, including rarities during passage periods. From a dune-top vantage point in winter truly huge numbers of waders of a variety of species pass eastwards to roost at Thornham Harbour. In an hour or so up to 25,000 Knot may fly past.

Holme is also the site of a bird observatory run by the Norfolk Ornithologists' Association. Its activities, including ringing, centre on an area of 2.5ha (6¼a) of pines among the dunes, but there are hides available for ordinary bird-watching.

Thornham Harbour is a large inlet with its own population of wildfowl and waders. It acts as a high-tide roost for the huge population of waders that utilize this part of the coast.

To the east lies the RSPB reserve at Titchwell. This was purchased in 1973, at which time it was one of the few spots in Britain still to hold Montagu's Harriers. Unfortunately these extremely scarce birds no longer favour even this well-protected area. Covering 170ha (420a) the reserve includes shingle beaches and dunes, some large areas of saltings, a substantial reed bed and large fresh and brackish marshes that are managed with typical RSPB efficiency. There is even a small copse with dense undergrowth that enables visitors to add to the substantial range of birds that can be seen.

The area now holds breeding Bearded Tit, Sedge and Reed Warblers, Water Rail, Avocet, Bittern and Marsh Harrier – a goodly collection of East Anglian specialities. In winter there are Short-eared Owls and Hen Harriers, as well as a good number of wildfowl including Brent Geese, Wigeon, Teal, Goldeneye, Red-breasted Merganser and Shelduck. During passage periods the combination of adjacent fresh and salt marshes provides an ideal habitat for a wide variety of waders.

The shoreline itself, though liable to disturbance, is still the home of breeding Little Terns, Ringed Plover and Oystercatcher, while in winter and passage periods the same area acts as a high-tide roost. At exceptional tides up to 30,000 Knot, Bar-tailed Godwit and Oystercatcher may concentrate here. The inter-tidal area is a haunt of numerous waders including Grey Plover, Turnstone and Sanderling in season.

Winter	Little Grebe, Brent Goose, Teal, Shelduck, Wigeon, Goldeneye, Red-breasted Merganser, Hen Harrier, Merlin, Knot, Bar-tailed Godwit, Sanderling, Turnstone, Oystercatcher, Grey Plover, Short-eared Owl, Lapland Bunting, Snow Bunting, Twite
Spring	Wood Sandpiper, Ruff, Black Tern, Little Gull
Summer	Bittern, Shelduck, Marsh Harrier, Shoveler, Gadwall, Water Rail, Avocet, Redshank, Ringed Plover, Oystercatcher, Common Tern, Little Tern, Bearded Tit, Sedge Warbler, Reed Warbler, Grasshopper Warbler, Reed Bunting
Autumn	Brent Goose, Shelduck, Hen Harrier, Knot, Bar-tailed Godwit, Black-tailed Godwit, Grey Plover, Greenshank, Wood Sandpiper, Little Stint, Curlew Sandpiper, Little Gull, warblers, flycatchers, Shore Lark, Snow Bunting, Twite

Holme Bird Observatory Leave the A149 north of Hunstanton signposted Holme-next-the-Sea. Proceed down Holme Beach Road and turn right just before the golf course. The observatory is open daily between 11.30 a.m.and 4.00 p.m. and permits may be obtained on arrival. Contact: The Warden,

Mr P.R. Clarke, Aslack Way, Holme-next-the-Sea, Hunstanton PE36 6LP. *Tel*: (048 525) 266.

Holme Dunes Follow route as above and contact the Warden at The Firs, Holme-next-the-Sea. *Tel*: (048 525) 240. The Reserve is open during the summer months by permit. Contact Norfolk NT, Cathedral Close, Norwich NR1 4DF. Unsold permits may be obtained on the day from the Warden at The Firs after 10.00 a.m.

Thornham Harbour Leave the A149 northwards at Thornham on to a track out to the old jetty. A seawall on the western side leads out to Thornham Harbour and the dunes overlooking Broad Water and the sea.

Titchwell No permits are required to visit the RSPB reserve. There is also a visitors' centre with free displays and information. Hides are open during daylight hours throughout the year, except for the Tern Hide which is open only during the summer. Leave Titchwell village westwards on the A149 and watch out for a tree-lined track on the right after 1km (½m). Proceed to car park beyond the visitors' centre. Non-members might repay RSPB generosity and gain much else besides by joining on the spot. The Warden is usually present on the reserve, but can be contacted at Three Horseshoes Cottage, Titchwell, King's Lynn PE31 8BB. *Tel*: (048 521) 432.

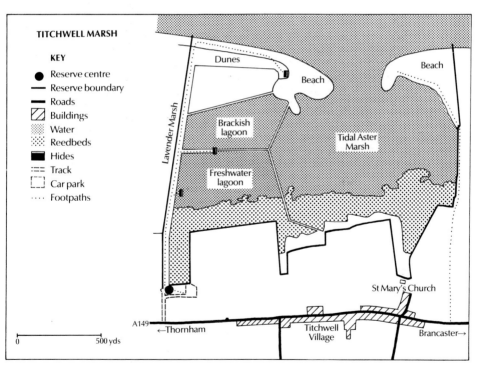

TITCHWELL MARSH

KEY
● Reserve centre
— Reserve boundary
▬ Roads
▨ Buildings
▦ Water
▦ Reedbeds
◼ Hides
⚌ Track
⊡ Car park
···· Footpaths

Minsmere*****   OS156

This is perhaps the best-known bird reserve in the country and certainly one of the richest in terms of species. In part this stems from its diversity of habitat, but also from its geographical position. The RSPB have created a series of large coastal lagoons collectively know as 'The

25

Scrape', dotted with islands suitable for nesting. By careful management of water levels this superb example of active conservation offers breeding sites at one time of the year and large feeding zones at others. 'The Scrape' is separated from the sea by a double seawall that enables visitors to walk along the shore without disturbing birds inside the reserve.

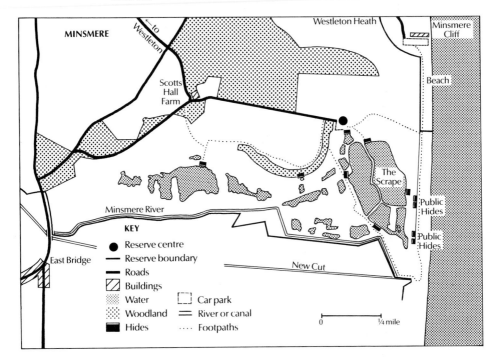

Inland the area becomes gradually drier, and what were once old grazing meadows, inundated as part of wartime coastal defence against invasion, now form a huge reed bed. All the East Anglian specialities breed here including Bittern, Bearded Tit, Water Rail, Marsh Harrier and masses of Sedge and Reed Warblers. To the north and west dry fields give way to open heathland that extends virtually to the village of Westleton some 5km (3m) from the sea. At the Westleton–Dunwich road Minsmere abuts the Westleton Heath NNR, 47ha (116a), and it is a poor winter that does not produce Great Grey Shrike and Hen Harrier.

Minsmere's woodlands are exquisite and in May they are alive with bird song, including all the regular summer visitors. Nightingale, Blackcap and Garden Warbler may all be heard and Redstarts, Tree Pipits and many more are to be seen. Along the edges of the reed beds Grasshopper Warbler reel away, while among the reeds and willows are Savi's and Cetti's Warblers.

Wildfowl, including Bewick's Swans, are regular in numbers in winter when Hen Harriers quarter the reeds and fields. If there are Rough-legged Buzzards about, Minsmere will have its share; Merlins are regular and Peregrines reasonably so. Spring and autumn brings floods of waders to 'The Scrape' including the odd rarity, while in summer Spoonbill and Purple Heron cause speculation, though as yet neither has bred. 'The Scrape' at this time is a mass of breeding terns with dense packs of Sandwich together with Common, and a few Little Terns that have a stronghold on the beach. There are masses of gulls and a healthy population of Avocets.

There are well-positioned and well-constructed hides mostly overlooking 'The Scrape' and reed beds, and along the shore is a massive two-storey-high public hide offering viewing space for perhaps 50 or more bird-watchers. On summer Sundays it may be thronged by the curious, but at other times bird talk rules.

Winter	Bewick's Swan, Wigeon, Pintail, Teal, Gadwall, Hen Harrier, Marsh Harrier, Merlin, Redshank, Turnstone, Snipe, Great Grey Shrike, Bearded Tit
Spring	Spoonbill, Garganey, Sanderling, Whimbrel, Spotted Redshank
Summer	Bittern, Marsh Harrier, Water Rail, Avocet, Redshank, Ringed Plover, Sandwich Tern, Common Tern, Little Tern, Black-headed Gull, Herring Gull, Grasshopper Warbler, Savi's Warbler, Cetti's Warbler, Bearded Tit, Nightingale, Nightjar
Autumn	Marsh Harrier, Water Rail, Avocet, Spotted Redshank, Greenshank, Wood Sandpiper, Little Stint, Curlew Sandpiper, Ruff, Bar-tailed Godwit, Black-tailed Godwit, Curlew, Snow Bunting

Permit details giving access for the current season may be obtained from the RSPB. This enables members (reduced prices) and non-members to explore the reserve along well-marked paths with access to all hides. To see 'The Scrape' permits are not required.

Open Days	Turn eastwards in Westleton on the B1125, between Blythburgh and Leiston, next to the village post office, and follow signs to the reserve.
Closed Days	Leave the Westleton–Dunwich road southwards signposted Minsmere to Dunwich Heath NT. A small parking fee is payable at summer weekends. Proceed as far as possible and park at the cliff top overlooking Minsmere to the south and the sea to the east, which may produce a diver or Fulmar in season and regularly has summering Scoter.

Walk southwards between the walls to public hides overlooking 'The Scrape' which are just beyond the reserve entrance.

Westleton Heath NNR May be explored on foot along various footpaths. These are usually sufficient to produce all the birds of the area. To leave the footpath a permit is required – please do not trespass. Best spots are northwards off the Westleton–Dunwich road.

Ouse Mouth*   OS131

South of Wolferton the coastline of The Wash is backed by saltings, extending in some places for up to 4km (2½m). This barrier has resulted in considerable neglect by bird-watchers and, as a result, it is still possible to wander along miles of seawall without meeting a soul. It is also possible to wander for miles with little in the way of ornithological reward. Nevertheless, there are birds here and at really high tides masses of waders may be forced over the saltings to seek refuge among the fields behind the seawall.

At Ouse Mouth birds can be seen at most times, and it is a significant area for wildfowl and waders and one that all the efforts made to explore may reward. Wigeon, Brent and a small flock of Pinkfeet may be seen along with most of the common waders and the occasional Short-eared Owl.

Winter   Pink-footed Goose, Brent Goose, Shelduck, Teal, Wigeon, Pintail, Scaup, Goldeneye, Oystercatcher, Grey Plover, Knot, Redshank, Bar-tailed Godwit, Curlew, Short-eared Owl

Ouse Mouth   Find the way through a maze of turnings, leave King's Lynn docks on the track running down the eastern wall of the River Ouse and continue northwards for 3km (2m) to the old lighthouse. Park and follow walls eastwards, then northwards out to Vinegar Middle. A wall continues northwards and rejoins the old wall west of Estuary Farm. For the ambitious and energetic the same wall can be followed to North Wootton or even Wolferton, both of which are connected by private tracks through farmland.

Terrington   Take the A17 west of King's Lynn and, after turning right (north) at West Lynn, continue through a network of lanes to the seawall near the Ouse Mouth. Terrington can also be reached by leaving King's Lynn in the same direction (west) and turning right (north) after 5km (3m) to Little London. Turn left, then right past The Dun Cow down a road signposted Terrington. After 2km (1¼m) turn right to Ongar Hill. Park at the seawall and walk leftwards towards Admiralty Point.

Scolt Head and Burnham**   OS132

At Scolt Head a huge sandy beach encloses a large area of saltings, broken at each end by the outlet of a river. The resulting island forms a natural haven for breeding birds and has been an NNR since 1954.

Scolt lies offshore between Brancaster and Burnham Overy, stretches 6km (3¾m) from east to west, and covers 425ha (1051a). Birds are varied and provide variety and excitement at all seasons. Outstanding are the breeding colonies of terns, which include 1400 pairs of Sandwich and 600 of Common at the western end.

Winter brings good numbers of wildfowl with the flock of over 1000 Brent Geese being the main attraction, along with huge numbers of waders. Passage brings a large variety of waders, terns (including Roseate) Kittiwakes, especially in July, and a fair number of passerines. But Scolt is really a summer place for those who like to see large breeding colonies of terns.

Burnham Overy has a charm and attraction of its own. It lies between two walls that enclose the estuary of the River Burn. Areas of saltings are intersected by numerous creeks, and a substantial area of mud is exposed on the eastern side out of Overy Staithe. The area is attractive to waders and Hen Harrier and Merlin in winter. Though not equipped with hides, this is a wild area where 'walking birders' feel at home.

Winter	Brent Goose, Wigeon, Goldeneye, Merganser, Eider, Hen Harrier, Merlin, Knot, Turnstone, Bar-tailed Godwit, Grey Plover, Short-eared Owl, Twite
Summer	Common Tern, Sandwich Tern, Little Tern, Short-eared Owl, Oystercatcher, Shelduck
Autumn	Peregrine, Bar-tailed Godwit, Whimbrel, Spotted Redshank, Turnstone, Grey Plover, Short-eared Owl, Roseate Tern, Sandwich Tern, Common Tern, Kittiwake.

Scolt Head NNR Access by boat from Brancaster Staithe which is on the main A149; watch out for signpost to Scolt Head, or via Overy Maritime Stores, East Harbour Way, Burnham Overy Staithe, Nr King's Lynn, Norfolk. *Tel*: (032873) 267. The boat trip can be made two or three hours either side of high tide. The best area is near the landing point. There are no restrictions on landing but please avoid the terneries during the breeding season. It is a good idea to contact the Warden at 26, The Close, Brancaster Staithe, King's Lynn, Norfolk PE31 8BS. *Tel*: (048521) 330 before visiting.

Burnham Overy On the eastern side turn north off the A149 opposite 'The Hero', Overy Staithe, to the quay. At the right-hand end a wall leads northwards past the largest areas of exposed mud towards the sandhills of Gun Hill. Continue to the sea and sandbanks. At high tide watch for waders flighting to Scolt Head.

To reach the western side watch out for an old windmill on the southern side of the A149 half a mile west of Overy Staithe, and for the delightful old maltings and water mill (Kingfisher) on the River Burn if coming from Burnham Norton. Opposite both mills, paths run down to the seawall which then leads out towards Scolt Head.

Snettisham and Hunstanton**** OS132

Though the Wash is one of the top three British estuaries for birds and one of the top dozen most important wetlands in Europe, at low tide the whole area can appear quite lifeless. However, as the tide rises, the flocks are pushed off their feeding grounds to flight to roost. As with other estuaries, the Wash is best visited some two or three hours before high water. At such times birds gather close inshore, feeding along a narrow stretch of mud and sand. They then fly along the coast in huge flocks to their favoured roosts. At Hunstanton this movement is mainly northwards to the roosts of Thornham Harbour and Scolt Head. At Snettisham the movements are mainly southwards.

Hunstanton, on the north-eastern corner of the Wash, is a Victorian seaside resort, and provides excellent winter bird-watching from the deserted promenade and cliff tops. It forms the northern limit for most of the duck found off Heacham and Long-tailed Duck can often be seen. It also attracts several marine species that are rarer to the south, notably the three divers and more unusual grebes, especially Black-necked. In autumn it is one of the main sea-watching points in Norfolk.

Southwards along the coast is Heacham, where, at low tide, large areas of sand and mud are exposed and there are mussel beds offshore that attract sea-duck. Vast flocks of wildfowl in the new year, with maxima in February–March, can be a mile or two north or south of Heacham. Maxima include 500 Scaup and, quite outstanding for southern England, 2000 Common and 200 Velvet Scoter and 40 Long-tailed Duck. High tide produces huge roosting flights of waders with Knot and Bar-tailed Godwit by the thousand. A small flock of a dozen or so Purple Sandpipers is regular between here and Hunstanton to the north.

Further south is Snettisham, where the muddy feeding grounds of waders lie immediately offshore. Snettisham is outstanding and the main attraction comes just before high tide when a huge movement of waders passes south down the coast. Maxima are 35,000 Knot, 10,000 Dunlin, 4000 Bar-tailed Godwit. The 1000 Sanderling in autumn are unique in the Wash area.

The old gravel pits to the south are an RSPB reserve frequented by wildfowl and form a major wader roost. Snow Buntings are often quite numerous, and Lapland Buntings and Shore Larks are regular. The pits with their islands and shingle banks can be seen from hides where one can watch the birds gather and disperse without disturbance. Knot, Oystercatcher, Redshank and Dunlin are often present in their thousands along with Grey Plover and Bar-tailed Godwit. During passage periods virtually anything can turn up here and Greenshank, Wood Sandpiper and Little Stint are all regular. Wildfowl also use the reserve with Pinkfeet (5000) and Brent (1000) and a regular herd of Bewick's Swans. Whooper Swans also winter. Breeding birds include Redshank, Ringed Plover and Common Tern.

Winter	Bewick's Swan, Whooper Swan, Brent Goose, Shelduck, Wigeon, Teal, Shoveler, Scaup, Scoter, Velvet Scoter, Long-tailed Duck, Goldeneye, Red-breasted Merganser, Eider, Knot, Bar-tailed Godwit, Grey Plover, Turnstone, Sanderling, Purple Sandpiper, Shore Lark, Snow Bunting, Twite
Spring	Redshank, Greenshank, Black-tailed Godwit
Summer	Shelduck, Redshank, Ringed Plover, Common Tern, Little Tern
Autumn	Ringed Plover, Greenshank, Wood Sandpiper, Green Sandpiper, Little Stint, Curlew Sandpiper, Ruff

Hunstanton	Lies on the A149 and the promenade is easily found. Walk northwards and climb the cliff steps to obtain better views of sea-duck and flighting waders. There is a cliff-top car park just north of the town.
Heacham	Just west of the A149 and well signposted 5km (3m) south of Hunstanton. Take either of two routes through the village to the beach.
Snettisham	On the A149 about 4km (2½m) from the sea. Drive westwards to the beach and watch waders from among the chalets. Drive southwards to the RSPB reserve, but do not park beyond the entrance sign. The reserve is open at all times free of charge, and there are hides available overlooking the pit. Snettisham can also be reached via Dersingham, also on the A149, where a footpath leads to a public hide. But there is no access into the RSPB reserve by this track. For advice and information contact: The Warden, School House, Wolferton, King's Lynn. *Tel*: (0485) 40129.

Southend* OS178

Though one of the least likely localities to be included in a bird book, the Southend area has always attracted birds. Since the Thames has been cleaned up its attractions have, if anything, increased. The Pier, over 2km (1¼m) of it, still survives and is a good place for watching seabirds, including skuas in September. To the west lies Leigh-on-Sea with its large inter-tidal areas extending as far as Canvey Point and with the NNR of Leigh Marsh on Two Tree Island sandwiched between. Here over 2000 Brent Geese winter along with 10,000 Dunlin and lesser numbers of Grey Plover and Redshank. Indeed this is a major wader roost and Turnstones commute between here and the nearby cockle sheds. Adjacent Bowers Gifford Marshes are worth a look, particularly for passage waders.

Winter	Brent Goose, Wigeon, Grey Plover, Redshank, Ringed Plover, Turnstone
Passage	Terns, skuas, waders
Southend Pier	From promenade in centre of town. The famous railway will run again from 1986.
Leigh-on-Sea	Access to shoreline on south side of railway from centre of Leigh.
Two Tree Island	Free access at all times via Leigh-on-Sea, but keep to marked footpaths; there is a hide.
Canvey Point	Free access, but beware being stranded at the Point by incoming tides.

Stour and Orwell Estuaries**** OS169

The Stour estuary lies on the Essex–Suffolk border and is broad and shallow. Diving duck are scarce but Wigeon are particularly numerous; they frequently reach 4000 and have totalled 13,700, making the Stour the most important spot on this coast for the species. Both godwits winter, and Black-tailed build up to 1000 in spring. The concentration of Mute Swans, up to 900, at the malthouses at Mistley in autumn is notable. Up to 500 Brent are regular and Shelduck are often abundant with up to 2500. Pintail find one of their few major wintering grounds here and may reach 1000 on occasion. Dunlin attain a maximum of over 10,000 and Grey Plover and Redshank also reach good numbers.

Best access is on the southern shore at the RSPB reserve of Stour Wood and Copperas Bay near Wrabness where the coppiced woodland holds typical species, including all three woodpeckers. There are excellent views over the estuary at one of its best points.

The estuary of the Orwell stretches from Harwich some 14km (8½m) inland to Ipswich. In places it is almost 2km (1¼m) wide and has larger areas of mud than the Deben to the north. Like that water it is narrowest in the lower reaches and most concentrations of birds occur at Pinmill or above. Black-tailed and Bar-tailed Godwits winter, and passage brings large numbers of several species of wader. There is much interchange with the Stour.

Winter	Mute Swan, Brent Goose, Shelduck, Teal, Wigeon, Shoveler, Pintail,

	Goldeneye, Pochard, Tufted Duck, Grey Plover, Turnstone, Dunlin, Knot, Redshank, Curlew, Bar-tailed Godwit, Black-tailed Godwit
Spring	Black-tailed Godwit
Summer	Mute Swan, Shelduck, Redshank
Autumn	Mute Swan, Knot, Dunlin, Redshank, Black-tailed Godwit, Whimbrel, Greenshank

There are four basic approaches to the Stour, all start from Manningtree Station on the A137 17km (10½m) south of Ipswich and north of Colchester.

Mistley Take the road to Manningtree from the station and continue, joining the B1352 to see the autumn gathering of Mute Swans.

Stour Wood and Copperas Bay Continue through Bradfield on the B1352 and take the second turning left after 4km (2½m). There is an inn on the corner. This road passes under the railway and a track leaves to the left after 200m (220yd) to Jacques Bay. Return to and continue along the metalled road to Wrabness Halt where a track leads off to the left to the RSPB reserve. The section from Copperas to Harwich is the primary haunt of Brent Geese and is viewed from the Parkstone Quay area.

Holbrook Bay On the Suffolk shore leave Manningtree station by the A137 northwards, keep right after 5km (3m) on the B1080 to Stutton. Turn right and then left to the church. Continue past the church to Holbrook Bay. Returning, turn right past the church to the B1080 then turn right to Holbrook. Turn right past Holbrook church to Harkstead in 4km (2½m). Turn right down to Holbrook Bay on the eastern shore.

Orwell Estuary Much more difficult to work. Leave Ipswich by the A137, turn left after 4km (2½m) on to the A138 and enjoy good views of the estuary on your left for 2km (1¼m). The only other point of access is from Pinmill, turning left at Chelmondiston. Footpaths to east and west give good views of the best parts.

Walberswick**** OS156

A large part of this exceptionally rich area is an NNR, extending from the southern shore of the Blyth estuary to the centre of the great reed beds of Westwood Marshes. Ornithological interest, however, extends northwards to include the whole of the Blyth's inter-tidal banks together with the splashy grazing that lies to the north towards Reydon, while to the south Corporation and Dunwich Marshes back the shore between Walberswick and Dunwich. Within its boundaries there are estuarine mud banks, damp grazing marshes, fresh and salt marshes, reed beds, sandy heaths, old pine coverts, marram-lined dunes and the seashore. Such a diversity of habitats combines with its strategic position, little more than 160km (100m) from the coast of Holland, to produce a wealth of species and one of the top 'big day' areas in Britain.

In cross section the dune-lined shore with its Little Terns and Ringed Plovers protects an area of open pools of varying levels of salinity. These are the home of passage waders and flocks of wintering Twite, Snow Bunting and Shore Lark. Moving inland the influence of salt (which permeates through the beach) is reduced and fresh pools and dykes hold breeding Redshank and other 'fresh' waders such as Greenshank and Wood Sandpiper on passage. Areas of rough grass between pools are a favoured haunt of Short-eared Owls. Beyond the embanked Dunwich River, a huge reed bed stretches inland for 3–4km (2–3m) broken here and there by areas of open water which the Nature Conservancy Council has considerably extended. This is the heart of the reserve and home to a number of birds including Marsh Harrier, Bittern, Bearded Tit, Cetti's and Savi's Warblers and hosts of Sedge, Reed and Grasshopper Warblers. Inland still the marsh has been invaded by a growth of willow and other scrub which gives way to an old wood known as Blythburgh Fen. It is a wet, tangled jungle of a place, impenetrable and even dangerous to those who do not know it. Fortunately it holds no birds that cannot be better seen elsewhere. At the western edge of the Fen the land is sandy and well drained, and heathland birds such as Stonechat, Nightingale and Nightjar appear. Inland arable land may still hold a few pairs of Stone-curlew.

To the north the Blyth is one of the most viewable of all estuaries. It is neither so daunting in size that nothing can be seen, nor so small that a single bird-watcher can disturb all the birds. Shelduck, Grey Heron and Cormorant are present throughout the year. There are Common Terns in summer and wildfowl in winter, but in spring and autumn the Blyth offers excellent collections of migrant waders. Spotted Redshank, Greenshank, Grey Plover, Whimbrel, both godwits and so on can be seen, and Spoonbill and Avocet are far from irregular.

The posts and banks that break the surface of the mud banks are the remnants of walls that embanked the Blyth until 1926. At that time exceptional floods broke through to flood the rough grazing on either side and return the estuary to something like its former state. Downstream the river remains embanked and is lined by the damp, splashy grazing beloved by wildfowl. Geese, Wigeon, Teal, Shoveler and Bewick's Swans are regular visitors and there are Ruff, Green Sandpiper and Black-tailed Godwit in autumn.

Mid-May is undoubtedly the best for a large day-list with totals of well over a hundred species quite possible. August to October is a particularly good period, including the bulk of autumn passage and the arrival of winter visitors. The latter include good numbers of Marsh and Hen Harriers, Short-eared Owl, duck, waders and rarities.

Winter Shelduck, Wigeon, Teal, Gadwall, Shoveler, Bewick's Swan, Hen Harrier, Marsh Harrier, Merlin, Short-eared Owl, Water Rail, Bar-tailed Godwit, Curlew, Spotted Redshank, Great Grey Shrike, Snow Bunting, Shore Lark, Twite

Spring Shelduck, Redshank, Black-tailed Godwit, Whimbrel, Stone-curlew

Summer Bittern, Water Rail, Cetti's Warbler, Savi's Warbler, Bearded Tit

Autumn Red-throated Diver, Wood Sandpiper, Green Sandpiper, Greenshank, Little Stint, Ruff, Black-tailed Godwit, Spotted Redshank, Grey Plover, Sandwich Tern, Little Gull, Snow Bunting, Shore Lark

The whole of the area and all the best habitats can be explored by road, track and public footpath, and there is no need to trespass on the NNR or private land. Indeed, during the spring and summer unauthorized tramping about may seriously interfere with the breeding of many of the more sensitive species.

Blyth West	From the A12 some 550m (600yd) north of Blythburgh from a lay-by on the west side of the road. Cross and view over the fenced bank.
Blyth South	Via track immediately north of The White Hart, Blythburgh which leads to a path that follows the old course of the narrow gauge Southwold Railway. Keep strictly to path and access to NCC public hides.
Reydon Quay	Signposted from A1095 Southwold road. Access to dykes and grazing marshes north of embanked River Blyth on foot only.
Walberswick	Plentiful car-parking by forking right just past The Anchor Hotel and continuing straight towards the sea. Walk southwards behind (not on) the beach wall, all the way to Dunwich.
Westwood Marshes	Take embankment due east of ugly red-brick building on Dingle Hill from beach path. Follow to windmill and thereafter keep right with reeds on either side, through excellent scrub to road. Turn right back to village. A car park courtesy NCC at Hoist Covert enables this route to be reversed.
Westwood Lodge	Leave Walberswick and fork left before the church on road to Hoist Covert. Continue to Westwood Lodge and park as requested. Views southwards over huge reed bed. No trespassing.
Dunwich	Leave B1125 at Westleton to beach car park. Walk northwards with pools on left.

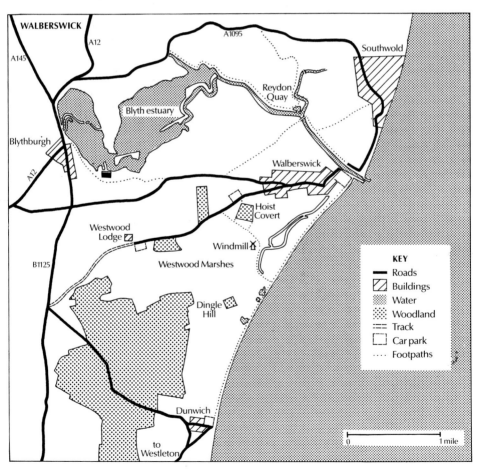

Walton-on-the-Naze*** OS168

Large, difficult-to-work area of creeks, saltings and islands on the Essex coast immediately north of Walton-on-the-Naze. In practice, bird-watching is confined to the south and east, and the huge Horsey Island is strictly private. Among the major attractions is the flock of Brent Geese that have built up to reach a maximum of 2500. Shelduck, Wigeon and Teal are all numerous and Pintail may reach 250 at times. In really hard winters outstanding numbers of duck may occur, including 25,000 Wigeon and 12,000 Shelduck. Other duck include Pochard, Scoter, Long-tailed Duck and a decent number of Red-breasted Merganser. Waders may be abundant with up to 10,000 Dunlin, together with lesser numbers of Redshank, Curlew and Grey Plover.

Summer is generally rather quiet, but Shelduck, Redshank, Ringed Plover, Common Tern and Little Tern (c. 40 pairs) all breed. At migration times good numbers of other waders may pass through, including both godwits (up to 500 Black-tailed), Greenshank, Whimbrel, Ruff and Spotted Redshank. At these times attention is usually concentrated on The Naze where the bushes that line the cliff tops may, on occasion, be alive with migrants. Walking northwards towards Stone Point the broken seawall holds the only regular flock of Purple Sandpipers along this coast, while Stone Point itself is a regular haunt of Snow Bunting, Twite, and a good sea-watching spot for skuas.

Winter	Brent Goose, Shelduck, Teal, Wigeon, Pintail, Shoveler, Pochard, Goldeneye, Scoter, Long-tailed Duck, Red-breasted Merganser, Merlin, Golden Plover, Grey Plover, Turnstone, Dunlin, Knot, Sanderling, Purple Sandpiper, Oystercatcher, Redshank, Bar-tailed Godwit, Curlew, Short-eared Owl, Shore Lark, Snow Bunting, Twite
Spring	Black-tailed Godwit
Summer	Shelduck, Redshank, Snipe, Ringed Plover, Common Tern, Little Tern
Autumn	Ringed Plover, Redshank, Greenshank, Whimbrel, Little Stint, Curlew Sandpiper, Arctic Skua, warblers, chats, flycatchers

Access is awkward, but good views can be obtained at a number of spots, and many birds can be seen without undue effort. All routes start by following main roads to Clacton, but leaving the A133 at Weeley and joining the B1033 towards Frinton and the B1034 to Walton.

The Naze Reached by following the cliff footpath northwards. It continues as far as Stone Point, but this involves crossing several tidal creeks – beware being marooned. At the first creek follow the seawall along the south side to overlook Walton Channel.

Hamford Water Leave Walton on the B1034 toward Kirby le Soken, but turn right down track after 3km (2m) to reach the start of 'The Wade' (a tidal track to Horsey Island – private). Turn left and walk along seawall for up to 8km (5m). Skipper's Island is a reserve of the Essex NT that can be visited by prior arrangement.

Wells**** OS132

Wells-next-the-Sea is a rather quaint, little town on the north Norfolk coast that is the jumping-off point for Wells Harbour with its geese and the excellent Holkham NNR covering 3925ha (9700a). Its main street is flanked on one side by candy floss joints and fish-and-chip shops, and on the other by tidal banks beloved of Brent Geese. It is possible for a glutton to indulge all three.

The road to the Harbour follows the western (left) bank of the straightened river, passing a football pitch on the left beloved of Richard's Pipits. After 2km (1¼m) it terminates at a large car park. At this point the mouth of the Harbour is protected by a seawall from which up to 6000 Brent Geese may be seen between October and March. To the west lies Holkham NNR and access is unrestricted (save to farmland). Autumn often produces a string of rarities in and around the belt of pines. In the middle is a small pool that regularly attracts all the birds of the area to drink and bathe, but its location is impossible to describe, and recourse must be made to asking (or following) other bird-watchers. The pines extend in a crescent to Holkham Gap and most birds are found in the open areas or among the birch and elder scrub that backs them to the south. Recorded rarities have included Red-breasted Flycatcher, Radde's, Dusky, Arctic, Greenish and Barred Warblers, while Pied Flycatcher and Redstart are regular. Parrot Crossbills have bred.

To the north the sand flats extend out over 1km (½m) at low water and are the haunt of a good collection of open shore waders in all but the summer months.

Away to the south a column stands out above an area of woodland. This is a monument to Thomas William Coke, one of the pioneers of the agricultural revolution of the early nineteenth century. It stands in the grounds of Holkham Hall, a splendid and imposing pile still in private hands. The woodlands are excellent for birds and, in front of the Hall, is a large lake and headquarters of a large flock of Canada Geese. In winter large numbers of wildfowl, especially Wigeon, find a safe refuge here. Do not tresspass – permits may be obtained – see below.

Winter	Brent Goose, Wigeon, Teal, Curlew, Oystercatcher, Turnstone, Bar-tailed Godwit, Knot, Crossbill
Spring	Common Tern, Sandwich Tern, Little Tern, Crossbill
Summer	Egyptian Goose, Greylag Goose, Ringed Plover, Oystercatcher
Autumn	Migrant and rare warblers and chats

Holkham NNR Turn northwards from Wells jetty (off A149) along the west side of the river signposted to the Harbour. Park in car park at end and examine the mouth of the river for geese and other wildfowl. Continue westwards behind the pines watching for migrants, or for groups of other bird-watchers either whooping in delight or walking purposefully. Ask where the pool is.

Walk westwards as before but at the entrance to the NNR fork right and head towards the beach. Find a vantage point and settle down with a telescope, preferably when the tide is rising.

Holkham Hall Leave Wells westward on the A149 to Holkham. Obtain a permit in advance from Holkham Estates, Holkham, Nr Wells. The Hall is open to the public at certain times during the summer months.

Holkham Gap Opposite the entrance to the Hall, Lady Ann's Road runs from Holkham village to Holkham Gap. Access by vehicles is allowed by Lord Leicester (not a right of way) and a parking fee is charged. From here one can walk eastwards through the pines as above; or westwards towards Overy Staithe.

Yare Valley*** OS134

Between Norwich and Yarmouth the Yare is bounded north and south by high embankments protecting grazing marshes. Just a few km east of Norwich these are broken by extensive areas of fen and broad, and it is here that the RSPB established their Strumpshaw Fen Reserve in 1976. Based on the old Strumpshaw Broad which once covered 6½ha (16a), the reserve extends over 143ha (353a) along the north bank of the Yare between Brundall and Buckenham. It thus lies adjacent to both Rockland Broad in the south and Surlingham Broad to the west.

By 1976 Strumpshaw Broad was little more than an open pool set in the midst of heavily overgrown fen and reed. It was invaded by high tides in winter and this facilitated its maintenance as a reed swamp. Elsewhere reed had succumbed to a natural invasion of scrub and, ultimately, woodland carr, so that a succession of habitats was already created. There is also a large area of grazing marshes including the regular wintering ground of a flock of Bean Geese – one of only two remaining in Britain. This well-known flock had attracted bird-watchers for years, but disturbance was always a hazard and the RSPB did well to include one of their favoured areas within the reserve.

Other birds here in winter include Hen and Marsh Harriers, Short-eared Owl, Wigeon and Teal and sometimes wild swans, Smew and Goosander. Bearded Tit and Water Rail are present in good numbers and the range of habitat makes for a good variety of summer birds including Snipe and Redshank, Savi's, Cetti's and Grasshopper Warblers, Woodcock, all three woodpeckers, Yellow Wagtail and Common Tern. Soon after acquiring Strumpshaw Fen the RSPB was able to purchase a further 20ha (49a) of fen that included one of the strongholds of the rare Swallowtail Butterfly.

The larger areas of open water of Rockland and Surlingham Broads nearby were always an attraction to bird-watchers in their own right. Both have always been known as hard-weather resorts of a variety of wildfowl, particularly in the new year, and both are worth more than a glance by any visitor.

Downstream grazing marshes line both banks, and from time to time the geese and other wildfowl move up and down the valley. The marshes at Cantley are regularly good and the pools to the east of the village may be worth a look.

Winter Bean Goose, Wigeon, Teal, Water Rail, Marsh Harrier, Hen Harrier, Short-eared Owl, Great Grey Shrike, Siskin

Summer Little Grebe, Great Crested Grebe, Marsh Harrier, Water Rail, Shoveler, Gadwall, Pochard, Redshank, Snipe, Woodcock, Common Tern,

Lesser Spotted Woodpecker, Kingfisher, Grasshopper Warbler, Savi's Warbler, Cetti's Warbler, Yellow Wagtail, Bearded Tit

Autumn Migrants

Strumpshaw Fen Leave Norwich on the A47 eastwards to Blofield. Turn right to Brundall and at a T-junction in 1½km (1m) turn left towards Strumpshaw. The reserve is on the right: report to the reception hide at Staithe Cottage, Low Road. The reserve is open several days each week throughout the year. Contact RSPB for details. There is a public hide overlooking the Bean Geese fields (OS Ref: TG342067) which is open from October to March — best time is in the new year.

Surlingham and Rockland Broads Lie south of the Yare and can be reached by taking the A146 over the Yare and forking left onto a minor road at Trowse Newton. Take a left at Bramerton and follow signs to Surlingham. Continue to the foot ferry and walk westwards (left) along the Yare to the Broad. Return to Surlingham and take a left in the village to Rockland St Mary. Take a left at a T-junction to Rockland Broad which can be viewed from the south.

The Ferry at Reedham is a delightful method of transferring from the north to the south of the Yare. It lies downstream of the area and may, on occasion, prove worthwhile for birds.

East Midlands

Bedfordshire, Cambridgeshire, Hertfordshire, Leicestershire, Lincolnshire, Northamptonshire, Nottinghamshire

1 Donna Nook and Tetney Haven
2 Covenham Reservoir
3 Saltfleetby-Theddlethorpe
4 Gibraltar Point
5 The Wash
6 Nottingham Gravel Pits
7 Wisbech Sewage Farm
8 Nene Washes
9 Castor Hanglands
10 Rutland Water
11 Charnwood Forest
12 Eyebrook Reservoir
13 Stanford Reservoir
14 Northampton Reservoirs
15 Ouse Washes
16 Grafham Water
17 Wicken Fen
18 Fowlmere
19 The Lodge
20 Tring Reservoirs

Castor Hanglands*   OS142

Castor Hanglands is an area of heath, with scrub and woods, that is now an NNR. It lies on the edge of the Fens and is well served with maps to show visitors where they may and may not go without a permit. There is a wide range of breeding and wintering species, making for nice bird-watching without anything outrageous.

Winter   Sparrowhawk, Redpoll, Siskin
Summer   Long-eared Owl, Nightingale, Garden Warbler, Lesser Whitethroat, Blackcap, Grasshopper Warbler, Woodcock, Marsh Tit, Willow Tit

Leave the A47 at Ailsworth northwards on to an unclassified road. After 3–4km (2–3m) there are conifers on the left in new plantations. Past here a path leads westwards to the reserve notice board. OS Ref: TF118023

Charnwood Forest**   OS129

To the north-west of Leicester is an area of good bird-watching that includes high heathland dotted by small woods with a series of reservoirs to the east. Though Charnwood Forest is privately owned much can be seen from roads and footpaths, and the county trust has a reserve at Charnwood Lodge where habitats include moorland, heath and woodland. Birds here include Woodcock, Sparrowhawk and warblers. The reservoirs at Cropston and Swithland may not be huge, but they do attract a variety of passage migrants as well as winter wildfowl. One of the best ways of viewing Cropston is from the adjacent Bradgate Park where some moorland-type species can be seen, while nearby Swithland Wood has a good cross-section of woodland birds. Swithland Reservoir lies to the north.

Winter   Great Crested Grebe, Bewick's Swan, Wigeon, Pintail, Teal, Tufted Duck, Pochard, Goldeneye, Sparrowhawk, Siskin, Redpoll
Summer   Woodcock, Whinchat, Redstart, Wood Warbler

Leave Leicester westwards signposted M1 and watch for the B5327 to Anstey. This leads to the B5325 and a right turn to Cropston. The reservoir can be viewed from the road across the dam. Bradgate Park and Swithland Wood are open to the public. For Swithland Reservoir leave the A65 at Mountsorrell north of Leicester and navigate through a maze of roads with OS map. Find the road running along the north-eastern edge and over the dam.

Covenham Reservoir*   OS122

Lying only a few km from the Lincolnshire coast this reservoir has quickly built up a good reputation with local bird-watchers. It has a good population of wildfowl in winter and, despite its artificial banks, regularly attracts a good variety of passage waders. Oddities such as divers and the rarer grebes turn up from time to time and there is a sizeable gull roost. Autumn Black Terns and Little Gulls are regular.

Winter Red-throated Diver, Cormorant, Slavonian Grebe, Pochard, Goldeneye, Scaup
Passage Greenshank, Wood Sandpiper, Little Stint, Ruff, Little Gull, Black Tern

Leave the A16 eastwards at the Z-bend 2km (1¼m) north of Utterby and continue for 4km (2½m) to the public car park at the north-west corner of the reservoir. View from the track around the perimeter wall.

Donna Nook and Tetney Haven** OS113

A large area including tidal sand that has proved a good deal more than Lincolnshire's answer to Spurn Point. Though much of Donna Nook is a military area, there is a reserve and an area of good beach and shoreline that attracts waders, gulls, terns and passage migrants. Indeed this is one of the best places in the county for producing rarities with Ortolan Bunting and Richards Pipit virtually annual. Beaches and dune scrub in the north and south are the principal rarity haunts, though the central part, with its enclosed grassy marsh and pools, attracts many fresh waders. All the usual waders occur in winter and Dotterel are more or less annual on the seabank fields in spring.

Tetney is similar, but with even larger areas of foreshore. A wide variety of waders occurs including a good range of autumn species. In winter there is a major wader roost here. The area is an RSPB reserve of particular importance to the Little Tern.

Winter Brent Goose, Shelduck, Mallard, Hen Harrier, Merlin, Grey Plover, Knot, Dunlin, Sanderling, Curlew, Snow Bunting, Lapland Bunting
Spring Dotterel
Summer Ringed Plover, Little Tern
Autumn Greenshank, Green Sandpiper, Wood Sandpiper, Curlew Sandpiper, Common Tern, Arctic Tern, Shore Lark, Richard's Pipit, chats, fly-catchers, warblers, Snow Bunting, Lapland Bunting

For the northern part of the reserve take Marsh Lane northwards from North Somercotes on the A1031 and park at the end. Walk eastwards along the edge of the dunes. All other tracks and roads to the dunes in this area are strictly private. Central areas can be reached from the car park down the track from the brick tower by the A1031 half-way between North Somercotes and Saltfleet. For southern areas park in the car park at the end of Sea Lane in Saltfleet. For Tetney park at Tetney Lock and walk along the southern bank to Northcoats Point.

Eyebrook Reservoir** OS141

Flooded in 1940 this well-established reservoir remains one of the best in the area, despite competition from Rutland Water and Grafham.

Trout have made the reservoir a favourite haunt of fishermen, but other than for this summer sport the water is strictly protected and holds excellent numbers of winter wildfowl and passage waders. An area of marsh-like habitat at the northern end near the inlet is always worth a good look and frequently produces waders and Bewick's Swan. Wigeon and Mallard are the most numerous of a diverse duck population.

Winter Great Crested Grebe, Bewick's Swan, Canada Goose, Mallard, Wigeon, Teal, Shoveler, Gadwall, Pochard, Tufted Duck, Goldeneye, Goosander

Passage Greenshank, Redshank, Wood Sandpiper, Green Sandpiper, Ruff, Little Stint, Curlew Sandpiper, Black Tern, Common Tern

Leave the A47 southwards at Uppingham on the A6003 to Caldicote or take that road northwards from Kettering. Turn westwards to Stoke Dry and then to the reservoir.

Fowlmere*   OS154

A disused watercress bed that has become a reed swamp and which is now an RSPB reserve. Surrounded by intensive arable farming the marsh, reed bed and surrounding scrub act as an oasis for breeding and passage birds.

Summer Little Grebe, Water Rail, Reed Warbler, Sedge Warbler, Whitethroat, Lesser Whitethroat, Blackcap

Winter Hen Harrier, Green Sandpiper, Kingfisher, Fieldfare, Redwing, Redpoll, Siskin

Leave Royston northwards on the A10 to Melbourne. Turn right towards Fowlmere where the reserve lies south of the village at OS Ref: TL407461.

Gibraltar Point***   OS122

Gibraltar Point is the site of a bird observatory and field research station strategically situated on the northern shore at the mouth of the Wash 5km (3m) south of Skegness. It is an LNR and, though the emphasis is on migration, winter brings numbers of divers, grebes and sea-duck, while there is usually a large flock of Snow Buntings, and a few Shore Larks and Lapland Buntings. Passage waders pass through and terns and skuas are noted offshore, often in some numbers. Almost anything can turn up here.

Winter Divers, sea-duck, Hen Harrier, Rough-legged Buzzard, Great Grey Shrike, Oystercatcher, Bar-tailed Godwit, Knot, Shore Lark, Snow Bunting, Lapland Bunting

Spring Waders, chats, warblers

Summer Little Tern, Ringed Plover
Autumn Pink-footed Goose, Whimbrel, Bar-tailed Godwit, Green Sandpiper, Wood Sandpiper, Spotted Redshank, Curlew Sandpiper, Ruff, Commic and Black Terns, skuas, chats, warblers, flycatchers, rarities, diurnal migrants

Leave Skegness southwards to Gibraltar Point. Accommodation is available at the Observatory which is used as a base for ringing courses. Write to: The Warden, Gibraltar Point Bird Observatory and Field Station, via Skegness, Lincs.

Grafham Water** OS153

When flooded in the 1960s this was the largest inland water in England and an obvious attraction to wildfowl and passage birds. Intensive leisure exploitation has prevented the area from fulfilling its potential. It has, however, built up a good population of winter duck when fishing has stopped and sailing is reduced. Mallard, Teal, Wigeon and Tufted Duck all reach good numbers and Goldeneye and Goosander are regularly present. Spring and autumn brings a good variety of terns and waders, though the nature reserve at the shallow western end is disturbed.

Winter Mallard, Teal, Gadwall, Wigeon, Shoveler, Pochard, Tufted Duck, Goldeneye
Summer Great Crested Grebe, Little Grebe, Water Rail, Shoveler, Gadwall, Garganey, Shelduck, Redshank, Ringed Plover, Little Ringed Plover
Passage Common Sandpiper, godwits, Greenshank, Redshank, Common Tern, Black Tern, Little Gull

Leave the A1 at Buckden westwards on the B661. There are many good car parks around the reservoir, and there is a hide reached from the sailing club car park. Access to the reserve is by permit only.

The Lodge* OS153

The Lodge, Sandy, Bedfordshire, is the headquarters of the RSPB replete with 42ha (104a). Since its purchase in 1961 the grounds have become a well-managed bird reserve. The oaks and Scot's pines are rich in typical woodland birds, and there are more open areas of sandy heath and birch scrub, as well as three ponds. An artificial, polythene-lined lake has added considerably to the birds to be found here. Careful management has encouraged over 130 species to appear, and an average of some 50 species breed. All three woodpeckers, the typical warblers, Spotted Flycatchers, Goldcrests and so on provide good opportunities to learn more about regular woodland birds. Despite the wealth of expertise watching out of the windows and during lunch breaks, comparatively few rarities have been recorded – though Marsh

43

and Hen Harriers, Osprey, Black Tern and Whimbrel show that the staff do keep an eye open from time to time.

Summer   Woodcock, Lesser Spotted Woodpecker, Tree Pipit, Redstart, Lesser Whitethroat, Blackcap, Garden Warbler, Redpoll

Leave Sandy on the A603 and the entrance is well marked on the right after 3km (2m). It is open weekdays 9.00 a.m. to 5 p.m. throughout the year. On summer Saturdays 10.00 a.m. to 5.00 p.m.; and to members and guests only 10.00 a.m. to 5.00 p.m. on summer Sundays. *Tel*: (0767) 80551.

Nene Washes**   OS142

After the Somerset Levels and the nearby Ouse Washes, the floods along the Nene, between Peterborough and Guyhirn, are the most important floodlands in Britain. Though overshadowed by their more famous neighbour to the south, the Nene Washes are significant both for their wintering and breeding birds. Indeed they act as safety nets for birds driven by high water from the Ouse Washes. The number of breeding wildfowl thus varies considerably. Though much of the area is now arable the RSPB have established a reserve near Whittlesey that protects some of the best floodland.

Winter brings up to 6000 Wigeon, 3000 Teal, 1200 Pochard and 2000 Pintail. Golden Plover and Lapwing are abundant, and in spring the flock of Bewick's Swans may build up to 1000. Hen Harrier and Short-eared Owl are also found. In summer, apart from duck, there are Yellow Wagtail and Sedge Warbler.

Winter   Bewick's Swan, Wigeon, Teal, Pintail, Pochard, Hen Harrier, Golden Plover, Short-eared Owl
Summer   Duck, Yellow Wagtail, Sedge Warbler

Leave Peterborough eastwards on the A47 and turn right on the B1040 at Thornley. Though much can be seen from the road, the reserve can be visited via The Warden, 59 Headlands Way, Whittlesey, Cambs.

Northampton Reservoirs**   OS141

The reservoirs at Pitsford, Ravensthorpe and Hollowell are mature waters lying a few km north of Northampton and are noted bird haunts in an otherwise rather thin area. Pitsford is one of the country's top birding reservoirs with large flocks of diving duck, especially Pochard, and Bewick's Swan are regular. Tern and wader passage is often very good, and a winter gull roost attracts the occasional Glaucous. Hollowell and Ravensthorpe lie close together to the west. Of the two Hollowell is generally best, but Ravensthorpe should not be ignored. A good duck population winters. Hollowell has good numbers of most common duck and regularly produces some of the scarcer species.

Winter	Bewick's Swan, Canada Goose, Mallard, Wigeon, Shoveler, Pintail, Tufted Duck, Pochard, Goldeneye, Goosander
Summer	Great Crested Grebe, Little Grebe, Redshank, Sedge Warbler
Passage	Little Ringed Plover, Green Sandpiper, Wood Sandpiper, Curlew Sandpiper, Greenshank, Ruff, Common Tern, Black Tern

Pitsford Leave Northampton northwards on the A50 and keep right on the A508 after 3km (2m). Turn right at Brixworth to the causeway. OS Ref: SP783701.

Hollowell Leave Northampton northwards on the A50 and turn left to Hollowell after 15km (9¼m). Fork right in the village and continue towards Guisborough. The reservoir can be seen on the right. Access by permission of Anglian Water Authority, Cliftonville, Northampton.

Ravensthorpe Leave Hollowell opposite the main entrance and continue to the causeway across the reservoir. OS Ref: SP675712.

Nottingham Gravel Pits* OS129

Around Nottingham the Trent Valley is rich in gravel deposits and the construction industry has created a series of gravel pits that have become immediately inundated. They offer some of the best bird-watching in this part of the country with duck and Canada Goose flocks often reaching good numbers and passage migrants including waders and terns. There are new pits being created continuously and, while they are all worthy of exploration, the older mature pits generally attract larger numbers and a greater variety of birds. Those at Attenborough are a Nottinghamshire TNC reserve, but other well-established pits can be found at Gunthorpe, Hoveringham and Radcliffe. Though not a gravel pit, Martin's Pond west of the city is an LNR with grebes and Water Rail, passage waders and a good breeding population.

Winter	Great Crested Grebe, Shoveler, Pintail, Wigeon, Teal, Tufted Duck, Pochard, Goldeneye, Goosander, Water Rail, Green Sandpiper, Snipe
Summer	Little Ringed Plover, Yellow Wagtail, Grasshopper Warbler, Reed Warbler
Autumn	Greenshank, Green Sandpiper, Common Sandpiper, Dunlin, Black Tern, Common Tern

Attenborough Take the A6005 (former A453) southwards from Nottingham and then from Beeston Rylands to Attenborough. Past the station there is a car park at the Strand. This area is a reserve, keep to footpaths. OS Ref: SK521343.

Gunthorpe Leave Nottingham on the A612 northeast toward Lowdham. Turn right to Gunthorpe. At the bridge, park on the right and walk upstream beside the Trent. Cross a bridge where a tributary joins the Trent and bear right. This gives good views of the pits.

Hoveringham Leave Nottingham on the A612 to Lowdham. Turn right and then left to Caythorpe. After a sharp corner turn right through Hoveringham. As the road bends beyond the village watch for a stream and a bridle path on the right.

Martin's Pond Leave Nottingham westward on the A609 and turn right into Russell Avenue, Wollaton after 1km (½m). The reserve is at the end of the road, access via a public footpath.

Ouse Washes***** OS143

When the Fenland south of the Wash was drained, 'washes' were created where surplus water could be stored until it could be accommodated in the newly straightened rivers. They are thus a safety valve.

The Ouse Washes traditionally flood in February and March and are then the haunt of one of the greatest collections of wildfowl and waders in the country. However, since 1964 large areas of this splendid wetland have been acquired by conservation bodies and the Washes are now managed as much for the birds as they are for flood control. The result is that a splendid wetland has been converted into a series of absolutely first-class bird reserves.

Today the RSPB, the Cambridgeshire and Isle of Ely Naturalists' Trust (CAMBIENT) and the Wildfowl Trust own over half of the total 1100ha (2700a). Since 1952 Black-tailed Godwits have bred and now number over 50 pairs. Ruff returned soon after, and Black Terns have done so erratically. In 1975 a pair of Little Gulls bred. Nine species of duck together with the more usual waders and Short-eared Owls breed among the total of 50 species to be found here in the summer.

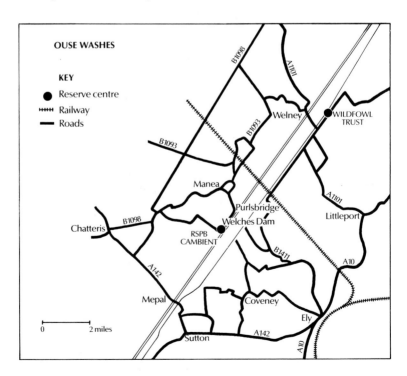

Wildfowl in winter remain the primary attraction. Pintail (3500), Shoveler (1000), Teal (7500), Pochard (5500), and Mallard (7000) make this a site of international importance, but 42,500 Wigeon represent a quarter of the UK total for this species. Some 20 per cent of the world population of Bewick's Swan winter along with lesser numbers of Whoopers. The deeper waters of the cuts attract all three sawbills, and there are good numbers of great Crested Grebes.

During passage periods a variety of waders and terns may be seen, including numbers of Black Terns, Wood and Green Sandpipers, Greenshank, Little Stint and others.

Winter   Bewick's Swan, Whooper Swan, Wigeon, Pintail, Teal, Pochard, Shoveler, Hen Harrier, Golden Plover, Ruff, Redshank, Short-eared Owl

Spring   Greenshank, Snipe, Black Tern, Little Gull, Little Owl

Summer   Black-tailed Godwit, Ruff, Redshank, Snipe, Little Owl, Redpoll

Autumn   Greenshank, Little Stint, Curlew Sandpiper, Ruff, Black-tailed Godwit, Black Tern

RSPB and CAMBIENT Reserves   Leave the A142 at Chatteris eastwards on the B1098. After 10km (6m) turn right to Manea. Continue to Welches Dam where there is a visitor's centre and access to the Barrier Bank which has nine different hides open free of charge at all times. Please read the simple rules carefully to avoid disturbing the birds and also your own chances of good views.

Wildfowl Trust   Return to Manea and continue northwards on the B1093 to Welney. Cross the Washes eastwards, stopping for views over the surrounding floods, and then turn left to the Trust's observatory and hides. On winter evenings the wild swans can be seen by floodlight. There are unescorted visits daily and warden-escorted visits on Saturdays and Sundays. *Tel*: Ely 860711.

Rutland Water**   OS141

The largest inland water in England occupying 1200ha (3000a) to the west of the A1 near Peterborough. This huge lake is inevitably subject to considerable disturbance, but attracts large numbers of duck as well as passage waders and terns. Teal, Shoveler, Pochard, Goldeneye all winter and Bewick's Swans are often present. Despite its size most of the area can be seen from surrounding roads and car parks and is almost cut in half by a long peninsula extending from the west. The northern part is partially a nature reserve, though this does not mean that birds are confined to this section.

Winter   Great Crested Grebe, Teal, Wigeon, Shoveler, Tufted Duck, Pochard, Goldeneye, Goosander

Passage   Wood Sandpiper, Green Sandpiper, Spotted Redshank, Greenshank, Ruff, Snipe, Turnstone, Common Tern, Black Tern, Little Gull

Leave the A1 westwards near Stamford on the A606 to Oakham. Turn southwards on the A6003 and left at Manton on an unclassified road to Edith Weston and northwards to Empingham. There are car parks and view points at various places along this route. Access to the reserve is via the interpretive centre of the Lincolnshire and Rutland NT at Lyndon Hill, itself worth a visit.

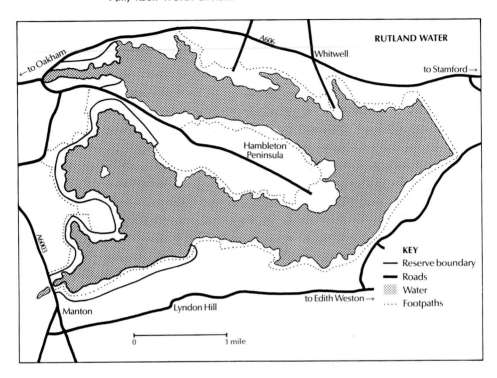

Saltfleetby-Theddlethorpe**   OS122

This NNR covers some 8km (5m) of coastline between Saltfleet Haven and Mablethorpe and offers a wide variety of habitats from dunes, scrub and grassland to a large freshwater marsh, saltmarsh and open sand and mud flats. Formerly a bombing range this area has now become popular with birders and produces a good variety of interest at all seasons. In winter the common waders are often abundant and a variety of wildfowl include Brent Goose. Hen and Marsh Harriers are regular, and Snow Buntings flit along the shore. The marsh area attracts Water Rail to breed and during passage there are terns and skuas, a variety of waders and a fair passage of small birds.

Winter Brent Goose, Hen Harrier, Marsh Harrier, Knot, Snow Bunting
Spring Marsh Harrier, waders, small migrants
Summer Shelduck, Water Rail, Ringed Plover, Snipe, Redshank, Short-eared Owl
Autumn Sandwich Tern, Common Tern, Arctic Skua, Greenshank, Wood Sandpiper, Little Stint, chats, flycatchers, warblers

There are about six tracks leading from the A1031 to public car parks distributed along the length of the reserve. The most popular and varied habitat is at the Rimac entrance, 2km (1¼m) south of Saltfleet. The only restrictions on access are because of RAF regulations on their bombing range. *Tel*: (050 783) 632.

Stanford Reservoir* OS140

Stanford offers birding in what is otherwise a rather dull area just·east of the M1 at its junction with the M6. It may not be brilliant, but it is better than nothing. Winter brings a good selection of wildfowl, though in no great number, while passage produces waders and a few terns.

Winter Great Crested Grebe, Wigeon, Shoveler, Pochard, Goosander
Passage Common Sandpiper, Green Sandpiper, Common Tern, Black Tern

Leave the M1 at Exit 20 eastwards on the A427 toward Market Harborough. Turn right in North Kilworth and continue through South Kilworth. Turn left toward Welford and view from the bridge.

Tring Reservoirs* OS165

These old reservoirs were constructed on the site of a former marsh to supply the Grand Union Canal and were made ornithologically famous by the breeding of the Little Ringed Plover in 1938, the first in Britain. They are now an NNR and are visited by the staff of the BTO and British

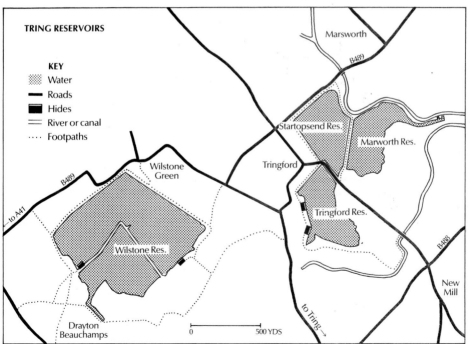

Museum (Nat.Hist.) Bird Room, which are nearby. Wildfowl are good here with Teal and Shoveler, as well as the three common species, all present throughout the winter. Bewick's Swan and Goosander appear and there is a flock of Greylags during the summer as well as ground-nesting Herons. Passage waders were good in autumn, but have recently declined. It is one of these places that produce birds partly because of intensive watching.

Winter   Bewick's Swan, Mallard, Teal, Wigeon, Shoveler, Pochard, Tufted Duck, Goosander

Summer   Great Crested Grebe, Little Grebe, Greylag Goose, Grey Heron, Pochard, Shoveler, Reed Warbler

Passage   Ringed Plover, Little Ringed Plover, Greenshank, Green Sandpiper, Little Stint, Curlew Sandpiper, Black Tern, Common Tern

Leave the A41 between Tring and Aylesbury northwards on the B489 at Aston Clinton. Footpaths run around all four reservoirs, and there are hides and a nature trail.

The Wash – Lincolnshire***   OS122/131

The Wash is one of Europe's top estuaries and holds enormous numbers of birds at all seasons. Huge numbers of waders pause here in autumn and, though some move on, many remain to be joined by hosts of wildfowl. Up to a quarter of a million waders may use the area each year.

Outstanding are the flocks of Brent that occur around the Nene and Welland outfalls and those of Pinkfeet that flight to roost near the Nene. Both species number about 3000, but between 5000 and 10,000 may occur sometimes. Shelduck and Wigeon flocks too can be huge here.

Waders are always present, but high-tide roosts occur at Wainfleet, Bennington, Welland Mouth, Holbeach St Matthew and Dawsmere. These often involve tens of thousands of birds with up to 70,000 Knot and 40,000 Dunlin dominant. They may be joined by 15,000 Oyster-catchers and 6000 Redshank (autumn). Of course, such numbers do not occur all at once, or at a single site, but they do give a clear indication of the possibilities.

Unfortunately the shoreline is fringed by extensive saltings a km or more wide, so that the visitor is often confronted by a low horizon of olive-green saltmarsh without a single bird in sight. The problems are daunting, but the birds are there. Careful planning, especially to coincide with periods of the highest tides, is the best bet. At such times even the saltings are covered by the sea, and tens of thousands of waders are forced over the sea wall to roost on the adjacent fields.

As if this were not enough The Wash also attracts many predators including Marsh and Hen Harriers, Merlin, Short-eared and Long-eared Owls, plus about half the British winter population of Twite.

Winter   Bewick's Swan, Pink-footed Goose, Brent Goose, Shelduck, Wigeon, Teal, Pintail, Shoveler, Scaup, Red-breasted Merganser, Hen Harrier,

	Marsh Harrier, Merlin, Oystercatcher, Grey Plover, Turnstone, Dunlin, Knot, Sanderling, Redshank, Bar-tailed Godwit, Curlew, Short-eared Owl, Twite
Summer Passage	Oystercatcher, Redshank, Common Tern, Black-headed Gull Ringed Plover, Whimbrel, Greenshank, Redshank, Black-tailed Godwit

Access is everywhere awkward, and the most that can be achieved is a sample of birds present at high tide — preferably the highest tides.

Nene Leave the A17 at Sutton Bridge on the western side of the river. Take the more westerly road northwards, not the one alongside the river. Good for geese.

Holbeach Leave the A17 at Chapelgate northwards on to the B1359. Leave this left after 4km (2½m) signposted Holbeach St Matthew. Continue through the village and along banks to the sea wall. Walk out to Flushing Creek Wall. Wildfowl and wader roosts.

Kirton and Frampton Marshes Follow minor roads east from the A16 at Wyberton to the sea bank and Frampton Marsh. Leave the A16 eastwards on a minor road at Kirton to the sea bank at Marine Villa for Kirton Marshes. Wader roost, huge Black-headed gullery, raptors.

Boston Point and Frieston Shore Leave Boston south-eastwards on a maze of lanes to Fishtoft. At Nunn's Bridge explore southwards on the eastern shore along Hobhole Drain where Long-eared Owls roost in winter in thick hedges. Return to the bridge, cross and continue to the sea wall. Walk for 2km (1¼m) to Boston Point for a wader roost. Return to Fishtoft, turn right to Frieston and then to Frieston Shore. Walk northwards.

Wrangle-Friskney Large numbers of tracks lead from the A52 to the shore. Some are private and very muddy. A metalled track 2km (1¼m) north of Wrangle past Marsh Farm seems satisfactory.

See also Gibraltar Point.

Wicken Fen* OS142/143

Wicken Fen is a small remnant of what the original Fens might have been like. It has been maintained intact by its owners, the National Trust, by manipulation of the water levels and is now an impenetrable wilderness of sedges, reeds and thorn, intersected by wide rides.

A mere of 4ha (10a) has been excavated on the neighbouring Adventurer's Fen and the whole was declared a sanctuary in 1957. The area is attractive at all seasons but principally in winter for duck, and in summer for breeding marsh birds, though passage periods often bring a touch of the unusual including Hobby, Great Grey Shrike and the occasional Spotted Crake.

Winter	Hen Harrier, Wigeon, Shoveler, Bittern, Bearded Tit, Great Grey Shrike
Summer	Great Crested Grebe, Water Rail, Snipe, Woodcock, Redshank, Grass-hopper Warbler, Sedge Warbler, Reed Warbler, Long-eared Owl

The Fen is reached from either the A142 westwards, or the A10 eastwards on to the B1085. The village of Wicken lies roughly half-way between these roads. At the western end of the village turn southwards for 300m (328yd) down a track marked Wicken Fen. For advice and information contact: Warden's House, Lode Lane, Wicken, Ely CB7 5XP for permit. Open daily with access to tower hide.

Wisbech Sewage Farm* OS143

For long a famed haunt of waders and their watchers, Wisbech Sewage Farm has, like so many others, undergone a thorough modernization. Instead of large flooded fields and delightful, if smelly, settling beds there are now filters and pumps. A small area does, however, remain, and there are plans afoot to persuade the appropriate authorities to declare this remnant a monument and bird reserve. Should these efforts succeed then a nineteenth-century process will be preserved for posterity and waders will still come to the farm.

Wisbech is best during spring and autumn when sandpipers and stints gather in good numbers, often with a rarity tagging along. American waders are far from unknown here and up to 150 Curlew Sandpipers have been counted.

Spring Wood Sandpiper, Green Sandpiper, Spotted Redshank, Greenshank, Temminck's Stint

Autumn Curlew Sandpiper, Little Stint, Ruff, Spotted Redshank, Greenshank, Wood Sandpiper, Green Sandpiper

Leave Wisbech northwards on the A47, turning left on an unclassified road at Walpole Highway. Follow signs to Walpole St Peter, keeping left to Walpole Island. Here a track leads to the embankment along the Ouse past the northern edge of the Farm. Turn southwards to the best areas.

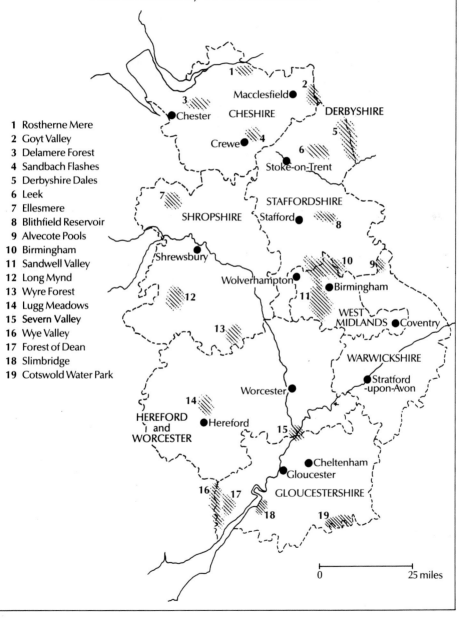

West Midlands

Cheshire, Derbyshire, Gloucestershire,
Herefordshire, Shropshire, Staffordshire,
Warwickshire, Worcestershire

1 Rostherne Mere
2 Goyt Valley
3 Delamere Forest
4 Sandbach Flashes
5 Derbyshire Dales
6 Leek
7 Ellesmere
8 Blithfield Reservoir
9 Alvecote Pools
10 Birmingham
11 Sandwell Valley
12 Long Mynd
13 Wyre Forest
14 Lugg Meadows
15 Severn Valley
16 Wye Valley
17 Forest of Dean
18 Slimbridge
19 Cotswold Water Park

Alvecote Pools*   OS140

Extensive areas of mining subsidence along the River Tame have created this series of shallow pools that lie east of Tamworth and provide a wealth of rich habitat including open water, reed marsh, damp bog and thorn. The area is a reserve of the West Midland Trust for Nature Preservation.

The commoner duck are frequently present in large numbers. Wader passage is heavy, especially in autumn when Black Terns also pass through. The reserve is extensively used by school parties for field work and by fishermen in winter, and is an excellent example of co-operation of different interests.

Winter Teal, Wigeon, Tufted Duck, Pochard, Snipe
Spring Waders, terns
Summer Snipe, Redshank, Reed Warbler, Lesser Whitethroat, Kingfisher
Autumn Little Ringed Plover, Common Sandpiper, Greenshank, Ruff, Black Tern, 'Commic' terns

Leave Tamworth eastwards on the A51 and turn left under the railway viaduct on to an unclassified road signposted Amington. Continue to the pools, most of which can be seen from the road at OS Ref: SK254047. Excellent bird-watching with a permit from the West Midland TNP.

Birmingham*   OS139

The visitor to Birmingham is well served by motorways by which to make his escape. To the north Blithfield Reservoir is a major attraction, while to the west the Wyre Forest is a splendid summer spot. If time is short he may have to settle for one of the smaller and closer reservoirs such as Bittell or Bartley Reservoirs in the south, or Cannock, Gailey or Belvide to the north. All hold winter wildfowl and the odd passage wader or tern, but Cannock, set in an uncomprisingly industrialized landscape, does have the wilds of Cannock Chase immediately to the north. Here it is even possible to find Red Grouse, Redstart and Wood Warbler.

Winter Canada Goose, Teal, Wigeon, Pochard, Goldeneye
Summer Great Crested Grebe
Passage Ringed Plover, Snipe, Common Sandpiper, Green Sandpiper, Greenshank

Bartley Leave Birmingham to Selly Oak and turn right through a maze of lanes to Bartley Green. Take the narrow road from the roundabout south past the western end of the reservoir.

Bittell Leave the M5 at Exit 4 eastwards on the A38 and turn southwards (right) to Barnt Green. At the causeway across the smaller pool stop, and turn sharp right up a narrow lane to view the upper reservoir.

Gailey Leave the M6 at Exit 12 and view from the A5. Permits can be obtained from the West Midland Bird Club.

Cannock Leave the A5 just east of its junction with the A452 near Brownhills. Turn north into Wilkin Road or Hednesford Road and after 1km (½m) turn right on to an industrial track to the reservoir. For Cannock Chase continue northwards.

Belvide Leave Cannock westwards on the A5. The reservoir lies to the south after 10km (6m) and can be seen from the road and via a track at the western end.

See also Sandwell Valley.

Blithfield Reservoir** OS128

This large Staffordshire water has always been highly rated by reservoir birders and has maintained its place as one of the top ten such waters in the country. Flooded in 1952, it has Teal and Wigeon numbering over 1000 and twice as many Mallard. Shoveler, Pochard and Tufted Duck are regular, and Bewick's Swan are frequently present. Its natural banks attract waders, and Black Terns are as regular as anywhere in this region.

Winter Great Crested Grebe, Bewick's Swan, Canada Goose, Mallard, Teal, Shoveler, Wigeon, Pochard, Tufted Duck, Goldeneye, Goosander, Snipe

Spring Little Ringed Plover, Common Tern, Black Tern

Autumn Whimbrel, Little Stint, Curlew Sandpiper, Green Sandpiper, Wood Sandpiper, Greenshank, Redshank, Ruff, Little Gull, Black Tern, Common Tern

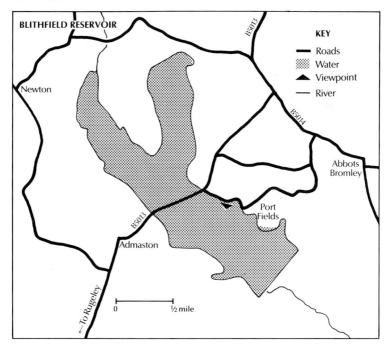

55

Leave Rugeley northwards on the B5013 to the reservoir causeway in 7km (4¼m). A road southwards on the east side gives good early morning views. OS Ref: SK058238.

Cotswold Water Park* OS163

Extensive gravel extraction south of Cirencester has created an important series of pits and a major wetland in this part of the country. In all some 400ha (1000a) have been created, offering good numbers of winter duck, including really significant flocks of Pochard. In summer Little Ringed Plover are really quite numerous. Passage waders and terns can be good, with Black Tern quite regular.

Winter   Teal, Gadwall, Wigeon, Pochard, Tufted Duck, Goldeneye
Summer   Great Crested Grebe, Little Grebe, Tufted Duck, Little Ringed Plover
Passage   Common Sandpiper, Green Sandpiper, Redshank, Greenshank, Common Tern, Black Tern

Leave Cirencester southwards on the A419 and turn right to South Cerney. Explore with the aid of OS. Follow minor roads eastwards to a further group of pits between Fairford and Lechlade south of the A417. Exploration is the key as birds tend to move about, depending on disturbance.

Delamere Forest* OS117

Lies largely north of the Chester–Northwich road, the A54, and is basically a conifer forest with small areas of mixed and deciduous woodland. It offers good birding, particularly in summer, when a good variety of species can be found including Crossbill, Hawfinch and Pied Flycatcher. The whole is Crown property with extensive Forestry Commission areas.

Summer   Long-eared Owl, Nightjar, Redstart, Pied Flycatcher, Tree Pipit, Hawfinch, Siskin

Leave Chester eastwards on the A51 and fork left on to the A54 just before Tarvin. Fork left again on to the A556 beyond Kelsall. At the crossroads with the B5152 turn left. Cross the railway at Delamere Station and turn left after 1½km (1m). Explore the forest along numerous tracks and paths that are clearly marked on both sides of the road.

Derbyshire Dales* OS119

Of all the beautiful valleys of this southern outpost of the Pennines, Lathkill Dale and Dovedale are the gems. Both have fine, tumbling young streams with wooded banks and both are beautiful and good for birds. Dovedale is the most frequented by tourists. Dipper, Grey

Wagtail, Redstart and Wood Warbler breed and Sparrowhawk may frequently be seen.

Summer Sparrowhawk, Dipper, Grey Wagtail, Wheatear, Redstart, Tree Pipit, Wood Warbler

Dovedale Leave Ashbourne northwards on the A515 and turn left after 2km (1¼m). There is a car park near Thorpe and foot access northwards.

Lathkill Dale Leave Bakewell westwards and turn left toward Alport on a minor road that crosses the valley. Explore along good footpaths.

Ellesmere* OS126

Around and to the south-east of Ellesmere lie a group of natural lakes that offer some of the best birding in Shropshire. Largest is Ellesmere itself, right next to the town and very picturesque. It is, of course, well used in summer, but has winter duck. Other meres include Cole Mere, White Mere, Blake Mere, Crose Mere and Newton Mere. All are worth a look, and in autumn Black Tern and Black-necked Grebe pass through.

Summer Great Crested Grebe, Little Grebe, Canada Goose, Reed Warbler, Sedge Warbler

Autumn Black-necked Grebe, Common Sandpiper, Green Sandpiper, Common Tern, Black Tern

Winter Wigeon, Shoveler, Pochard, Goldeneye, Goosander

Ellesmere Adjacent to the town.

White Mere 2km (1¼m) south on A528.

Cole Mere Turn left from A528 at north end of White Mere and after 1½km (1m) turn left in village to track along southern side of the Mere.

Blake Mere Stop at junction of A528 and A495 and walk eastwards along canal towpath.

Newton Mere Turn left from A528 on A495 and take first right to south side of the Mere.

Forest of Dean* OS162

The National Forest Park consists of a huge area that has been forested since time immemorial. The birds here represent as complete a hardwood community as can be found anywhere in the country. Though the whole is worth exploring, the best area lies in the south-west where, naturally enough, the RSPB established their Nags-head Reserve. Notable is a large population of Pied Flycatchers along with Wood and other warblers, Buzzard, Sparrowhawk and, along the stream, Grey Wagtail and Dipper.

Summer Buzzard, Sparrowhawk, Nightjar, Raven, Dipper, Grey Wagtail, Tree Pipit, Greater Spotted Woodpecker, Lesser Spotted Woodpecker, Pied Flycatcher, Redstart, Wood Warbler, Grasshopper Warbler, Siskin, Hawfinch

57

The forest lies between the rivers Severn and Wye and between the A4136 to Monmouth and the A48 to Chepstow. Access is generally unrestricted. The RSPB's Nagshead Reserve is found by leaving the A48 northwards to Parkend and continuing from there westwards on the B4431 for 1km (½m) to OS Ref: SO606080.

Goyt Valley*   OS118

From its origins high on Goyt's Moss the river drops down via Errwood and Fernilee Reservoirs to Taxal near Whaley Bridge. This beautiful valley is justly famous and attracts many visitors apart from bird-watchers. As a result it is now partially a traffic-free zone. The stream holds Dipper, Grey Wagtail and Common Sandpiper while the woods are alive with chats and warblers. The open moors have Curlew, Golden Plover and Red Grouse.

Summer Great Crested Grebe, Little Grebe, Red Grouse, Curlew, Golden Plover, Woodcock, Common Sandpiper, Short-eared Owl, Kingfisher, Great Spotted Woodpecker, Lesser Spotted Woodpecker, Dipper, Grey Wagtail, Whinchat, Wheatear, Ring Ousel, Redstart, Tree Pipit, Wood Warbler

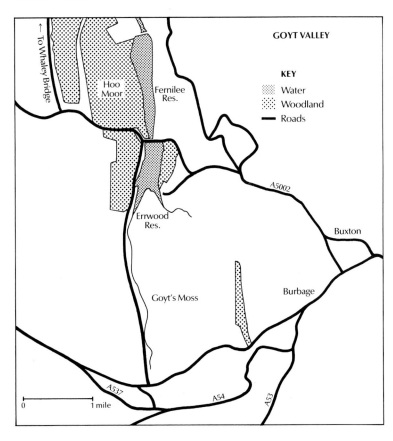

Leave Buxton westwards on the A53 and turn right on the A54 and right again on the A537. After 200m (220yd) turn right and in 400m (440yd) right again. There is a car park at the north end of Errwood Reservoir. Walk down one side of the valley and return along the other.

Leek*   OS118

The hills around Leek are disected by a series of deeply cut valleys that are beautiful, well-wooded and full of birds. Over the years the RSPB has built up a considerable holding in the area with the famous Coombs Valley as its centrepiece. The Society also has reserves at Rough Knipe and Booth's Wood. Coombs Valley lies along the Coombs Brook, and its birds are typical of such upland wooded valleys. The Sparrowhawk is the major predator with typical birds including all three woodpeckers, Pied Flycatcher, Wood Warbler, Grey Wagtail, Dipper, Woodcock and Kingfisher.

Summer   Sparrowhawk, Woodcock, Tawny Owl, Long-eared Owl, Dipper, Kingfisher, Great Spotted Woodpecker, Lesser Spotted Woodpecker, Green Woodpecker, Grey Wagtail, Tree Pipit, Pied Flycatcher, Redstart, Wood Warbler, Willow Warbler

Leave Leek south-eastwards on the A523. Take left turn signposted Apesford and the reserve entrance is on the left after 2km (1¼m). Booth's Wood and Rough Knipe are approached via the A520 turning left to Consall and continuing on a public footpath.

Long Mynd*   OS137

Situated in the south-west of Shropshire, near the Welsh border, the upland qualities of this extensive area of moorland give it a bird population with closer affinities to that country than to neighbouring England. The wooded valleys and streams hold the usual species.

Summer   Red Grouse, Ring Ouzel, Whinchat, Grey Wagtail, Dipper, Pied Flycatcher, Wood Warbler, Redstart

Leave Shrewsbury southwards on the A49 and turn right on to the B4370 to Church Stretton. Carding Mill Valley is worth exploring and the whole area is of generally unrestricted access.

Lugg Meadows*   OS149

The meadows border the River Lugg to the north-east of Hereford, just before it joins the Wye. They are divided into Upper and Lower Meadows and lie north and south of the A465. In winter the meadows flood, and wildfowl are plentiful. A few waders including Jack Snipe occur most years.

Winter   Wigeon, Teal, Pintail, Shoveler, Pochard, waders

Leave Hereford on the A465 or A438 and stop at Lugg Bridge; there is a path along the river bank.

Rostherne Mere**   OS109

Largest and most famous of the Cheshire Meres, Rostherne is 132ha (326a) in extent, surrounded by dense scrub and reeds and is best known as a refuge for large numbers of duck. It is an NNR with no public access. Mallard are particularly numerous, but Teal, Wigeon, Pintail and Shoveler also occur in good numbers. There is a moult gathering of Canada Geese and a substantial gull roost in winter. In summer it holds Great Crested and occasional Little Grebe, Reed Warbler and Canada Goose. Passage brings a few terns including Black. A total of 161 species have been seen.

Winter   Canada Goose, Mallard, Wigeon, Teal, Shoveler, Pintail, Tufted Duck, Pochard, Gadwall, Goldeneye, Goosander, Water Rail
Summer   Great Crested Grebe, Little Grebe, Canada Goose, Tufted Duck
Passage   Bewick's Swan, Whooper Swan, Common Tern, Arctic Tern, Black Tern

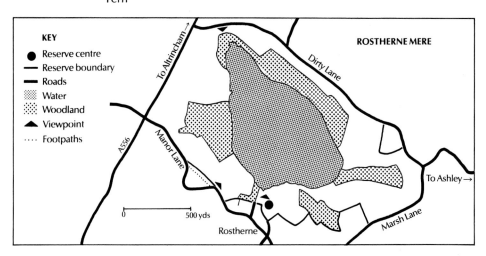

Leave the M56 at Exit 8 and follow the A556 toward Altrincham. Turn right along Manor Lane to Rostherne village. The mere can be viewed from the churchyard where there is also the A.W. Boyd Memorial Observatory. Permits to use the hide can be obtained on an annual basis (for a fee) from the Manchester Ornithological Society, 13 Kingston Drive, Sale M33 2FS, but are unnecessary for a casual visit; views can be obtained from several places along the surrounding lanes. Nearby Tatton Park Mere at Knutsford also holds birds, but is much disturbed by leisure activities.

Sandbach Flashes**   OS118

This area lies between Elworth and Elton Hall, north-west of Crewe and 3km (2m) from Sandbach and comprises four large sheets of water, created by subsidence due to salt mining, surrounded by marsh and wet pasture. A wide variety of species breed and the flashes are the best inland place in the region for wader passage.

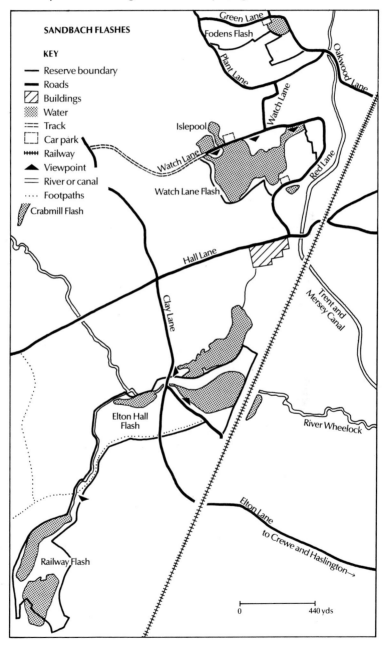

SANDBACH FLASHES

KEY

— Reserve boundary
▬ Roads
▨ Buildings
▦ Water
≡≡ Track
☐ Car park
⊢⊢⊢⊢ Railway
▲ Viewpoint
= River or canal
···· Footpaths
▨ Crabmill Flash

0   440 yds

Winter Wigeon, Pochard, Goldeneye
Summer Great Crested Grebe, Tufted Duck, Teal, Redshank, Common Sandpiper, Little Ringed Plover
Autumn Green Sandpiper, Greenshank, Ringed Plover, Spotted Redshank, Little Stint, Curlew Sandpiper, Ruff

The flashes are managed as a nature reserve by the Cheshire CT. Permits are neither issued nor necessary for ordinary bird-watching which is perfectly adequate from the maze of lanes in the area. Leave Middlewich southwards on the A533 alongside the Trent and Mersey Canal to Sandbach. Continue straight on and follow the unclassified road before turning left to the first of the flashes. Follow the OS for the other flashes. Members of the Cheshire CT may obtain a detailed map and access notes from the secretary. There is access off the M6 at Exit 17.

Sandwell Valley*   OS139

Sandwell lies just 7km (4¼m) from the heart of Birmingham and offers good birding to a huge number of visitors. Indeed it is nothing less than a green oasis surrounded by urban sprawl. A large lake together with pools, marsh and scrub attract good numbers of birds and the RSPB manages a section of the valley as a reserve with an impressive nature centre. Though primarily seen as an educational centre there are always birds of interest.

Spring Green Sandpiper, Wheatear, Yellow Wagtail
Summer Great Crested Grebe, Little Grebe, Canada Goose, Tufted Duck, Little Ringed Plover, Sedge Warbler
Autumn Waders
Winter Snipe, Jack Snipe, Long-eared Owl

The Sandwell Nature Centre lies near the junction of the M6 and M5 to the north-west of the city. Up-to-date details of access from the RSPB.

Severn Valley*   OS150

The lower reaches of the Severn Valley are often flooded in autumn and winter and attract duck in quite decent numbers along with a variety of passage waders. The best area is around the disused canal at Coombe where even a few Whitefronts may appear from time to time. To the north the area around Tewkesbury has long been famous for its meadows with summer visitors such as Reed Warbler, Yellow Wagtail and notably Marsh Warbler, for which it is the British stronghold. Unfortunately it is not possible to be more precise about the location of these birds.

Winter White-fronted Goose, Wigeon, Teal, Shoveler, Golden Plover

Summer	Curlew, Yellow Wagtail, Reed Warbler, Sedge Warbler, Marsh Warbler, Corn Bunting
Passage	Green Sandpiper, Redshank

Coombe Hill West of the M4 at Exit 10. Just at the junction of the A38 and the A4019 a track leads westwards to the canal. Seek permission to walk the towpath from a cottage near the end of the track.

Tewkesbury West of the M4 at Exit 9. Turn westwards immediately north of the Abbey on to a road that runs alongside the Avon. Watch for fellow-birders in mid-late June.

Slimbridge** OS162

Home of the Wildfowl Trust, founded by Peter (now Sir Peter) Scott in 1946. Though the collection of wildfowl here is second to none, the major attraction is the flock of Whitefronts that were the main reason for Sir Peter's choosing this area in the first place. Though numbers have recently declined this is still one of the largest flocks in Britain and regularly contains the odd rarer bird. Lesser Whitefront and Red-breasted Geese are the value birds here. Peak time is January and February. Bewick's Swans have been encouraged and now feed on the Swan Lake under floodlights. Exactly what effect this has on their metabolism one can only guess, but they come back year after year, up to 600 of them. Wigeon and Teal are numerous and a Peregrine usually winters on the saltings.

Winter Bewick's Swan, White-fronted Goose, Peregrine

Leave the M5 at Exit 13 or 14 and join the A38 southwards or northwards respectively. Follow signs westwards to the Trust, which is open every day except Christmas Day from 9.30 (Sunday 12.00). Tower hides give views over the geese grounds, but Trust members may get closer if accompanied by a warden. Entrance fee. *Tel*: (045 389) 333.

Wye Valley* OS162

A fabulously beautiful valley that may be walked for its entire length from Chepstow to Monmouth, or in various shorter sections. The valley is wooded, with meadows and steep limestone outcrops here and there, and offers a good range of woodland and riverside birds.

Summer Buzzard, Sparrowhawk, Peregrine, Raven, Dipper, Grey Wagtail, Tree Pipit, Great Spotted Woodpecker, Lesser Spotted Woodpecker, Red-start, Wood Warbler, Willow Warbler

Tintern Parva on the west bank is a good starting point walking upstream to Brockweir and Bigsweir Bridge, where there are extensive woods on the western bank. There are many forest walks and trails to be explored. The A466 runs along the valley. Symonds Yat is a noted beauty spot and Peregrine watch-point.

63

Wyre Forest*

OS138/139

This is an old, predominantly deciduous forest with interesting areas of conifers, heath and an attractive stream. It is partly NNR and partly LNR with a Forestry Commission centre at Callow Hill. Among an excellent range of breeding species are Woodcock, all three woodpeckers, Hawfinch and Pied Flycatcher.

Summer Woodcock, Dipper, Kingfisher, Great Spotted Woodpecker, Lesser Spotted Woodpecker, Pied Flycatcher, Wood Warbler, Siskin, Hawfinch, Crossbill

Leave Kidderminster westwards on the A456 and turn right on the B4194 at Bewdley. Footpaths facilitate exploration and there are helpful signs at OS Ref: SO750760 and elsewhere.

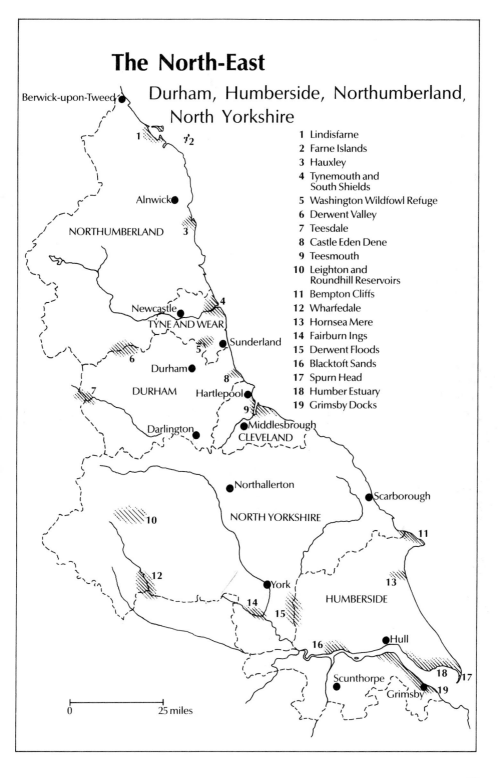

The North-East

Durham, Humberside, Northumberland, North Yorkshire

Berwick-upon-Tweed

1   Lindisfarne
2   Farne Islands
3   Hauxley
4   Tynemouth and
    South Shields
5   Washington Wildfowl Refuge
6   Derwent Valley
7   Teesdale
8   Castle Eden Dene
9   Teesmouth
10 Leighton and
    Roundhill Reservoirs
11 Bempton Cliffs
12 Wharfedale
13 Hornsea Mere
14 Fairburn Ings
15 Derwent Floods
16 Blacktoft Sands
17 Spurn Head
18 Humber Estuary
19 Grimsby Docks

Alnwick

NORTHUMBERLAND

Newcastle
TYNE AND WEAR
Sunderland
Durham
DURHAM
Hartlepool

Darlington
Middlesbrough
CLEVELAND

Northallerton
Scarborough

NORTH YORKSHIRE

York
HUMBERSIDE

Hull

Scunthorpe
Grimsby

0   25 miles

Bempton Cliffs** OS101

Bempton, now a reserve of the RSPB, has for long been known as one of the major seabird breeding stations on the east coast and the home of the only British mainland colony of breeding Gannets. Eight separate species regularly breed on the chalk cliffs including huge numbers of Kittiwakes — over 80,000 pairs if nearby Flamborough Head is also included. Guillemots, Razorbills, and Puffins also run to four figures, though Fulmars are surprisingly scarce with only 400 pairs. Gannets first nested in the 1920s, and for many years the colony remained very small. Then in the late 1970s numbers suddenly took off and over 300 pairs bred in 1981.

To the north lies Filey Brigg, a 2km (1m) promontory of hard rocks that sticks out into the sea and which, at low tide, is a mass of pools holding Turnstone, Sanderling and Purple Sandpiper. At migration times it is an excellent watchpoint for terns, skuas and gulls, while in winter divers and the rarer grebes are regularly present.

To the south Flamborough Head offers similar vantage points for sea-watching as well as holding an attractive collection of cliff-nesting seabirds. This area has the advantage of sufficient cover to hold passerine migrants.

Winter Divers, Black-necked Grebe, Slavonian Grebe, Scoter, Eider, Snow Bunting
Summer Fulmar, Gannet, Shag, Kittiwake, Guillemot, Razorbill, Puffin
Autumn Divers, Manx Shearwater, Gannet, terns, skuas, gulls, Redstart, Pied Flycatcher, Ring Ouzel

Take the B1255 from Bridlington and turn left signposted Bempton after 3km (2m). Continue through Bempton and follow RSPB signs along Cliff Lane. From the car park walk towards the cliff tops and explore to left and right. The RSPB has established observation points and an information centre. There are daily boat trips along the foot of the cliffs from Bridlington.

Blacktoft Sands*** OS106

This RSPB reserve lies at the confluence of the Rivers Ouse and Trent on the upper part of the Humber estuary. Inevitably its ornithology is closely linked with that of the river with large numbers of waders and wildfowl finding a refuge at high tide. Blacktoft does, however, have one of the largest reed beds in the country and it is this that brought the RSPB here, and it is the core of the reserve. In summer it is alive with Reed and Sedge Warblers and the population of Bearded Tits represents over 10 per cent of the British total. Water Rail also breed and sometimes Marsh Harriers do as well, though they are close to their northern limit here. Blacktoft hit the headlines in 1983 when Black-winged Stilt bred (only the second time ever), but there is no reason to suppose that they will return.

Areas of rough grass have, in typical RSPB fashion, been converted from a comparative ornithological desert to wader-rich lagoons with islands suitable for breeding birds. Gadwall, Snipe, Redshank, and Little Ringed Plover now nest. In autumn the water level is lowered to provide feeding for the newly fledged waders as well as a variety of birds of passage. Avocet, Spotted Redshank, Wood Sandpiper and others occur at this time.

In winter the normal waders and wildfowl of the upper Humber can be seen and the lagoons form an important roost for wildfowl and waders. Hen Harriers winter and up to seven roost in the reeds. Merlin and Short-eared Owl also winter, while most years a pair of the latter stop on to breed.

Winter Pink-footed Goose, Teal, Mallard, Shelduck, Hen Harrier, Merlin, Knot, Dunlin, Redshank, Short-eared Owl

Summer Gadwall, Teal, Marsh Harrier, Water Rail, Little Ringed Plover, Redshank, Snipe, Bearded Tit, Sedge Warbler, Reed Warbler, Grasshopper Warbler, Redpoll

Autumn Greenshank, Wood Sandpiper, Green Sandpiper, Little Stint, Curlew Sandpiper, Avocet

Leave the A161 southwards from Goole and take a left at Swinefleet on to minor roads to Reedness, Whitgift and Ousefleet. The reserve entrance is on the left at OS Ref: SE843232 after 1km (½m). There are public hides.

Castle Eden Dene* OS88/89

An LNR under the care of Peterlee New Town and the largest of Co. Durham's coastal denes. This is basically a 5km (3m) long, wooded valley with mature trees in the western and central sections being replaced by scrub near the sea. Important for breeding birds that are otherwise scarce in the area; Nuthatch, Redstart, Wood Warbler, Tree Pipit and Grey Wagtail fall into this category. Whitethroat and Grasshopper Warblers frequent the scrub. Unfortunately this is so dense that migrants are seldom seen and few rare birds have been produced.

The Dene reaches the sea between Horden and Blackhall – one of the ugliest shorelines in Britain. Coal waste has been dumped over the former sandy shoreline for years in a massive act of corporate vandalism. The main attractions are the large gull flocks of late summer that include up to 300 Little Gulls in mid-August, but extend from mid-July to early October. Kittiwakes are the most numerous species, but there are always terns present and a few Arctic Skuas in attendance.

Along the back of the beach the 'fresh' pools often hold the Little Gulls as well as small numbers of passage waders.

Summer Nuthatch, Treecreeper, Great Spotted Woodpecker, Wood Warbler, Whitethroat, Grasshopper Warbler, Sedge Warbler, Redstart, Tree Pipit, Grey Wagtail, Yellow Wagtail

Autumn Little Gull, Kittiwake, Arctic Tern, Sandwich Tern, Arctic Skua, Ruff, Greenshank, Green Sandpiper, Little Stint, Curlew Sandpiper

Leave the A1086 eastwards on minor roads to Blackhall Rocks. There are three footpaths leading southwards from the suburbs of Peterlee into Castle Eden Dene, and a visitors' centre is open on weekdays. OS Ref: NZ410387.

Derwent Floods* OS105/106

The River Derwent runs southwards through a low-lying valley to join the River Ouse south of York. For generations it flooded its banks every winter and even today, following extensive drainage operations, it still floods between Bubwith and Wheldrake. Part of this area is now a reserve of the Yorkshire NT. The floods usually last for 6–8 weeks in February and March and are then the resort of a flock of Bewick's Swan plus large numbers of duck. At other times of the year there is little of interest.

Winter Bewick's Swan, Whooper Swan, Mallard, Teal, Wigeon, Pintail, Pochard, Tufted Duck

Leave Selby northwards on the A19 and turn right 2km (1¼m) past Barlby onto the A163. Continue to Bubwith and inspect the river northwards just before the village. On occasion many birds can be seen from here. In 2km (1¼m) turn left on the B1228. Most of the area can be seen from this and minor roads leading to Aughton, Ellerton, East Cottingwith and Storwood.

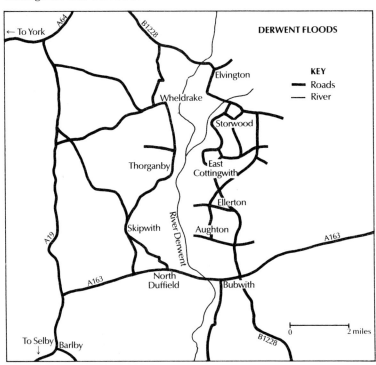

Derwent Valley*   OS87

The Derwent Reservoir, built in the mid-1960s, is among the few inland wetlands of note in this part of the country. It holds a good population of up to 800 duck of 5 species, including a significant flock of Wigeon. Goosander are regular and an Osprey is often present in spring. Short-eared Owl and Hen Harrier may be seen in winter.

Downstream lies an excellent woodland area with oak and beech forming a home for Redstart, Wood Warbler and Pied Flycatcher. Chopwell Woods, further down the valley, has Hawfinch, Crossbill and Siskin, while Hamsterley Mill has Lesser Spotted Woodpecker.

Winter	Wigeon, Teal, Goldeneye, Pochard, Goosander, Hen Harrier, Short-eared Owl
Spring	Osprey
Summer	Lesser Spotted Woodpecker, Pied Flycatcher, Redstart, Wood Warbler, Hawfinch, Crossbill, Siskin

Take the A694 south-westwards from Newcastle to Hamsterley and take a right into Chopwell Woods. Continue to Consett and take the A68 northwards turning left on the B6278 and right on the B6306 for Derwent Reservoir. Public access across private road along the dam.

Fairburn Ings***   OS105

The mining subsidences in the Aire Valley have created a series of pools the most famous of which are the Fairburn Ings (Ings is the old Viking word for water meadows). Owned by the National Coal Board, these shallow pools were declared an LNR in 1957 and accorded the status of a statutory Bird Sanctuary in 1968. The whole 247ha (610a) is now administered by the RSPB, though the Coal Board retain tipping rights and the Water Authority need the Ings as 'washlands'. Nevertheless, and in spite of the difficulties of continually changing water levels, Fairburn Ings is now one of the most important wetland sites in this part of the country. There are deep-water areas with islands that are safe breeding places for ducks and gulls, shallow floods flocked by waders on passage, and overgrown marshes with invading scrub. Some 240 species have been recorded of which 70 have bred. The breeders include Great Crested Grebe, Teal, Shoveler, Gadwall, Tufted Duck, Pochard and the occasional Garganey as well as Redshank, Snipe and Little Ringed Plover and Sedge and Reed Warblers, the latter near their northern UK limit. Passage waders include Ruff, Spotted Redshank, Greenshank, Wood Sandpiper and Green Sandpiper and passage of Black Terns and Little Gulls is regular. The former has attempted to breed.

Winter	Goldeneye, Goosander, Whooper Swan, Snipe, Redshank, Siskin, Redpoll
Spring	Arctic Tern, Black Tern, Common Tern, Little Gull
Summer	Great Crested Grebe, Little Grebe, Garganey, Teal, Shoveler, Gadwall,

Pochard, Tufted Duck, Black-headed Gull, Redshank, Snipe, Little Ringed Plover, Sedge Warbler, Reed Warbler, Blackcap, Garden Warbler

Autumn   Black Tern, Little Gull, Greenshank, Ruff, Spotted Redshank, Green Sandpiper, Wood Sandpiper, Common Sandpiper

There is a public footpath from the centre of Fairburn village which itself lies immediately west of the A1 some 7km (4¼m) north of the M62 intersection. Three public hides are situated along the cut and river bank footpaths and an information centre is open at weekends. On the northern boundary there is a minor road leaving Fairburn westwards from which most areas can be viewed and with a substantial layby for 15–20 cars.

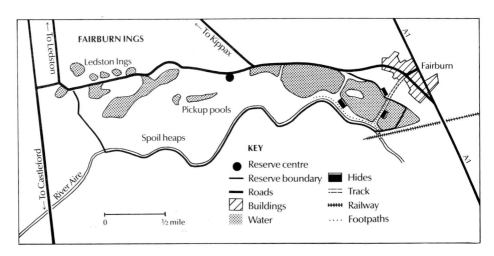

Farne Islands***   OS75

The Farnes consist of some 30 mostly low-lying islands some 3–8km (2–5m) off the Northumberland coast. Famous as one of the world's oldest bird sanctuaries (thanks to St Cuthbert), they now attract huge numbers of trippers throughout the summer months. Despite being often overrun by people, the birds continue to prosper and have become remarkably tolerant. Common, Arctic and Sandwich Terns all nest, and there are still a few pairs of the rare Roseate to be found. Stacks and cliffs hold the usual auks, and there are large numbers of Eider. Photographed by all who visit are the flat-topped stacks, the Pinnacles, off Staple Island, where 1000 Guillemots cram together to breed.

Summer   Fulmar, Shag, Eider, Kittiwake, Sandwich Tern, Common Tern, Arctic Tern, Roseate Tern, Guillemot, Razorbill, Puffin, Rock Pipit

Passage   Divers, Whimbrel, Turnstone, Purple Sandpiper, Arctic Skua, Great Skua

The Islands are owned by the National Trust and two, Inner Farne and Staple Island, may be visited throughout the year. Times are restricted during the breeding season. Boats ply from nearby Seahouses and the National Trust has an information centre at 16 Main Street. The Warden is at The Sheiling, 8 St Aidan's, Seahouses, NE68 7SR.

Grimsby Docks* OS113

The docks lie immediately north of the town at the mouth of the Humber. In winter the calm waters offer a refuge to many sea-duck and the extensive mud flats and a sewage outfall attract thousands of gulls, including the occasional Iceland and Mediterranean, and good flocks of waders including large numbers of Curlew.

Winter Eider, Scaup, Long-tailed Duck, Curlew, Turnstone, gulls, Iceland Gull, Mediterranean Gull

Most of the docks can be seen from the public roads, and access to the shore is via No.3 Fish Dock.

Hauxley** OS81

Hauxley lies on a peninsula 3km (2m) south of Amble with Coquet Island, the RSPB reserve, offshore. This is best known for its colonies of terns, including Roseate, but is not open to visitors. Fortunately many of its birds can be seen from Hauxley. The peninsula also attracts many migrants, including its fair share of rarities, and sea-watching may be rewarding especially in autumn for shearwaters and skuas.

Summer Sandwich Tern, Common Tern, Arctic Tern, Roseate Tern
Passage Divers, Fulmar, Manx Shearwater, Sooty Shearwater, Gannet, terns, Arctic Skua, Great Skua

Leave Alnwick southwards on the A1068 to Amble and continue on an unclassified road towards Radcliffe. After 2km (1¼m) turn left at Hauxley and continue to Low Hauxley. The continuation of this road southwards to Bondicarr is a public footpath – the surrounding land is strictly private.

Hornsea Mere*** OS107

A simple glance at a map is sufficient to establish Hornsea Mere as a likely place for birds. At this point the coast runs approximately north–south and, facing the North Sea, must inevitably receive migrants, particularly in autumn. The Mere, however, lies immediately behind the coast and acts as a magnet to migrating birds of all types. Add to this its nutrient-rich water, and an ideal bird resort is established.

Not surprisingly the RSPB purchased Hornsea, and it is now a well-run reserve with attractions at all seasons. About half the total area is open water with extensive reed beds and sedge covering the rest, mainly at the western end. The reserve also includes adjacent farmland as well as woods to the west and north, so the variety of species that can be seen is always large.

Winter brings regular numbers of duck with several hundred each of Teal, Wigeon, Gadwall, Shoveler, Pochard and Tufted Duck. Mallard may reach 2500 and Goldeneye are particularly numerous in late winter. Severe conditions often bring divers, grebes and sea-duck in search of refuge. Bearded Tit and Bittern may also appear.

Summer birds include Water Rail and Reed Warbler (here at one of their most northerly sites) as well as Sedge Warbler, Sparrowhawk, Great Spotted Woodpecker, Treecreeper and other typical woodland birds. In late summer a large flock of moulting Mute Swans is present.

Passage periods bring a wide variety of birds including many 'fresh' waders and hosts of passerines that invariably include rarities. Black Terns are regular and there is a gathering of up to 50 Little Gulls at this time.

Winter Divers, grebes, Water Rail, Bittern, Mallard, Teal, Wigeon, Gadwall, Shoveler, Pochard, Tufted Duck, Goldeneye, Goosander, Bearded Tit
Summer Shoveler, Gadwall, Sparrowhawk, Water Rail, Reed Warbler, Sedge Warbler, Great Spotted Woodpecker, Treecreeper
Autumn Greenshank, Little Stint, Curlew Sandpiper, Green Sandpiper, Black Tern, Little Gull

Leave Hornsea village westwards on the B1244 which gives good views at various points. There is a car park at the western end and much can be seen nearby. On the south side a footpath runs westwards from Kirholme Point which is just south of Hornsea, turning right off the B1242 just before the railway bridge. Escorted visits start at the information centre here every afternoon. Contact the Warden, Keepers Cottage, Warsand, Hull, North Humberside HU11 5RJ.

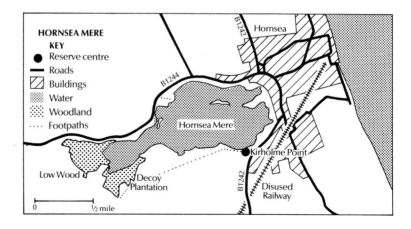

Humber Estuary**** OS106/107/112/113

The Humber forms one huge bird-watching area that is best treated as a single unit, even though several individual sites are well-known birding spots in their own right. To this end only Spurn Head and Blacktoft Sands have been treated separately – the first because it is primarily a bird observatory, the second because its habitat and RSPB status introduce many non-estuarine species.

Effectively, the Humber estuary stretches eastwards from Goole to the sea, though from a bird viewpoint it is only when joined by the River Trent at Blacktoft that it really becomes interesting. The north bank is particularly well endowed with mud flats and the huge area between Sunk Island and Kilnsea is an outstanding wader haunt. By and large the inner estuary holds most of the wildfowl, while waders can be found throughout.

Starting at the head of the estuary, Blacktoft (which see) has an important wader roost. Next downstream is the Humber National Wildfowl Refuge at and around Bramfleet, which holds a declining flock of up to 900 Pinkfeet plus good numbers of surface-feeding duck that include the largest British aggregation of Mallard. Reads Island also has good wildfowl numbers, but is largely inaccessible. This was formerly a major Pinkfeet roost when this species was more abundant on the Humber. The sands at Cherry Cobb form a major wader roost, and there are even larger numbers at Skeffling and Spurn. On the southern shore most waders gather south of Grimsby and have been treated under Tetney and Donna Nook.

Pinkfeet apart, the Humber holds 6000 Mallard, 1000 Shelduck, 2500 Wigeon plus lesser numbers of Teal and Pintail. Most important of the waders are Knot and Dunlin, with the former's total of over 22,000 representing an important proportion of the UK total. Curlew and Redshank also reach good numbers, and Grey Plover (particularly in autumn), Sanderling and Turnstone are always to be seen.

Winter also brings a wide variety of other species including wild swans and sheltering sea-duck, divers and grebes. The odd raptor may well be present, particularly during passage periods when waders include Greenshank, Spotted Redshank and reasonably regular Avocet. One of the best spots for these and other non-estuarine species are the North Killingholme Haven Pits on the southern shore, north-west of Grimsby.

Altogether the Humber is a splendid place for birds and one that the new road bridge has made considerably more accessible.

Winter	Red-throated Diver, divers, grebes, Bewick's Swan, Whooper Swan, Pink-footed Goose, Shelduck, Mallard, Wigeon, Teal, Shoveler, Pintail, Grey Plover, Knot, Dunlin, Sanderling, Curlew, Redshank, Turnstone
Spring	Spoonbill, Greenshank, Spotted Redshank, Avocet, Little Gull, Black Tern
Autumn	Grebes, Ruff, Green Sandpiper, Wood Sandpiper, Greenshank, Spotted Redshank, Little Stint, Curlew Sandpiper
Wildfowl Refuge	Leave the A63 at Scalby and drive southwards 7km (4¼m) to the estuary at Faxfleet. Walk eastwards or drive westwards (OS Ref:

SE804242 and SE936263) for views over the refuge. Do not trespass on the sanctuary.

Read's Island Though there is no access much can be seen by leaving the A1077 10km (6m) west of South Ferriby, signposted Whitton. There are also views off the A1077 itself, west of South Ferriby.

Cherry Cobb These sands and their waders can be viewed by leaving the A1033 just east of Thorngumbald, itself east of Hull. Follow minor roads to Stone Creek House and walk westwards along the estuary bank.

Kilnsea This is reached by leaving the A1033 at Patrington southwards on the B1445, but many observers go all the way to Spurn (which *see*).

North Killingholme Haven Pits These are found by taking the road signposted West Docks and Ferry Terminal in Immingham to the roundabout at the end of the A160 from Brigg. Turn right under the railway bridge, then immediately left along a straight road for 3km (2m) before turning right along the Haven road to the Humber bank. The pits can be viewed from the road.

Leighton and Roundhill Reservoirs* OS99

These comparatively small upland reservoirs in North Yorkshire are ranked eighth among English reservoirs for wildfowl. There is much coming and going between the two, but upwards of 2000 duck of 9 species, including an outstanding flock of Goosander occur.

Winter Teal, Wigeon, Shoveler, Pochard, Goldeneye, Goosander

Leave the A1 north of Boroughbridge westwards to Ripon and take the A6108 to Masham. Take a poorly marked minor road to the left of the reservoirs, both of which can be well seen from the highway. Permits may be obtained from Yorkshire Water Authority, North Central Division, 182 Otley Road, West Park, Leeds LS6 5PR.

Lindisfarne**** OS75

The Lindisfarne area, including Ross Links and Budle Bay to the south, is one of the best birding spots in northern England. The centrepiece is the huge inter-tidal area between Holy Island and the coast, including the Holy Island Sands and Fenham Flats, with an outstanding collection of winter wildfowl and waders. Wigeon number nearly 22,000 and represent over 10 per cent of the British total. Almost as significant are the 4400 Bar-tailed Godwits that winter here. Knot and Dunlin, 10,000 each, are the dominant waders. Outstanding, however, is the comparatively small flock of 640 Brent Geese, but being the Pale-bellied form this represents virtually the whole UK population of the Spitzbergen breeding population. The area also has the largest English flocks of Whooper Swan (360), Greylag (1000), Eider (2500) and Long-tailed Duck (250). Most of these birds frequent the Fenham Flats and Budle Bay areas.

On the open sea, especially off Skate Road, there are many sea-duck as well as grebes, with Slavonian and Red-necked being regular features, along with all three divers. Passage periods bring a variety of waders and terns, but breeding birds are comparatively few, doubtless because of the pressure of holiday-makers at this remarkably beautiful and historical spot.

Winter Red-throated Diver, Black-throated Diver, Great Northern Diver, Slavonian Grebe, Red-necked Grebe, Whooper Swan, Brent Goose, Greylag Goose, Shelduck, Wigeon, Eider, Long-tailed Duck, Scoter, Velvet Scoter, Goldeneye, Scaup, Red-breasted Merganser, Oyster-catcher, Ringed Plover, Grey Plover, Turnstone, Dunlin, Knot, Sander-ling, Bar-tailed Godwit, Curlew, Purple Sandpiper

Passage Barnacle Goose, Pink-footed Goose, Greenshank, Whimbrel, Little Stint, Wood Sandpiper, Spotted Redshank, Arctic Tern, Common Tern, Arctic Skua, Great Skua

The whole of the area is an NNR, but permits are unnecessary to see the main areas.

Budle Bay Park at Bamburgh Castle and walk northwards along the coast to Budle Point, turning inland to Heather Cottages and beyond to a footpath striking southwards to Budle. Return by the same route or inland along the B1342.

Skate Roads Leave the A1 eastwards at Belford on a minor road signposted Easington. Cross the railway and take the next left to Ross. A footpath leads across Ross Links to the sea.

Fenham Flats From Ross (above) return to Elwick and take a footpath due north to

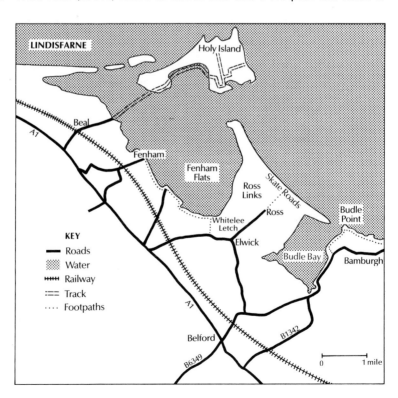

Whitelee Letch. Or 8km (5m) north take an unclassified road eastwards to Fenham. A footpath leads southwards along the shoreline.

Holy Island This is connected to the mainland by a tidal causeway. Leave the A1 at West Mains signposted Holy Island and continue across the flats to the island. Check tide times or be prepared to be marooned or flooded out. Tides do nasty things to Range Rovers let alone Rolls Royces.

Spurn Head*** OS113

Spurn is a well-established Bird Observatory, with a resident warden, that offers accommodation to students of bird migration and especially ringers and would-be ringers. It lies at the southern point of the Spurn Peninsula, a 5km (3m) long bar of sand and shingle at the mouth of the Humber. The area is also a reserve of the Yorkshire NT. Though waders and wildfowl are numerous these are covered under the Humber Estuary (which see). The main attractions of Spurn are migrants and, while falls of small birds are regular in autumn and rarities turn up from time to time, sea-watching is exceptionally good. Terns gather in early autumn and passing skuas regularly stop over to harry them. Other seabirds including shearwaters and petrels can be seen.

Autumn Manx Shearwater, Sooty Shearwater, Gannet, Scoter, Eider, Arctic Tern, Common Tern, Sandwich Tern, Little Tern, Great Skua, Arctic Skua, chats, warblers, flycatchers, Great Grey Shrike

Leave Hull eastwards on the A1033 and fork right at Patrington on the B1445 to Easington. Continue on unclassified roads to Kilnsea and then southwards to Spurn. There is an admission fee to the reserve. Accommodation at the Observatory is on a hostel basis – bookings to The Warden, Spurn Bird Observatory, Kilnsea, via Patrington, Hull, HU12 0UG.

Teesdale* OS92

Scene of a heated political debate between conservationists and ICI in the 1960s, Upper Teesdale now boasts the useless Cow Green Reservoir, rather fewer alpine flowers and much the same bird popula-tion as previously. The typical upland fauna includes Red Grouse, Golden Plover, Curlew, Snipe and Ring Ouzel with Dipper and Grey Wagtail along the streams. There are, however, decent leks of Black Grouse at Langdon Beck, Mickleton Moor and by the Swinhopeburn road. Twite occur at Langdon Beck, Grassholm Reservoir and at Gains o' the Beck, both in Lunedale.

To the east lies Hamsterley Forest with Hawfinch at The Grove and good numbers of Crossbill and Siskin. Pied Flycatcher, Wood Warbler and Redstart are summer visitors along with Nightjar. Green Wood-pecker is regular, and Merlin may be seen on the surrounding moors.

Summer   Sparrowhawk, Merlin, Black Grouse, Red Grouse, Golden Plover, Snipe, Curlew, Common Sandpiper, Short-eared Owl, Green Wood-pecker, Nightjar, Grey Wagtail, Dipper, Whinchat, Wheatear, Pied Flycatcher, Redstart, Wood Warbler, Ring Ouzel, Hawfinch, Crossbill, Siskin, Twite

Upper Teesdale   Explore roads to the west and south of Middleton-in Teesdale with Langton Beck off the B6277.

Hamsterley   Lies to the east via the B6282 north of Woodland.

Teesmouth***   OS93

Heavily industrialized and extensively reclaimed, the estuary of the Tees and its surroundings nevertheless continues to produce good bird-watching. In winter there are substantial flocks of duck including 1000+ of Shelduck (on Seal Sands) together with numbers of Teal, Wigeon, Pintail, Shoveler and Pochard. Goldeneye is also regular. Up to 10,000 each of Knot and Dunlin may be present with lesser numbers of Redshank, Turnstone, and notably Sanderling and Bar-tailed God-wit. During passage periods the marshy pools around the estuary – Long Drag, Saltholme Pool and Dorman's Pool – attract a good range of waders including Little Stint, Curlew Sandpiper and Whimbrel. Rarities have a remarkable habit of appearing and it is a poor autumn that does not produce at least one Pectoral or White-rumped Sandpiper or a Wilson's Phalarope.

The RSPB reserve at Cowpen Marsh is an area of open shallow waters surrounded by grazing marshes that regularly produces many of the wildfowl and waders found in Teesmouth. Seaton Snook Sands near the river mouth attracts gulls and terns in the late summer, and skuas are invariably present. In winter Glaucous, Iceland and Mediterranean Gulls are regular among hordes of commoner species, and wild swans, Merlin, Short-eared Owl and Snow Bunting are often present.

To the north the headland's parks and gardens at Hartlepool remain one of the best spots for small migrants on the north-east coast. Autumn sees a regular combing of the area by local watchers who turn up scarcities such as Bluethroat, Wryneck, Black Redstart, Barred Warbler, Firecrest and Red-backed Strike with the occasional Red-breasted Flycatcher and Icterine Warbler. At sea all four skuas may be seen with Arctic Skua sometimes in their hundreds. Petrels are regular and Sabine's Gull almost so. Winter brings divers and grebes to Hartlepool docks.

A little way inland lies Hurworth Burn Reservoir, once a regular haunt of Little Gulls, but unfortunately no longer attractive to these birds, though occasional flocks do appear. However, there is a good passage of autumn waders including Green Sandpiper and Spotted Redshank, while winter brings a good variety of duck usually including Red-breasted Merganser and Goosander together with the occasional wild swan. Water Rail can often be seen at this season and Turtle Dove is something of a local speciality in summer.

Winter Black-throated Diver, Red-necked Grebe, Whooper Swan, Bewick's Swan, Shelduck, Wigeon, Teal, Pochard, Tufted Duck, Goldeneye, Red-breasted Merganser, Goosander, Merlin, Glaucous Gull, Iceland Gull, Mediterranean Gull, Short-eared Owl, Snow Bunting

Autumn Storm Petrel, Leach's Petrel, Little Stint, Ruff, Whimbrel, Curlew Sandpiper, Greenshank, Spotted Redshank, Green Sandpiper, Wood Sandpiper, Temminck's Stint, Arctic Tern, Sandwich Tern, Arctic Skua, Great Skua, Little Auk

Teesmouth Walk southwards along the beach from Seaton Carew to North Gore, along the seawall or across the North Gore Sands from a road owned by the Tees and Hartlepool Port Authority. One can watch over Seal Sands from a public hide opposite RSPB car parks on the A178 between Middlesbrough and Hartlepool. Alternatively access may be obtained to the South Gare breakwater via a private road owned by the British Steel Corporation and Tees and Hartlepool Port Authority. There is also access along the beach from Redcar.

Tynemouth and South Shields** OS88

Though primarily thought of as a heavily urbanized industrial area, the mouth of the River Tyne has always proved a popular place for bird-watchers in the north-east. In particular, there is a good passage of seabirds in autumn that includes shearwaters, skuas, terns and auks and regularly produces scarce birds. Passage of wildfowl between September and November is good, and Barnacle Geese are fairly regular in late October and early November – presumably birds that have missed the Solway. The huge winter gatherings of gulls at Tynemouth invariably include Glaucous, Iceland and Mediterranean and have produced Ross' on at least two occasions. There are also good concentrations of terns in late summer. Small migrants are often interesting with Tynemouth Park producing rarities in the heart of the urban area. To the south Marsden Quarry and Marsden Hall are equally productive and have turned up good birds such as Radde's and Yellow-browed Warblers, Tawny Pipit and Little Bunting recently. Black Redstart, Firecrest and Wryneck are seen annually. Nearby there is a decent seabird colony at Marsden Cliffs with 4000 pairs of Kittiwakes and a variety of gulls plus Fulmar. Kittiwakes also nest on the quayside warehouses in Tynemouth itself. Further south, Whitburn Observatory near Souter Point is another sea-watch point and the cliff-top fields have wintering Snow Buntings plus the occasional Shore Lark and Lapland Bunting. Nearby Whitburn Steel has an area of inter-tidal rocks with Sanderling, Purple Sandpiper and Turnstone; Roseate Terns are regular in the late summer.

Finally the Cleadon Hills with their farmland and golf course are a regular stop-over for Dotterel in spring.

Spring Dotterel
Summer Cormorant, Fulmar, Kittiwake, gulls
Autumn Manx Shearwater, Sooty Shearwater, Gannet, Brent Goose, Barnacle

Goose, Arctic Skua, Great Skua, Arctic Tern, Roseate Tern, Black Redstart, Firecrest

Winter Red-throated Diver, Turnstone, Purple Sandpiper, Sanderling

Most spots are easily found with the aid of the OS map, and a thorough search of the area makes for a good day's birding.

Marsden Leave South Shields southwards on the A183 and park at the Marsden Grotto pub. A footpath extends north and south with Marsden Hall and Marsden Quarry in open ground to the south.

Whitburn Bird Observatory Continue south on A183 to Souter Point, but not when rifle range is in use.

Tynemouth Eastwards from the docks for seawatching and gulls.

Holywell Pond Leave Tynemouth northwards on the A192 and stop at Holywell Pond after 5km (3m). A public footpath leads along the southern side for winter wildfowl. Key available to members of Northumberland Wildlife Trust: *Tel*: (0632) 320038.

Seaton Sluice and St Mary's An area of coast for breeding seabirds and passage just 3km (2m) north-east of Holywell Pond.

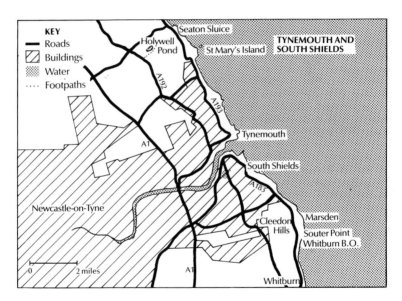

KEY
— Roads
▧ Buildings
░ Water
···· Footpaths

Washington Wildfowl Refuge*   OS93

Like other Wildfowl Trust Refuges, Washington boasts a first-class collection of captive wildfowl in a series of artificial lagoons. There is also a marsh that brings in wild birds and their watchers. The planted reed bed regularly produces Reed Warbler, though not yet breeding, and Water Rail are regular in winter. Passage waders include good numbers of Greenshank as well as the occasional Temminck's Stint and Black-tailed Godwit. Odd rarities turn up, but rather less frequently

79

now that the nearby Barmston Pond (an area of mining subsidence) is past its best. This area is, however, still worthy of a look.

Winter   Water Rail, Tufted Duck, Teal
Summer   Little Ringed Plover
Autumn   Greenshank, Wood Sandpiper, Green Sandpiper, Ruff, Spotted Redshank, Little Stint

Take the A1231 to Washington and turn southwards, following signs to the refuge. OS Ref: NZ330565.

Wharfedale*   OS104

To the north-west of Bradford the moors and dales are no distance away, and moorland birds can be seen within a short drive of the conurbation. Rombalds Moor lies immediately south of Ilkley and is mainly rough grass and bracken, though with sufficient areas of heather to hold Red Grouse. Other typical upland birds also breed, including Golden Plover, Dunlin and Ring Ouzel.

A short distance up the valley lies Bolton Abbey which, with its woods, is part of the Chatsworth estate. This offers typical wood and streamside birds of the area, including Pied Flycatcher, Common Sandpiper and Dipper.

Summer   Sparrowhawk, Red Grouse, Golden Plover, Redshank, Snipe, Dunlin, Curlew, Common Sandpiper, Woodcock, Dipper, Ring Ouzel, Kingfisher, Grey Wagtail, Redstart, Pied Flycatcher

Rombalds   Can be reached southwards from Ilkley and is generally of free access.
Moor
Bolton Abbey   Continue westwards on the A65, forking right on the B6160. Join and then leave the A59 and continue past Bolton Abbey to a car park on the right after 1km (½m). Small fee. There is an excellent footpath north-westwards along the river bank to Barden Bridge. Cross and walk back along the other bank.

The North-West

Cumbria, Greater Manchester,
Lancashire, Merseyside, South Yorkshire
West Yorkshire

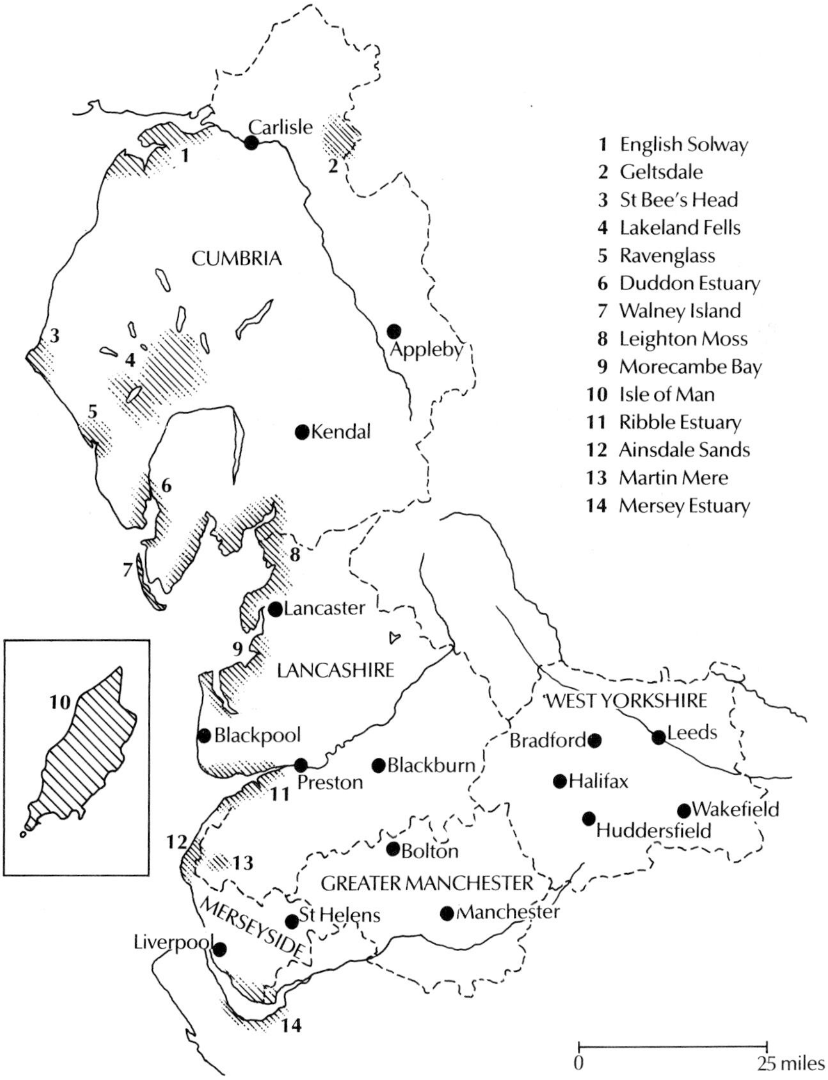

1 English Solway
2 Geltsdale
3 St Bee's Head
4 Lakeland Fells
5 Ravenglass
6 Duddon Estuary
7 Walney Island
8 Leighton Moss
9 Morecambe Bay
10 Isle of Man
11 Ribble Estuary
12 Ainsdale Sands
13 Martin Mere
14 Mersey Estuary

Carlisle

CUMBRIA

Appleby

Kendal

Lancaster

LANCASHIRE

WEST YORKSHIRE

Blackpool

Bradford

Leeds

Blackburn

Halifax

Preston

Wakefield

Huddersfield

Bolton

GREATER MANCHESTER

MERSEYSIDE

St Helens

Manchester

Liverpool

0   25 miles

Ainsdale Sands** OS108

Situated immediately north of Formby, Ainsdale Sands is an NNR which overlaps slightly with the Southport Sanctuary to the north. Habitats include the sea, the sandy shore, the dunes and slacks, and the extensive stands of Austrian pines. Numerous waders are found on the comparatively narrow shore, and the dune slacks, notably Massam's Slack in the south-west of the reserve, have thickets of sea-buckthorn that attract many breeding and migrant passerines. There is a good passage of seabirds.

Winter	Scoter, Bar-tailed Godwit, Knot, Sanderling, Snipe
Spring	Waders, passerines, chats
Summer	Nightjar, Long-eared Owl, Redpoll, Shelduck, Whinchat, warblers
Autumn	Black-tailed Godwit, Bar-tailed Godwit, Sanderling, Turnstone, auks, terns, Arctic Skua, passerines

Access to the reserve is by permit away from special footpaths, but there is a path to the shore which is of free access. From Freshfield Station in Formby walk up the road on the landward side of the railway. This continues as a footpath and crosses the railway line and is then known as Fisherman's Path. It runs through the reserve and the interesting Massam Slack to the shore.

Though outside the reserve, there is a road to Ainsdale-on-Sea to the north that is a favourite sea-watching spot.

Duddon Estuary** OS96

An area of inter-tidal sand immediately north of Barrow-in-Furness that has not been studied anywhere near as thoroughly as its dominant neighbour, Morecambe Bay, to the south. It does, however, have good waders with many Oystercatcher and Dunlin. There are also good numbers of Redshank and up to 2000 Sanderling on passage. There is a flock of Greylags here as well as good numbers of Shelduck, Pintail and Red-breasted Merganser.

In summer this is an important area for Little Tern (c.50 pairs) which has declined at the nearby Ravenglass Sanctuary.

Winter	Greylag Goose, Shelduck, Pintail, Wigeon, Teal, Red-breasted Merganser, Oystercatcher, Ringed Plover, Dunlin, Redshank, Curlew, Knot, Turnstone, Bar-tailed Godwit
Summer	Little Tern
Passage	Sanderling, Greenshank, Green Sandpiper

Millom	Cross over the railway near the station and turn left; turn left again under a railway bridge and follow a track to the shore. A footpath then heads along the back of the saltings.
Greenroad	Leave the A5093 north of Millom at The Green, turn right to Greenroad Station and continue to the shore.
Foxfield	Leave the A595 at Broughton-in-Furness southwards to Foxfield. A level crossing south of the station leads to the shore.

Dunnerholme Leave the A595 3km (2m) north of Askam westwards to Marsh Grange. Continue over the railway to Dunnerholme Ho and the shore.
Askam Turn westwards in the village to the shore.

In general the eastern shore is more productive than the west.

Geltsdale*   OS86

The RSPB created a reserve covering several thousand acres of moorland some 20km (12½m) east of Carlisle in 1983. Though similar to the surrounding landscape, the area is managed so as to provide optimum conditions for birds and offers most of the typical upland species found in this part of the country. Peregrine, Hen Harrier and Buzzard are present throughout the year. Goosander, Dipper, Redstart, Pied Flycatcher breed along with Dunlin and Golden Plover. Whooper Swans use mainly Tindale Tarn.

Winter Whooper Swan, Hen Harrier, Buzzard, Peregrine
Summer Goosander, Teal, Hen Harrier, Buzzard, Sparrowhawk, Peregrine, Merlin, Red Grouse, Dunlin, Common Sandpiper, Golden Plover, Woodcock, Short-eared Owl, Dipper, Grey Wagtail, Tree Pipit, Whinchat, Spotted Flycatcher, Grasshopper Warbler, Sedge Warbler

Leave Carlisle eastwards on the A69 to Brampton. Turn right on the B6413 to Castle Carrock and explore eastwards with the map. Access is restricted to paths along the river and to paths along the old railway lines.

Lakeland Fells*   OS89/90

The Fells lie at the heart of the Lake District centred on the Scafell area. Though noted for their beauty and as a centre of a NP, the Fells are not outstanding for birds, but do hold the bulk of breeding Ravens and Peregrines in northern England. Large numbers of the former gather at the top of Helvellyn. The usual upland species breed. The eastern Fells are lonely and desolate and hold some of the more interesting species. The Golden Eagle has returned to breed in the Lake District and will continue to do so if left in peace.

Summer Buzzard, Peregrine, Wheatear, Ring Ouzel, Pied Flycatcher, Redstart, Wood Warbler

The bird-watcher need not venture to the tops for his birds, but some climbing up of screes may be necessary for Ring Ouzel. Otherwise the valleys are best, and none better than Borrowdale. South of Keswick on the B5289 walk from the Bowder Stone southwards, up Stonethwaite Beck for delicious woodland. Continue to Seatollar and walk up to Seathwaite past excellent woodland and then up to Sty Head with Wheatears all the way. Grasmere is another good centre for Easedale

83

has most of the typical species including Ring Ouzel above Easedale Tarn.

Youth Hostels are ideally situated and other accommodation ranges up to the highest quality. No one should venture on to the hills unprepared and without Wainwright's Guide to the appropriate area. These guides are available in local shops and are invaluable to walkers.

Leighton Moss*** OS97

This marsh became an RSPB Reserve in 1964 and is now one of the most famous in the country. Large open waters are surrounded by the largest reed bed in the north offering perfect conditions to a variety of marsh birds more usually associated with East Anglia. Bittern breed in good numbers, and there is a healthy population of Bearded Tits along with Sedge, Reed and Grasshopper Warblers. Water Rails flourish as do Woodcock, and there are many woodland species to help build up the list.

Passage periods bring Ospreys and Marsh Harriers and many species of 'fresh' waders including Spotted Redshank, Greenshank and Ruff among others. Winter sees a variety of wildfowl including good numbers of Pintail and Shoveler together with Gadwall, Wigeon and Goldeneye.

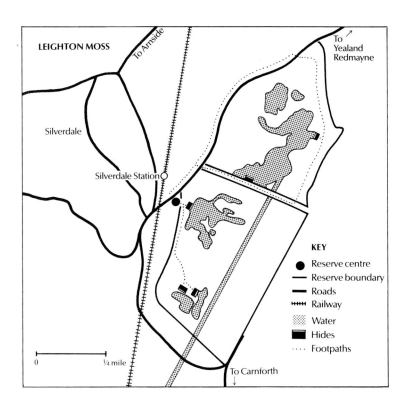

Winter Teal, Pintail, Shoveler, Wigeon, Gadwall, Tufted Duck, Pochard, Goldeneye, Bittern, Water Rail, Bearded Tit
Spring Marsh Harrier
Summer Bittern, Water Rail, Bearded Tit, Sedge Warbler, Reed Warbler, Grasshopper Warbler
Autumn Osprey, Greenshank, Spotted Redshank, Ruff

Leave the M6 at Exit 35A and take the A6 northwards to a minor road westwards to Yealand Redmayne. Follow signs towards Silverdale. The marsh will be seen on the left and there is a car park with access to a public track that crosses the marsh, with public hides. Visit the reserve by permit from the warden at the reserve centre and shop.

Isle of Man* OS95

Few birders visit the Isle of Man for birds alone, save for those *en route* to the observatory on the Calf of Man. This small island lies at the southern tip of Man and has been an observatory since 1952. Over the years it has had its share of rarities, though to be fair it does not exactly enjoy a perfect situation. It has some excellent seabird colonies and also a good colony of Choughs.

Elsewhere the Ayres and Point of Ayre in the north are largely sandy with good wader flocks, and divers and duck on the sea. Ballaugh Marshes are the best wetland on Man and hold decent numbers of wildfowl and waders. In the south-east the Castletown area is good for waders and there are Great Northern Divers in Derbyhaven with Choughs feeding along the shoreline. Waders frequent Douglas Bay and Spanish Head in winter where there are breeding auks.

Summer Fulmar, Razorbill, Guillemot, Puffin, Kittiwake, Chough
Winter Great Northern Diver, Goldeneye, Red-breasted Merganser, Curlew, Golden Plover, Turnstone, Purple Sandpiper
Passage Whimbrel, Turnstone, Knot, Bar-tailed Godwit, Sanderling, Curlew Sandpiper, Little Stint, Common Tern

All the areas mentioned are of straightforward access with the aid of a good map. The Calf of Man Bird Observatory has a resident warden and can accommodate up to ten visitors. Details from the Manx Museum, Douglas.

Martin Mere*** OS108

Once the site of the largest inland water in England, Martin Mere was drained and reduced to no more than a few splashy fields by the middle of the present century. Then, in 1969, the Wildfowl Trust purchased the area and created a new centre. Of course, a wildfowl collection was immediately established, but the wild Pinkfeet of Southport Sanctuary had always used the area and the Trust set about encouraging them. The area of winter flood was extended and shooting was banned. As a result the Pinkfeet have, on occasion, numbered over 18,000. Other wildfowl also responded and 10,000 Teal is one of the largest flocks in the country. Pintail, too, are significant with up to 2500 along with similar numbers of Wigeon. Passage waders are often good and there is a wintering flock of Ruff. Both Black-tailed Godwit and Ruff breed.

Winter   Pink-footed Goose, Mallard, Teal, Wigeon, Pintail, Gadwall, Pochard, Tufted Duck, Shoveler, Ruff
Summer   Little Ringed Plover, Ruff, Black-tailed Godwit
Passage Greenshank, Spotted Redshank, Wood Sandpiper, Ruff

Leave the A59 north of Ormskirk at Burscough Bridge, or the A565 at Mere Brow from where Martin Mere is signposted. Like other Wildfowl Trust refuges the area is open daily from 9.30 (12.00 Sundays). There is an admission charge that gives access to well-sited hides.

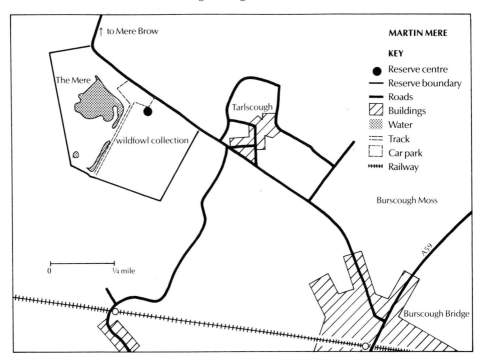

Mersey Estuary***   OS108/117

Near the mouth the Mersey is not only narrow and deep, but also flanked to both east and west by the industrial complex of Liverpool and Birkenhead. Inland the estuary widens out, and industrial development is less daunting. At low water huge mud banks are exposed, especially along the southern shore where they are backed by grazing marshes. The Manchester Ship Canal acts as a barrier in this area.

Large flocks of waders can be found including 35,000 Dunlin. Wildfowl are important, and the 7000+ Pintail form one of the largest flocks in the country. Wigeon, Teal and Shelduck are all numerous. During passage periods 'fresh' waders occur in numbers at several points, notably at Frodsham Lagoons (where dredgings are pumped) and on the adjacent marshes. This area around the Weaver bend is the best place for birds on Merseyside, and it is a great pity that it is so inaccessible.

Winter   Shelduck, Wigeon, Pintail, Shoveler, Teal, Dunlin, Redshank, Knot, Curlew, Short-eared Owl

Passage   Greenshank, Wood Sandpiper, Little Stint, Ruff

North   Garston Rocks are on the southern edge of Liverpool just west of the airport. Speke Hall (NT) lies to the east of the airport off the B5170. Continuing on this road leads to Hale Cliff and then in 2km (1¼m) to Hale where a minor road leads southwards past the church. Park and continue on foot to the estuary. The decoy here is a reserve of the Cheshire CT and Lancashire NT.

South   It is virtually impossible to gain access to the best area around Frodsham.

Morecambe Bay****   OS97/102

This splendid estuary is probably the most important in the country and of international significance for birds. It consists of the estuaries of the Wyre, Lune, Kent and Leven and has a truly huge area of inter-tidal sand and mud. Such a large area would, at first sight, seem totally daunting – and it is at low tide. Most birds, however, concentrate at particular feeding grounds and roosts and it is then, just before high tide, that the best can be obtained from the area. Huge swirling flocks of waders pour across the sky.

Up to 3000 Pinkfeet winter here, feeding on the Pilling and Cockerham Mosses and roosting in the Wyre-Lune reserve. Over 10 per cent of the UK Shelduck (some 6500) are found, and there are 4000 Wigeon, 3000 Teal and 500 Pintail together with good flocks of Eider, Scoter, Goldeneye and Red-breasted Merganser. Waders are, however, dominant with the 45,000 Oystercatcher and 80,000 Knot both being about a quarter of the UK total. The 50,000 Dunlin, 7000 Curlew, 8000 Bar-tailed Godwit, 7000 Redshank and 1500 Turnstone add to the winter spectacle. Passage numbers of some species are outstanding with 7000 Ringed Plover and 12,000 Sanderling being quite exceptional. Passage periods bring other waders species, often in very good numbers, along with a wide variety of other birds. Predators such as Merlin and Short-eared Owl are regular in numbers and Hen and Marsh Harriers and Peregrine appear from time to time.

Winter   Pink-footed Goose, Shelduck, Wigeon, Teal, Mallard, Pintail, Eider, Scoter, Goldeneye, Red-breasted Merganser, Hen Harrier, Merlin, Peregrine, Oystercatcher, Ringed Plover, Grey Plover, Knot, Sanderling, Dunlin, Bar-tailed Godwit, Curlew, Redshank, Turnstone, Purple Sandpiper, gulls

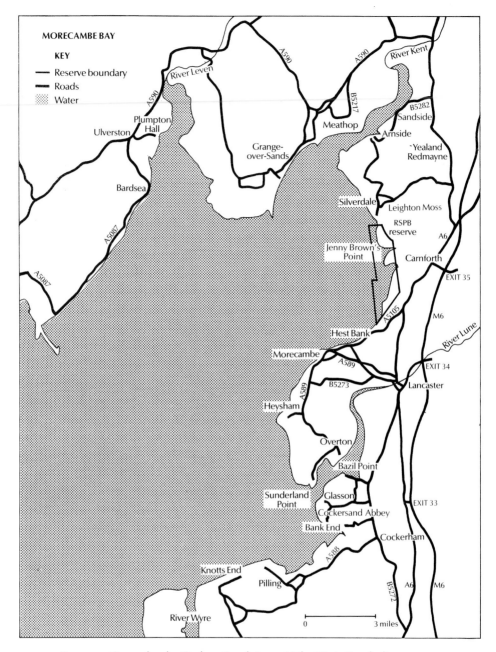

MORECAMBE BAY

KEY

— Reserve boundary
■ Roads
▓ Water

River Leven

A590

A590

River Kent

B5217

B5282

Plumpton
Hall

Ulverston

Meathop

Sandside

Arnside

Grange-
over-Sands

Yealand
Redmayne

Bardsea

Silverdale

Leighton Moss

RSPB
reserve

A6

Jenny Brown's
Point

Carnforth

A5087

A5087

EXIT 35

M6

A5105

River Lune

Hest Bank

Morecambe

A589

EXIT 34

A589

B5273

Lancaster

Heysham

Overton

Bazil Point

Sunderland
Point

Glasson

EXIT 33

Cockersand Abbey

Bank End

Cockerham

A588

Knotts End

Pilling

B5272

A6

M6

River Wyre

0   3 miles

Passage   Greenshank, Curlew Sandpiper, Little Stint, Sanderling

The tide at Morecambe Bay comes in remarkably quickly and is extremely dangerous as a result. There are also many hidden channels and creeks and areas of quicksand. The best advice is to watch from dry land at the right spots at the right time.

Hest Bank   At the southern tip of the RSPB Morecambe Bay reserve is one of the largest waders' roosts with 60,000 birds. Arrive 1½ hours before high tide. Take the A5105 northwards from Morecambe Bay to Hest Bank public car park. Walk under the railway bridge and turn northwards along a track. Contact the Warden, Warton, Carnforth LA5 9QD for advice on timing visits.

Morecambe The north end of the promenade is a good vantage point and the road northwards (A5105) gives excellent views at many places.

Pilling From Blackpool take the A586 eastwards turning left on to the A588 at Poulton-le-Fylde. Continue to Preesall and turn left to Knotts End at the north of the Wyre. A road leads eastward to Pilling for geese.

Cockerham Continue on the A588 toward Lancaster and turn left just beyond Cockerham to Bank End. Further north at Condor Green take a left-hand turning on the B5290 to Glasson. Walk to Fishnet Point.

Heysham Leave Morecambe southwards on the A589. At Heysham the road turns sharp right, continue straight on here to Overton. Footpaths lead to Bazil Point. From Overton drive westwards and turn left down the coast to Sunderland. A footpath leads to Sunderland Point.

Silverdale Leave the A6 westwards towards Yealand Redmayne and bear left to Silverdale (passing Leighton Moss – which see). In the village turn left to Jenny Brown's Point.

Kent The Kent estuary can be seen from the promenades at Arnside and Sandside and from the B5282. For the northern shore leave Grange-over-Sands eastwards on the B5278 and turn right on an unclassified road to keep to the coast after 1km (½m). This leads to Meathop Marsh and in a further 2km (1¼m) crosses a brook. A footpath strikes half right here to a footbridge over a cut and along the estuary.

Leven Leave Ulverston southwards on the A5087 to Bardsea. A path leaves the road to the east where it reaches the shore. Alternatively, leave Ulverston northwards on the A590 and turn right 200m (220yd) past the canal. Follow unclassified roads to Plumpton Hall where a footpath leads to the shore. Walk left under the railway bridge and out into the upper estuary

Ravenglass* OS96

A nature reserve situated on the Drigg Dunes, and the site of a Black-headed Gull colony that was formerly the largest in Britain. There are 10,500 pairs of these birds as well as 600 pairs of Sandwich and 20 pairs of Little Terns. The nearby Esk estuary has an interesting population of waders dominated by nearly 4000 Oystercatchers in autumn.

Summer Ringed Plover, Black-headed Gull, Sandwich Tern, Little Tern

Take a boat from Ravenglass village, just off the A595, with a permit obtained from Cumbria CC. No access during the last two weeks of May.

89

Ribble Estuary***** OS102

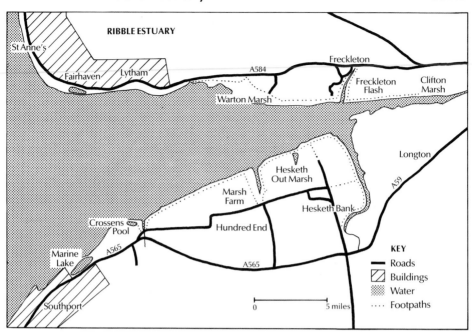

The Ribble vies with The Wash and Morecambe Bay as Britain's top estuary. It has huge inter-tidal sand banks and vast areas of salt marsh that combine to attract very large numbers of birds of a great variety of species. Wildfowl are outstanding with the flock of 14,000 Pinkfeet representing nearly a quarter of the world population. These birds commute between the Southport Sanctuary – a National Wildfowl Refuge established in 1956 – and Martin Mere, which is treated separately. For geese in numbers this is one of the most accessible sites in England. There are also large numbers of duck including 1500+ Pintail, one of the largest UK concentrations. It is, however, the waders that are outstanding here with 70,000 Knot representing the second-largest flock in Europe. Dunlin, Bar-tailed Godwit, Oystercatcher and Redshank are present in their thouands and there are also over 1000 Black-tailed Godwit (20 per cent of the UK total). About 2000 Sanderling winter, but on passage this number grows to over 6000. These birds can be found between Blackpool and Lytham. A recent addition has been the 160+ Bewick's Swans that graze the marshes. Summer sees good numbers of Common Terns, and passage periods bring fresh waders to areas like Crossens Pool and Hundred End.

Winter   Divers, grebes, Bewick's Swan, Pink-footed Goose, Shelduck, Wigeon, Teal, Pintail, Merlin, Oystercatcher, Ringed Plover, Golden Plover, Grey Plover, Knot, Sanderling, Turnstone, Dunlin, Bar-tailed Godwit, Black-tailed Godwit, Redshank, Short-eared Owl

Spring   Sanderling

Summer   Common Tern, Black-headed Gull

90

Autumn   Greenshank, Spotted Redshank, Little Stint, Curlew Sandpiper, Wood Sandpiper, Green Sandpiper, Ruff, Whimbrel

There are many access points, most of which are easy and provide car-side bird-watching. Different species favour different areas.

South Shore   Leave Southport northwards on the A565 and turn left at Crossens. Cross the dyke and turn left along the bank out to Crossens Pool. Return or continue along the bank to Marsh Farm and then out to Hundred End. Leave Hundred End northwards along the wall to Hesketh Out Marsh. Continue for a 10km (6¼m) walk to Hesketh Bank Station. **Note**: Do not ignore Marine Drive in Southport itself, between Marshside Road and Crossens, geese frequently fly overhead. Park at sand works.

North Shore   Fairhaven and Lytham have direct access from the promenade. Park at Fairhaven Lake. Freckleton Flash can be reached along the sea walls from Freckleton village. Then continue to Clifton Marsh. Warton Marsh lies east of Lytham and can be approached by footpaths from Warton Bank, Freckleton village and beside the customs building in Lytham. The latter route is probably easiest and gives good views at high tide.

North of St Anne's pier the tidal area narrows, and grebes and divers are regular, along with sea duck.

For geese explore the area inland between Southport and Formby enclosed by the A567 on a series of east-west minor roads. *See* Martin Mere.

St Bees Head**   OS89

The high, red sandstone cliffs here form one of England's most notable seabird breeding stations and the only mainland site of Black Guillemot. They number no more than half a dozen pairs, but are usually easily found on the water at the foot of the cliffs. Guillemot (2500 pairs) are dominant. The Head is also a good watch-point for migrants and Manx and Sooty Shearwaters; Gannet and skuas are regularly seen in autumn.

Summer   Fulmar, Kestrel, Kittiwake, Guillemot, Razorbill, Puffin, Black Guillemot, Raven

Autumn   Manx Shearwater, Sooty Shearwater, Gannet, Arctic Skua, Great Skua, Sandwich Tern, Common Tern, Arctic Tern

Several miles of cliff are now an RSPB reserve with observation points. Leave Whitehaven southwards on the B5345 and turn right after 3km (2m) to Sandwith. Walk from here to the cliffs. Alternatively walk northwards from St Bees village.

English Solway***   OS85

Inevitably, the English shore of the Solway does not attract nearly as many bird-watchers as the Scottish and the reasons are not hard to find. Though there are many birds, and good ones at that, the southern shore simply does not have the geese. Figures show up to 9000 Pinkfeet and 2500 Barnacles on this shore, but they occur only in March and April and doubtless come from Scotland. At other times the numbers are much smaller, especially of Barnacles. Other wildfowl occur only in moderate numbers. Waders are more plentiful with Knot and Oyster-catcher particularly numerous, but 4000 Bar-tailed Godwit, 3500 Curlew and 2000 Redshank are noteworthy. Up to 70 Greenshank also winter.

Winter Pink-footed Goose, Barnacle Goose, Shelduck, Scaup, Goldeneye, Red-breasted Merganser, Oystercatcher, Ringed Plover, Golden Plover, Knot, Sanderling, Dunlin, Bar-tailed Godwit, Black-tailed God-wit, Curlew, Redshank, Greenshank, Turnstone

Morecambe Bay Leave Silloth northwards to Skinburness and walk to Grime Point. Alternatively leave the B5307 at Kirkbride northwards to Whitrigg, turn left to Anthorn. Both spots require high tides and a telescope.

Inner Estuary Leave Carlisle westwards on the B5307 and fork right in 2km (1m) to Burgh-by-Sands. Turn right and watch for the monument to Edward I where a footpath leads to Burgh Marsh, a likely spot for geese. Rockcliffe, where most geese occur, is a flat open area best ignored.

Walney Island*** OS96

The southern half of this island is a nature reserve boasting the largest colony of ground-nesting Lesser Black-backed and Herring Gulls in Europe (c.60,000 pairs). It is also the southernmost Eider-breeding station in Britain, and three species of tern also breed. In winter and during passage periods the southern tip is also a major roost for the waders of Morecambe Bay and huge numbers descend on the point and adjacent Piel Island. Foulney Point across the bay on the mainland is another major wader roost.

Winter Red-necked Grebe, divers, Velvet Scoter, Scaup, Knot, Oystercatcher, Dunlin, Redshank, Curlew, Bar-tailed Godwit, gulls

Summer Ringed Plover, Redshank, Dunlin, Lesser Black-backed Gull, Herring Gull, Sandwich Tern, Common Tern, Little Tern

Cross the bridge to the island from Barrow. Access is by permit from South Walney Nature Reserve, Barrow-in-Furness, Cumbria. There is also a bird observatory here, details from The Warden, Coastguard Cottages, South Walney, Barrow LA14 3YQ. *Tel*: (0229) 41066.

The South-East

Kent, London, Surrey, East Sussex, West Sussex

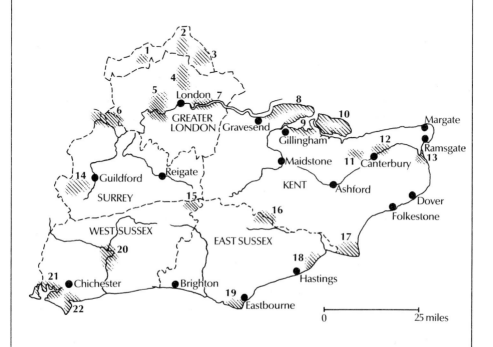

1	Hilfield Park Reservoir	**12**	Stodmarsh
2	Broxbourne Woods	**13**	Sandwich Bay
3	Epping Forest	**14**	Thursley and Ockley Commons
4	Lea Valley Reservoirs	**15**	Weirwood Reservoir
5	London	**16**	Bewl Bridge and Bedgebury
6	Middlesex Reservoirs	**17**	Dungeness
7	Inner Thames	**18**	Rye
8	North Kent Marshes	**19**	Beachy Head
9	Medway Estuary	**20**	Arun Valley
10	Sheppey	**21**	Chichester Harbour and Pits
11	Canterbury Woods	**22**	Pagham Harbour and Selsey Bill

Arun Valley*   OS197

Long famous as an area of winter floods that attracts good numbers of duck and Bewick's Swans, Amberley Wild Brooks survives under a permanent threat of drainage. Yet good numbers of Wigeon, Pintail, Gadwall and Teal can still be found with some fifty or so Bewick's Swans. The area also holds wintering Snipe, Redshank and Ruff. To the south is the Wildfowl Trust's Arundel Refuge with its collection of duck, geese and swans and the usual high-standard information centre. Wild birds occur regularly including duck, Water Rail and a good passage of waders. There are reed beds and mud banks with well-sited hides.

Winter Bewick's Swan, Wigeon, Pintail, Gadwall, Teal, Shoveler, Tufted Duck, Pochard, Water Rail, Bearded Tit, Kingfisher

Autumn Greenshank, Green Sandpiper, Wood Sandpiper, Little Stint

Amberley Wild Brooks Turn left off A29 south of Pulborough signposted Greatham and stop at Greatham bridge for wildfowl and waders. Parking is difficult so walking is advised from nearby Watersfield or Greatham villages.

Arundel Refuge Take the A284 north for 1km (½m) from Arundel. Well signposted from the town by-pass.

Beachy Head**   OS198/199

Standing 150m (500ft) above the waves, the white cliffs of Beachy Head attract good numbers of passage migrants as well as offering first-class opportunities for sea-watching. Whitethroat, Lesser Whitethroat and Blackcap are the main species, but flycatchers, chats and other warblers are also present. Visible movements of hirundines in autumn can be dramatic. Divers, skuas, Gannets and the occasional shearwater can be seen at sea along with a quite impressive passage of waders in spring.

Areas of cover are few in this downland landscape so that virtually every patch of bushes is worth a look. Bushes in the gardens around Birling Gap regularly hold migrants and this is the prime sea-watching site especially in spring. The small (but tall) plantation 2km (1¼m) to the east is also worth combing, and the fields here have the habit of turning up Tawny Pipit with some regularity in September. Whitebread Hollow, lined with bushes and scrub, regularly attracts migrant warblers, chats and flycatchers, and these in turn have attracted the attentions of a local ringing group.

To the west lies Cuckmere Haven, now included in the Seven Sisters Country Park complete with car park, information centre and concrete path to the Haven. Overrun by trippers throughout the summer months, there are still good areas for birds including a fenced-off 'scrape' area that, during passage periods, is good for waders.

To the north lies Arlington Reservoir covering 49ha (121a) where duck, grebes, terns and waders appear in season. A few good rarities have been turned up from time to time.

Spring	Red-throated Diver, Scoter, Ringed Plover, Redshank, Common Tern, Sandwich Tern, Pomarine Skua, Nightingale, Whitethroat, Blackcap
Summer	Sparrowhawk, Ringed Plover, Redshank, Kittiwake, Stonechat, Corn Bunting, Nightingale
Autumn	Greenshank, Ringed Plover, Grey Plover, Turnstone, Little Stint, Common Tern, Sandwich Tern, Arctic Skua, gulls, Spotted Flycatcher, Pied Flycatcher, Lesser Whitethroat, Redstart, Ring Ouzel
Birling Gap	Leave the A259 southwards at East Dean and watch for car park overlooking the sea on the right.
Whitebread Hollow	Stop at the western end of Eastbourne where the coast road takes a sharp inland turn and a worn white path leads directly ahead up the chalk down. Ignore it and walk seawards past a refreshment kiosk to the Hollow.
Cuckmere	Watch for sign Seven Sisters Country Park on A259 near Exceat Bridge. Park in car park and follow track to the sea and lagoons.
Arlington Reservoir	Turn northwards off A27 7km (4m) east of Polegate signposted Berwick Station. Beyond level crossing the reservoir is on the right – free car park leads to marked footpath.

Bewl Bridge and Bedgebury*   OS188

Opened in 1975, Bewl Bridge Reservoir has produced close on 200 species of birds, and the list grows year by year. Covering 312ha (770a) it is the largest freshwater in the area and, surrounded by the rolling hills and forests of the Weald, is as 'natural' a lake as anyone could wish. There are toilets and shelters judiciously placed around the perimeter and even neatly signposted trails with appropriate explanatory notes. If all this sounds a bit much, try a winter visit when wildfowl virtually have the place to themselves, or autumn when the lowered water level attracts a variety of passage waders.

Winter wildfowl include huge rafts of Pochard, up to half the Sussex total, as well as Tufted, Mallard, Gadwall, Wigeon and Pintail. The inevitable Canada Geese have moved in in numbers, and Garganey are regular in spring. Great Crested Grebe numbers may be impressive, and Whooper Swan, Red-crested Pochard and Ruddy Duck are often present.

Spring brings a passage of waders and terns, including Black Tern, and in autumn Green and Wood Sandpipers, Spotted Redshank, Greenshank and Little Stint are sometimes present.

Not far away is Bedgebury Pinetum, a collection of conifers owned by the Forestry Commission. Best known for its winter roosts of Hawfinches there are good woodland birds at all seasons including Crossbill, Sparrowhawk and Redpoll.

Winter	Great Crested Grebe, Little Grebe, Canada Goose, Mallard, Teal Wigeon, Shoveler, Pochard, Tufted Duck, Goldcrest, Hawfinch, Crossbill, Redpoll, Siskin, Brambling
Spring	Garganey, Common Sandpiper, Redshank, Snipe, Black Tern, Common Tern

Summer   Great Crested Grebe, Little Grebe, Crossbill, Redpoll
Autumn   Ringed Plover, Green Sandpiper, Wood Sandpiper, Common Sand-
            piper, Redshank, Spotted Redshank, Greenshank, Little Stint, Dunlin,
            Ruff, Black Tern, Common Tern

Bewl Bridge   Leave Tunbridge Wells southwards on the A21 to Lamberhurst and
            watch out for a turning on the right signposted Bewl Bridge about 2km
            (2m) beyond the village. A *Visitor Guide* has an excellent map of the
            area showing paths, trails and access at many points. Write for a copy
            to Recreation Office, Bewl Bridge Reservoir, Lamberhurst, Tunbridge
            Wells, Kent. The NR is administered by the Sussex TNC.

Bedgebury   Leave A21 eastwards 1km (½m) north of Flimwell. Continue along
            narrow lane to Pinetum on right. Large car park indicative of summer
            crowds. Many bird-watchers on Sunday afternoons in January.

Broxbourne Woods*   OS166

A large area of old mixed deciduous woods with some areas of open
heath and some new plantations.

Summer   Woodcock, Nightjar, Nightingale, Tree Pipit, Grasshopper Warbler

Leave Hoddesdon and the A10 westwards at a major fork on to
unclassified roads to Goose Green. There is a footpath through
Highfield, Cowheath and Broxbourne Woods.

Canterbury Woods*   OS179

The woods around Canterbury have long been famous for their
Nightingales and indeed it is a bird that is difficult to ignore on warm
summer nights. Over recent years the RSPB has established several
areas to the west of the town as reserves, notably at Church Wood,
Blean and nearby Bossenden Wood. Here, from the main A2, birds can
be heard and seen, but Church Wood is easily explored. Best time for
visiting is May and June.

Summer   Sparrowhawk, Nightjar, Great Spotted Woodpecker, Lesser Spotted
            Woodpecker, Nuthatch, Treecreeper, Tree Pipit, Nightingale, Redstart,
            Garden Warbler, Blackcap, Wood Warbler, Lesser Whitethroat, Haw-
            finch

Leave Canterbury westwards on the A2 and turn right after 2km (1¼m)
towards Rough Common. Church Wood can be entered at OS Ref:
TR 123593, access along public footpaths. The Warden, 32 Hillview
Road, Canterbury, CT2 8EX.

Chichester Harbour and Pits*** OS197

This huge estuary consists of four distinct channels that join together to form a comparatively wide exit to the sea. In the north-west it is joined to Langstone Harbour and birds often commute between the two. Unlike Langstone much of the surrounding land is undeveloped which, while making it a more attractive area, also has the result of making access considerably more awkward. The result is that the best access points are also the scene of sailing activity. Brent regularly number 5000, and there are good numbers of Wigeon, Teal and a small flock of Pintail. Waders are numerous with over 20,000 Dunlin and up to 1000 Knot – the largest south-coast flock. Godwits, Curlew and Redshank appear in good numbers. Slavonian Grebes winter, while on passage there are also Black-necked Grebes and the usual collection of waders and terns notable among which are up to 100 Greenshank.

As with all larger estuaries a variety of birds occur outside the breeding season including Merlin, harriers, Short-eared Owl and small migrants.

To the east, on the other side of Chichester, lies a series of gravel pits that have gained a significant reputation for producing interesting birds. They are often very good for passage terns and waders, particularly in autumn when Black Terns are regular.

Winter	Brent Goose, Shelduck, Wigeon, Teal, Pintail, Goldeneye, Ringed Plover, Grey Plover, Sanderling, Dunlin, Black-tailed Godwit, Bar-tailed Godwit, Curlew, Redshank
Summer	Great Crested Grebe, Common Tern, Little Tern, Ringed Plover
Passage	Spotted Redshank, Greenshank, Wood Sandpiper, Little Stint, Curlew Sandpiper, Curlew, Redshank, Black Tern, Common Tern

Access is available at a number of spots, remembering that the best wildfowl are at Thorney Deep and the best wader roost at Pilsey Island.

Hayling Island Leave the A27 southwards on the A3023 and scan from Langstone Bridge on the north side (*see* Langstone Harbour). Cross the bridge and turn left to North Hayling. At Tye a road leads to the seawall. Continue to South Hayling, turn left and explore the coast at Selsmore, Eastoke Point and Black Point.

Thorney Leave the A27 southwards to Thorney and continue to West Thorney, pausing at the wider channels along the way. Footpaths lead north and south along the seawall from the church. Southwards a walk of 1km (½m) leads to Longmere Point for waders.

Wittering Leave the Chichester by-pass southwards on the A285 to West Wittering. Continue to the beach and walk westwards to East Head. It is also possible to walk northwards along the eastern shore to West Itchenor – which is another access point off the A285.

Chichester Pits The Chichester by-pass gives access to most of the pits. Take the B2145 for terns at the first pit. Or the B2144 taking the first left and stopping at a wide track on the right. Cross the road and walk a track westwards viewing to the left for waders, terns and gulls. The OS map shows other pits and paths, but the two above are usually best.

Dungeness***** OS189

Dungeness has been a famous natural history site since the beginning of last century. Though the name applies strictly only to the southern end of the peninsular, it is here used to include the whole area between Rye and Hythe. It thus includes the bird observatory, the RSPB reserve, the once famous rarity haunts of The Wicks and The Midrips, the sheep walks of Walland and Romney Marshes, the wader feeding grounds at Greatstone and Littlestone, indeed the whole area enclosed by the Royal Military Canal created to keep Napoleon at bay. The area juts out into the Channel at a particularly favourable point to receive migrants coasting westwards along the southern shores of the North Sea. The shingle is some 6m (20ft) deep, and gravel extraction is a major industry. Large flooded pits have added significantly to the variety of Dungeness birds. Dry slacks are covered with brambles and dense bushes, offering a transitory home to the migrants for which Dungeness has always been famous. Towering above all else is the Dungeness Power Station – a monolithic structure that holds breeding Black Redstarts. Another part of the area, partially included in the RSPB reserve, is a Ministry of Defence range – out of bounds and decidedly noisy on occasion.

Nearby lies Dungeness Bird Observatory offering self-catering accommodation in comfortable dormitories and a handy base from which to explore the area and meet other birders. A warden is resident and 'Dunge', as it is affectionately called, undertakes an extensive ringing and migrant recording programme. Sea-watching is productive according to season with some heavy up-Channel movements of seabirds and waders in spring, notably Pomarine Skuas in the first week of May. 'The Patch' is the warm-water outflow from the Power Station cooling system and attracts a variety of seabirds to pause and feed. It is worth a look at any season, but in autumn invariably produces interesting gulls and terns. The Observatory has a hide overlooking 'The Patch' that is ideally sited for comfortable sea-watching.

The RSPB reserve covers 480ha (1190a) immediately north and west of the Power Station. At its heart lies Burrowes Pit with islands holding the most important seabird colonies in the south-east. The reserve has attracted some 270 species in its time. About 40–45 species breed, including colonies of Common and Sandwich Terns, and since 1920 about 12 pairs of Common Gulls – their only regular site in England. Mediterranean Gull breed regularly in small numbers. Wheatears still breed at specially created nest sites, but Stone-curlews have not done so since 1968. The creation of open water has led to colonization by Great Crested Grebes and a variety of waterfowl, while in winter duck as well as feral Greylag and Canada Goose are numerous. This is now one of the top spots for wintering Smew in the country.

The ARC (Amey Roadstone Company) Pit is an old-established one just south of the RSPB entrance on the main road south of Lydd. It can be watched only from the road, but has the habit of turning up good water birds at almost all seasons and should never be passed by. Spring and autumn regularly bring Black Tern and Little Gull, and in winter a variety of wildfowl include Ruddy Duck.

On the east coast Greatstone has an open sandy beach that attracts a good variety of waders, particularly when undisturbed in winter. Sanderling, Turnstone and Bar-tailed Godwit are regular.

Winter   Great Crested Grebe, Hen Harrier, Greylag Goose, Canada Goose, Bewick's Swan, Wigeon, Teal, Pintail, Pochard, Tufted Duck, Goosander, Smew, Short-eared Owl, Oystercatcher, Sanderling, Dunlin, Bar-tailed Godwit, Redshank, Grey Plover, Glaucous Gull

Spring   Scoter, Eider, Black-tailed Godwit, Pomarine Skua, Little Gull, Black Tern, Golden Oriole

Summer   Great Crested Grebe, Greylag Goose, Tufted Duck, Ringed Plover, Common Tern, Sandwich Tern, Little Tern, Roseate Tern, Common Gull, Mediterranean Gull, Sedge Warbler, Reed Warbler, Wheatear, Black Redstart, Yellow Wagtail

Autumn   Manx Shearwater, Mediterranean Gull, Sanderling, Oystercatcher, Green Sandpiper, Common Sandpiper, Curlew Sandpiper, Little Stint, Whimbrel, Redshank, Ringed Plover, Common Tern, Sandwich Tern, Roseate Tern, Black Tern, Arctic Skua, Ring Ouzel, Willow Warbler, Whitethroat, Firecrest, Pied Flycatcher, Spotted Flycatcher, Wheatear, Redstart, rarities

The major areas of interest are:

Dungeness Bird Observatory   Accommodation in small simple, but clean, dormitories with shower room, common room and lounge. 'Dunge' has improved no end since this book was first published. The Warden, Dungeness Bird Observatory, Dungeness, Romney Marsh, TN29 9NA. *Tel:* (0679) 21309.

Dungeness RSPB Reserve   Open to members free, non-members for a fee several days per week during the spring, summer and autumn, but less frequently in winter. Contact: The Warden, Boulderwall Farm, Dungeness Road, Lydd, Kent, which is on the right on the Dungeness road south of Lydd.

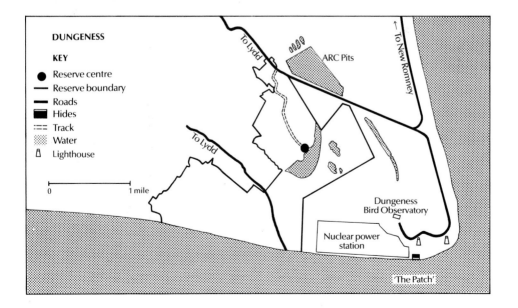

Greatstone Approached via New Romney where follow signs to Littlestone. Turn right along the coast road to Littlestone and watch over the beach at low tide.

Epping Forest* OS167

The forest lies on both sides of the A11 between Buckhurst Hill and Epping and is some 7km (4½m) long, by 2km (1¼m) wide. It offers a breath of fresh air to London's east-enders and some good woodland birding close to the city. Outstanding are Hawfinch and Redstart, but there is a good cross-section of breeding birds.

Summer Nightingale, Redstart, Tree Pipit, Wood Warbler, Grasshopper Warbler, Hawfinch, Redpoll

Leave London on the A11 – free access throughout.

Hilfield Park Reservoir* *OS176

Situated in the south-western corner of Hertfordshire just east of the M1 near Elstree. It is an important gull roost and regularly attracts good numbers of wildfowl in winter.

Winter Wigeon, Pochard, Tufted Duck, Goldeneye, Goosander, gulls

There is a public footpath reached by following signs to Elstree Airfield and parking just before the entrance. This leads through woodland and gives views southwards over the reservoir.

Inner Thames* OS177

The joint efforts of the Port of London Authority and the Greater London Council (at the time of writing soon to be abolished) have changed the inner Thames out of all recognition over the past 20 years. From an almost lifeless sewer the capital's river has become one of the more important bird zones in the country. From Woolwich to Gravesend the inter-tidal area is comparatively narrow, but it now supports populations of both wildfowl and waders in winter and of other species on passage. Of course, being so near London means that potential development is always a threat and even in the 1970s the Woolwich area was developed as the new town of Thamesmead. Nevertheless the river still holds birds, and the less than salubrious surroundings still attract their watchers.

Among the duck Pochard and Shelduck both top the thousand mark, while no less than 9000 Dunlin utilize this stretch along with Redshank, Grey Plover, Ringed Plover and a few Knot and Curlew. Many of the wildfowl frequent the old docks, whereas waders gather at Dartford

Marshes and Swanscombe where 100 Ruff spend the winter. This area is also a regular resort of passage waders.

Winter Shelduck, Teal, Pintail, Pochard, Tufted Duck, Grey Plover, Ringed Plover, Dunlin, Redshank, Knot, Curlew, Ruff

Access to the area can be awkward, but there is a shoreline footpath from Woolwich to Erith. Dartford Marshes can be reached via a minor road running eastwards on the east side of the River Darent and the north side of the railway from Dartford Station. Swanscombe is accessible off the A226.

Lea Valley Reservoirs** OS177

The Lea Valley is to north-east London what the Heathrow area is to west London. Large parts of the valley have been turned into reservoirs making it one of London's primary birding areas. Walthamstow Reservoirs consist of twelve pools and are the oldest. They are noted for their islands and, as a result, are good for breeding grebes and duck as well as a heronry. Winter duck flocks are often substantial with Tufted and Pochard reaching four figures. The William Girling and King George V reservoirs are larger, more modern and being adjacent share the same birds. Duck are less numerous, but often more varied with flocks of Goldeneye and Goosander regular. Passage brings a few waders and often Black Tern.

Winter Great Crested Grebe, Teal, Shoveler, Tufted Duck, Pochard, Goldeneye, Goosander, gulls

Summer Great Crested Grebe, Heron

Leave central London for the North Circular Road. Turn southwards at the Lea Valley and take Ferry Lane to Walthamstow Reservoirs. Alternatively turn northwards and take the road to Chingford between Girling and King George. Access strictly by permit only (*see* Barn Elms under London).

London* OS176/177

The London-based bird-watcher is, despite the urban sprawl, remarkably well off for birds. A series of open spaces provide stop-overs for a variety of migrants that could easily be overlooked in a more rural area. Wheatears, Willow Warblers, Chiffchaffs, Blackcaps and Spotted Flycatchers pass through in both spring and autumn, and watchers working their local open spaces regularly pick up Pied Flycatcher, Goldcrest and even Common Sandpiper. Places such as Hampstead Heath and Wimbledon Common hold good populations of breeding birds while the centre itself still has Black Redstarts. True quality watching is inevitably available at only a few sites, but Barn Elms Reservoirs are good by any standards, while the tiny reservoirs at Stoke Newington are not to be ignored.

Barn Elms has good winter flocks of Tufted and Pochard among which Gadwall, Wigeon and Goosander may be found. Passage brings Black and other terns and a few waders occur along the narrow banks.

Winter   Canada Goose, Pochard, Tufted Duck, Gadwall, Goosander
Summer   Skylark, Willow Warbler, Black Redstart
Passage   Chats, warblers, flycatchers

Barn Elms   Cross Hammersmith bridge southwards and turn left at the traffic lights into Merthyr Terrace. Continue to the end. A permit is required: write to Metropolitan Water Board, New River Head, Rosebery Avenue, London EC1.

Wimbledon Common   Cross Putney Bridge southwards and continue to the Common. At a large roundabout (A3) take the road to Wimbledon village and after 3km (2m) turn right to the Windmill. Explore in all directions.

Hampstead Heath   Follow roads northwards from the West End and watch for Hampstead signs. Continue to the Heath and explore from Jack Straw's Castle.

Medway Estuary***   OS178

At first sight the Medway is a decidedly daunting area, an impression that a glance at the OS map simply enforces. An intricate network of channels and creeks, mud banks, saltings and islands creates what is undoubtedly good bird habitat, but which seems quite impossible to explore adequately. Even the maps are always out of date as seawalls are breached and new areas enclosed. By sheer good fortune most of the best birds are concentrated and can be seen from a few well-chosen vantage points.

Dabbling duck are particularly important and concentrations of 10,000 Wigeon, 5000 Teal and 1000 Pintail are exceptional in this part of Britain. Up to 1000 Brent and 2500 Shelduck also occur along with smaller numbers of Bewick's Swans, Whitefronts, Goldeneye, Shoveler and Red-breasted Merganser. Waders are also important in winter when 10,000 Dunlin, 2500 Redshank and 1000 each of Oystercatcher, Ringed Plover, Grey Plover, Knot and Curlew may be present. Black-tailed Godwit may be less numerous but the average winter peak of 300 forms 6 per cent of the UK total.

There are, of course, other birds here in winter including Hen Harrier and Short-eared Owl, while during passage many waders and terns pass through.

Winter   Brent Goose, White-fronted Goose, Bewick's Swan, Shelduck, Wigeon, Teal, Pintail, Shoveler, Mallard, Goldeneye, Pochard, Tufted Duck, Red-breasted Merganser, Oystercatcher, Ringed Plover, Grey Plover, Turnstone, Dunlin, Knot, Redshank, Curlew, Black-tailed Godwit
Passage   Spotted Redshank, Greenshank, Curlew Sandpiper, Ruff, Bar-tailed Godwit, Black Tern

Most birds are concentrated on the Chetney Marshes and the adjacent mud flats and saltings to the west and on the Stoke Ooze area on the northern shore.

Chetney Leave the A249 north of Iwade, just south of Kingsferry Bridge en route to Sheppey on a minor road signposted Lower Halstow. Turn off this westwards and stop after 150–200m (160–220yd) where a track leads to Chetney Cottages. Follow this and fork off to the left to the seawall. Continue out to the main channel.

Stoke Take the A228 to Lower Stoke and thence to Stoke Lagoon (*see* North Kent) by the level crossing. Cross over and gain access to the seawall in 100–150m (110–160yd).

Middlesex Reservoirs**   OS176

Approaching London's Heathrow Airport from the air is one of the best ways of appreciating just how much wetland there is in this area of Middlesex. A string of gravel pits line the Colne Valley and are worth exploring, but pride of place must go to the reservoirs, some of which have been the happy hunting grounds for generations of London-based bird-watchers. Staines Reservoirs, in particular, have a large and varied population of migrants and winter visitors and are a noted haunt of rarities. Though duck dominate, Staines is a regular autumn haunt of Black-necked Grebe and Black Tern.

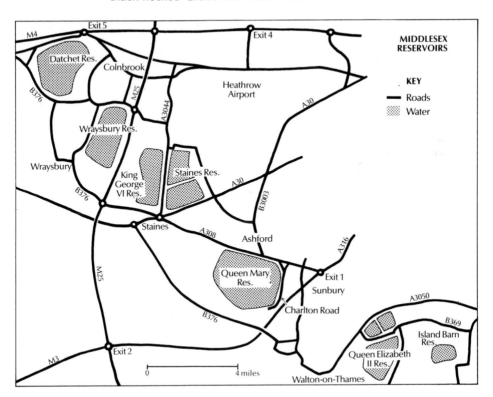

Closer in lies Queen Mary Reservoir which is so large that it has a causeway to break up the waves. Winter wildfowl often include the odd seaduck, and Goldeneye, and Goosander are regular. Of the newer reservoirs the Queen Elizabeth II at Walton-on-Thames has good numbers of duck with Shoveler reaching 500 and Wigeon regularly present. Newest of all is Datchet Reservoir right next to the M4. Here, too, winter duck are the primary attraction.

Winter Great Crested Grebe, Wigeon, Teal, Shoveler, Tufted Duck, Pochard, Goldeneye, Goosander, gulls

Autumn Black-necked Grebe, Black Tern

Staines Reached via A3044 north of Staines. Stop at a footpath leading up the side of the reservoir on the right. This leads to a causeway between the two pools of the reservoirs.

Queen Mary Take the A308 to Ashford. Stop at Charlton Road at the eastern corner of the reservoir and apply for entry to the building opposite the main gate 50m (55yd) down Charlton Road. Permits must be obtained from MWB (*see* Barn Elms under London).

Queen Elizabeth II Access by permit (as above) from the B369.

Datchet Leave the M4 at Exit 5 and turn southwards towards Colnbrook. Entrance by permit (as above).

North Kent Marshes*****   OS178

The North Kent Marshes are defined as that stretch of the Thames estuary extending from Cliffe in the west to the Isle of Grain in the east. For many years this has been a favourite haunt of London-based birders and its appeal remains, despite continued industrialization and the more insidious change from grazing to arable. A seawall separates the inter-tidal mud and sand from a huge area of fields intersected by drainage ditches.

The pits at Cliffe have been created by the extraction of clay for the cement industry and the result has been a series of mainly deep-water lagoons adjacent to the estuary. Inevitably they provide a refuge for diving duck as well as for divers, grebes and sea-ducks. Passage brings waders and regular Black Tern. At the present time this is also the main area for the flock of up to 1000 Whitefronts that regularly winter in North Kent.

To the east lie the major high-tide roosts at Egypt and St Mary's Bays and the RSPB reserve at Northward Hill. Though best known as Britain's largest heronry with over 200 pairs, this area also gives access to the marshes, and its hides enable the winter visitor to scan for harriers, Short-eared Owl, Merlin as well as for geese. There is, of course, a good population of typical woodland birds including abundant Nightingale, a pair of Long-eared Owls and all three woodpeckers.

Further east is Allhallows and nearby Yantlett Creek where passage waders are often interesting and where the regular species roost at high tide. Regular watchers always stop off at Stoke Lagoon.

Over the area as a whole waders are particularly important with 30,000 Dunlin, 1900 Curlew, 1000 Redshank and 700 Grey Plover in winter. This season also brings 2500 Shelduck, 1000 Wigeon, 1000 Mallard and several hundred Pintail, Shoveler, Pochard and Tufted Duck. Bewick's Swan are regular and there are always a few Gadwall and Goldeneye. Fieldfare and Redwing abound and there are usually a few Merlins on the hunt.

During passage periods there are waders everywhere and the intensity of watching regularly produces a few rarities.

Winter Red-throated Diver, Slavonian Grebe, Bewick's Swan, White-fronted Goose, Brent Goose, Shelduck, Wigeon, Teal, Shoveler, Pintail, Gadwall, Goldeneye, Merlin, Hen Harrier, Short-eared Owl, Long-eared Owl, Curlew, Dunlin, Grey Plover, Redshank, Ringed Plover, gulls, Fieldfare, Redwing

Summer Grey Heron, Redshank, Snipe, Lesser Spotted Woodpecker, Nightingale

Passage Slavonian Grebe, Black-necked Grebe, Garganey, Spotted Redshank, Greenshank, Wood Sandpiper, Green Sandpiper, Little Stint, Black Tern

Cliffe Leave Rochester northwards on the B2000 to Cliffe village. Continue as far as possible and then turn left on a rough track westwards. This leads those who care nothing for shock absorbers right out to the coastguard cottages. Proceed to the seawall and turn left around the pits and Cliffe Creek to Cliffe Fort and onwards around more pits cutting inland and then northwards to return to the coastguards.

Cliffe and Cooling From the coastguards (above) walk to the seawall and turn right with the Thames on the left. Before Egypt Bay there is a track across the marshes to Cooling. Alternatively, continue to Egypt and St Mary's Bays and turn right at the south-eastern corner of the latter to Swigshole and Northward Hill. It is a long way and best organized with two cars.

Northward Hill Proceed eastwards along minor roads from Cliffe to High Halstow. Park at the village hall and walk down Northwood Avenue to the footpath to the reserve. Free access to all except the heronry which can be seen from several hides. Continue to Decoy Farm and Swigshole to the Thames.

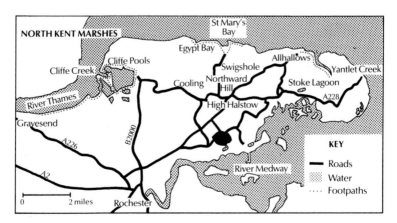

Allhallows Continue eastwards from High Halstow to Allhallows and park at the end of the road past the pub. Walk north-eastwards down a track to the seawall and turn right and thence to Yantlet Creek.

Pagham Harbour and Selsey Bill**** OS197

By any standards Pagham is a little gem, an estuary that attracts a wide variety of species but which is small enough to enable every nook and cranny to be fully explored in a day. Not surprisingly it is very popular with local and London-based watchers and has been an LNR since 1965.

In winter 1000 Brent Geese are based here along with good numbers of Pintail, Wigeon, Teal and Shelduck. Red-breasted Mergansers and Shoveler are also present, and a small flock of Eider are based at the harbour mouth regularly staying through the summer. Wader numbers may not be spectacular, but the variety is often good with Ringed Plover, Grey Plover, Turnstone, Dunlin, Redshank and Black-tailed Godwit invariably present. The flock of up to 1000 Ruff is the largest in the country. The same species also appear on passage but are then joined by Greenshank, Golden Plover, Bar-tailed Godwit, Little Stint, Curlew Sandpiper and Avocet. This is one of the more regular spots for the latter away from their Suffolk breeding sites. Many waders gather at the Ferry Pool at Sidlesham where they can be watched at close range while lorries thunder past the narrow (dangerous) pavement.

Ringed Plover and Little Terns breed and are joined by Common and Sandwich Terns in late summer. This is often a good time for unusual grebes and Slavonian regularly winter at Church Norton. The bushes at this site are combed every day in season and frequently produce good passerine rarities. 'The Severals' are a couple of pools just behind the beach that afford shelter to sea-duck in winter.

Selsey Bill was formerly the site of a bird observatory and is still noted as a fine site for sea-watching especially in spring when large numbers of waders and seabirds pass up-Channel. Early May sees a good number of Pomarine Skuas offshore – but dedication is required.

Winter Slavonian Grebe, Brent Goose, Wigeon, Teal, Pintail, Shelduck, Eider, Red-breasted Merganser, Grey Plover, Turnstone, Redshank, Black-tailed Godwit

Spring Avocet, Bar-tailed Godwit, Spotted Redshank, Greenshank, Little Tern, Common Tern

Summer Eider, Ringed Plover, Little Tern, Yellow Wagtail

Autumn Slavonian Grebe, Avocet, godwits, Grey Plover, Knot, Ruff, Little Stint, Curlew Sandpiper, Greenshank, Wood Sandpiper, Spotted Redshank

Sidlesham Ferry The reserve headquarters and information centre is at Sidlesham Ferry and is a convenient place to park for the Ferry Pond – arguably the finest little marsh in Sussex. A glass-fronted hide offers a viewpoint but the roadside is closer. Footpaths lead along the harbour wall in both directions. Access via B2145.

Church Norton Continue on B2145 taking a left to Church Norton where there is a car park. Walk to the estuary, past excellent bushes, and view one of the best parts of the inter-tidal area. Turn right to the shore and harbour mouth and right again to 'The Severals'.

Pagham Lagoon On the northern shore reached via B2166 out of Bognor Regis. A former gravel pit now heavily overgrown, but still attractive to many birds.

Selsey Bill Take B2145 to the Bill and settle down for sea-watching between mid-April and mid-May. Small migrants tend to be in people's gardens – be discreet, especially on hot days when sunbathing may reveal all.

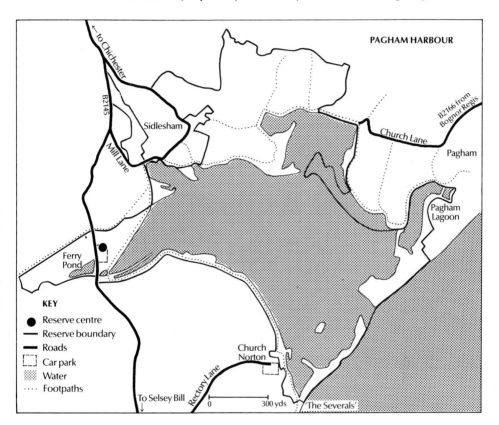

Rye***

OS189

Near Rye, in the south-eastern corner of Sussex, the sea has built up the huge shingle beach that culminates at nearby Dungeness. The outlet of the River Rother south of Rye Harbour is narrow and exposed mud is limited. However, the gravel extraction industry has created a series of pits behind the seawall that regularly attracts birds at all seasons including many breeding seabirds and the occasional rarity. This is Rye Harbour LNR, and there is a visitors' centre, hides and a permanent warden. Breeding terns include Common and Little and during passage periods waders are interesting especially at high tide. In winter the pits regularly hold a good collection of sheltering sea-duck, with Eider and Scoter offshore and Sanderling and other waders on the mud-lined shore.

Along the coast to the west is Pett Level – low-lying grazing marshes with areas of flood behind the shingle beach and coastal road. Much can be seen without trespassing on the fields, and birds include terns and waders. In autumn the Sussex Ornithological Society lowers the water level to produce an excellent wader marsh which regularly attracts a good variety of species, including rarities. The shoreline here has much mud at low tide and waders are always present as is a Mediterranean Gull or two.

Winter	Red-throated Diver, Pochard, Tufted Duck, Scoter, Gadwall, Shoveler, Wigeon, Teal, Oystercatcher, Grey Plover, Ringed Plover, Dunlin, Sanderling, Redshank, Turnstone, Bar-tailed Godwit, Curlew
Summer	Great Crested Grebe, Little Grebe, Oystercatcher, Ringed Plover, Redshank, Common Tern, Little Tern, Wheatear, Yellow Wagtail
Autumn	Oystercatcher, Grey Plover, Ringed Plover, Whimbrel, Dunlin, Sanderling, Little Stint, Spotted Redshank, Greenshank, Wood Sandpiper, Curlew Sandpiper, Common Tern, Sandwich Tern, Black Tern, Arctic Skua, Wheatear

Rye Harbour Leave westwards on the A259 and turn southwards signposted Rye Harbour on the outskirts of town. There is a car park at the end near the Harbour Inn with information centre and handy map. Walk westwards through the caravan park and continue over a small bridge on the left to the reserve.

Pett Level Take the A259 westwards and just before Winchelsea, turn left signposted Winchelsea Beach. Continue to coast and lagoons on right.

Sandwich Bay*** OS179

Sandwich and Pegwell Bays form the estuary of the River Stour immediately south of Ramsgate. Being sandy rather than muddy, they are not spectacular for waders, though Dunlin may build up to 1000 or more. The area is, however, strategically sited to receive migrants, and the Sandwich Bay Bird Observatory was established in 1961. Part of the area is a Kent NT reserve. Over the years the area has built up a reputation for producing both rarities and migrants in quantity. In spring waders and terns often include Gull-billed and in autumn all manner of rarities may occur.

Behind the coastal dunes lies the famous golf course and inland of that an area of grazing marshes intersected by dykes. Bushes around the houses immediately behind the beach are often productive.

Winter	Red-throated Diver, Teal, Wigeon, Bar-tailed Godwit, Dunlin, Redshank, Sanderling, Snow Bunting
Spring	Common Tern, Gull-billed Tern
Autumn	Wood Sandpiper, Greenshank, Ruff, Black-tailed Godwit, Little Stint, chats, flycatchers, warblers

Take the A256 or A257 to Sandwich and turn eastwards on minor roads toward Sandwich Bay. Turn left on foot after 1½km (1m) towards the Golf Club buildings and take the track to the left just before the entrance. Continue and bear right towards the shore or along the river bank.

Alternatively continue on the road, through the toll, to the Sandwich Bay Estate and the Bird Observatory. The Warden, Sandwich Bay Bird Observatory, Guildford, Sandwich Bay, Sandwich CT13 9PF, *Tel:* (0304) 617341, can supply details of accommodation, etc.

Sheppey*****   OS178/179

The Isle of Sheppey has for long been one of the most favoured bird-watching haunts in the south-east. It is a true island separated from the mainland by the Swale channel bridged only at Kingsferry. The Swale is lined by inter-tidal mud and attracts numbers of waders and wildfowl. Oystercatcher, Knot and Dunlin may all reach 5000, and Grey Plover, Redshank, Bar-tailed Godwit and Curlew almost as many. Wigeon are by far the most numerous of the wildfowl, but Mallard, Teal, Shelduck and Shoveler are also numerous. Up to 1500 White-fronted Geese and 2500 Brent Geese find a sanctuary here in winter. The resident Greylag Geese are the result of introductions.

Sheppey is also noted as a winter home of raptors including regular Hen and Marsh Harriers, Peregrine and Short-eared Owl. Most winters bring a few Rough-legged Buzzard, and this is one of the most reliable sites for this species. Sea-duck and divers are regular with Red-breasted Mergansers building up to decent numbers. A few Snow and Lapland Buntings are usually present. During passage periods all the usual waders pass through, including good numbers of Spotted Redshank, Greenshank, Ruff, Black-tailed Godwit and Whimbrel. Skuas are regularly present in autumn.

Shellness is a nature reserve, a noted high-tide roost and migration watch-point. Access is restricted in part, but much can still be seen without violating the reserve. The Swale can be worked from Harty Ferry, where there is a handy pub.

Elmley, once a long hard slog along sea walls, is a reserve of the RSPB and by far the best bird haunt in the area. From the comfort of well-sited hides one can watch over an area of shallow water, created by damming and pumping operations, as well as over the sea wall to the Swale. Here geese, duck, Bewick's Swan and numerous waders can be seen in the New Year, and waiting for raptors to put in an appearance becomes more a pleasure and less an ordeal on what can be a very bitter coastline. Wader passage is quite outstanding in both spring and autumn, and breeding birds, especially wildfowl (including Pintail) are abundant. The dukes, fleets and seawalls of Sheppey are marvellous in winter and Elmley is the best spot of all.

Winter Red-throated Diver, Bewick's Swan, White-fronted Goose, Greylag Goose, Brent Goose, Wigeon, Teal, Mallard, Shoveler, Pintail, Red-breasted Merganser, Hen Harrier, Marsh Harrier, Merlin, Rough-legged

Buzzard, Peregrine, Short-eared Owl, Knot, Dunlin, Oystercatcher, Grey Plover, Golden Plover, Redshank, Turnstone, Bar-tailed Godwit, Lapland Bunting, Snow Bunting

Spring Garganey, Pintail, Wood Sandpiper, Spotted Redshank, Common Sandpiper, Greenshank, Curlew, Whimbrel, Ruff, Knot, Little Stint, Temminck's Stint

Summer Pochard, Pintail, Teal, Wigeon, Gadwall, Greylag Goose, Canada Goose, Common Tern, Redshank, Ringed Plover

Autumn Marsh Harrier, Hen Harrier, Peregrine, Curlew Sandpiper, Little Stint, Wood Sandpiper, Green Sandpiper, Spotted Redshank, Greenshank, Black-tailed Godwit, Bar-tailed Godwit, Ruff, Grey Plover, Ringed Plover, Common Tern, Sandwich Tern, Arctic Skua, Snow Bunting

Access from London via the M2 (Exit 5) or M20 (Exit 11) striking northwards on the A249 to Kingsferry Bridge.

Shellness Follow signposts on the A250 to Leysdown and continue straight through until a gate with 'Private' notice bars the way. Walk directly to the sea across rough ground. Along this beach is a huge gathering of waders at high tide, with wildfowl offshore. Turn southwards and walk along the beach to Shellness for more waders and especially seaduck. The area is a reserve of the Kent NT.

Harty Ferry A road southwards between Leysdown and Eastchurch is signposted Ferry Inn. Turn down and continue for 1½km (1m) before turning sharp left over Capel Fleet. This is always worth investigating for duck and autumn waders. The road then runs parallel to the Fleet for another 2km (1¼m) before turning right and then right again down to the Ferry Inn, for waders, duck and White-fronts.

Elmley Cross Kingsferry Bridge and take the track on the right after 1km (½m). Then take the next left and proceed for 3km (2m) to Kingshill Farm, where RSPB signs are displayed. There is a charge to non-members, and the reserve is open on specified days throughout the year. A walk of 3km (2m) is required to reach the hides and the Swale shore.

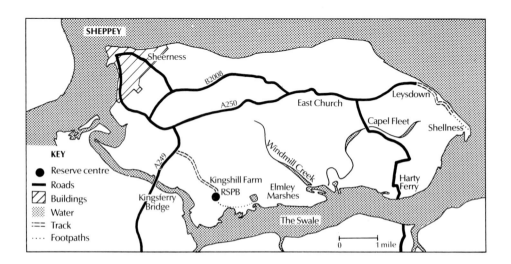

Stodmarsh****   OS179

Stodmarsh is notable for being the largest fresh marsh in Kent, a legacy of mining subsidence in the area. Lying in the Great Stour valley, some 7km (4m) downstream from Canterbury, the marsh is traversed by a wall which runs from the village to the river bank, making a natural viewing point. Also the winter floods which tend to occur further down the valley at Grove Ferry help to make this whole area a great attraction for wildfowl.

But Stodmarsh is still best known as the first port of call for scarce species like Cetti's and Savi's Warblers, as they colonize from the Continent. Both species were proved breeding here before anywhere else, and there are many eager eyes searching for the Penduline Tits (already seen) and Fan-tailed Warblers that seem destined to colonize the country quite soon. Bearded Tits are abundant, Marsh Harriers regular, Short-eared Owls breed and Hobby is a regular visitor. There are many small birds along the track from the reserve entrance to the marsh.

A little way upstream lies another area of subsidence at Westbere that is not a reserve. This has equally large reed beds and holds much the same birds while Savi's Warbler and Kingfisher are regular.

Winter	Wigeon, Teal, Shoveler, Pochard, Pintail, Gadwall, wild swans, Hen Harrier, Marsh Harrier
Spring	Marsh Harrier, Garganey, Ruff, Black Tern
Summer	Hobby, Common Tern, Short-eared Owl, Cetti's Warbler, Savi's Warbler, Sedge Warbler, Reed Warbler, Grasshopper Warbler, Bearded Tit, Redpoll
Autumn	Black Tern

Stodmarsh	Leave Canterbury eastwards on the A257 and turn left after 4km (2½m) on to unclassified roads to Stodmarsh. In the village turn left past the 'Red Lion' at a tiny triangle of green down a farm track to the NCC Car Park. After 250m (275yd) turn right along a bank, across a dyke, and then left along the wall from which views can be obtained over the whole area. Many watchers walk all the way to Grove Ferry relying on public transport for the return journey.
Westbere	Leave Canterbury on the A28 and turn right to Westbere after 7km (4¼m). Park and walk through the village to the level crossing. Beyond is a public footpath giving access to the reed beds and lagoons (wellingtons essential).

Thursley and Ockley Commons*   OS186

These two sandy Surrey heaths are among the most exciting places to watch birds near London. The variety of habitat together with the occurrence of scarce species makes a visit at any season productive. A wide range of breeding species includes Dartford Warbler while in winter Great Grey Shrike is regular.

Winter Hen Harrier, Great Grey Shrike
Summer Hobby, Tufted Duck, Curlew, Snipe, Redshank, Woodlark, Nightingale, Redstart, Dartford Warbler, Grasshopper Warbler

Leave the A3 westwards at Milford on the B3001 to Elstead. Turn left and park near the Hammer Pond. The Surrey TNC have a warden at 8 Holmfield Cottages, Highfield Lane, Thursley, Godalming, Surrey. *Tel:* (0252) 702513.

Weirwood Reservoir*   OS187

Although the south-east now has two larger reservoirs, Weirwood remains the best freshwater area south of the Thames. It lies 3km (2m) south of East Grinstead, has natural, gently sloping banks, and is more or less surrounded by woodland. Winter duck are quite numerous and passage periods bring waders, especially to the marshy shallows at the western end, and Black Tern. It is a poor autumn that does not produce an Osprey.

Winter Great Crested Grebe, Teal, Wigeon, Pochard, Tufted Duck
Passage Osprey, Common Sandpiper, Green Sandpiper, Black Tern, Common Tern

Take the B2110 from East Grinstead and turn left immediately. Pass Saint Hill and later turn left on a metalled road to the reservoir. A footpath runs eastwards. Return to the road and continue to western end of reservoir and the marsh.

South

Berkshire, Buckinghamshire, Hampshire, Oxfordshire, Wiltshire

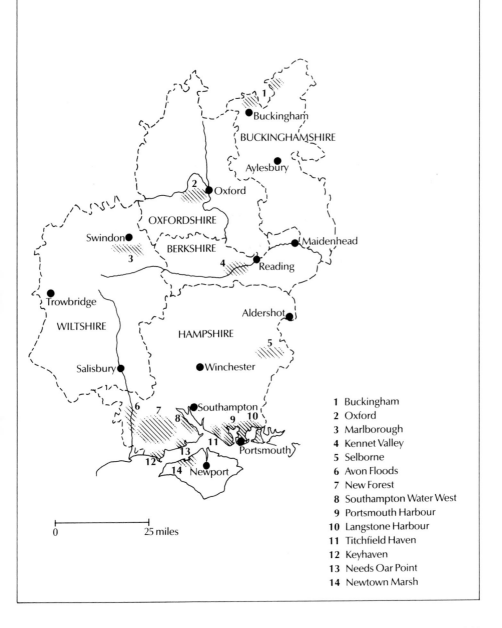

1 Buckingham
2 Oxford
3 Marlborough
4 Kennet Valley
5 Selborne
6 Avon Floods
7 New Forest
8 Southampton Water West
9 Portsmouth Harbour
10 Langstone Harbour
11 Titchfield Haven
12 Keyhaven
13 Needs Oar Point
14 Newtown Marsh

Avon Floods* OS196

Around Harbridge and Blashford the Avon regularly floods in winter and this, together with the extensive gravel diggings at the latter, makes it one of the most important wildfowl haunts in the county. Dabbling ducks are to be found there together with a flock of 600–1200 White-fronted Geese. Brent Geese are also becoming regular along with up to 250 Bewick's Swans. Diving duck are found on the pits.

Winter   Teal, Wigeon, Shoveler, Brent Goose, Bewick's Swan, White-fronted Goose, Pochard, Tufted Duck

Leave Ringwood northwards on the A338 and take the third turning on the right, a cul-de-sac. A footpath at the end leads through the gravel pits. Views of others from the A338. Continue to Blashford where a track leads left down to the flood area. At Ibsley, 3km (2m) north, turn left to Harbridge and observe floods from the road. All of the area is private, and trespassing can only do the birds harm. Be patient and sensible please.

Buckingham* OS152

In the north of Buckinghamshire lie Foxcote Reservoir and Stanton Low Gravel Pits. Both offer opportunities for birding in what is otherwise a wetland-free zone. Foxcote has a good collection of wildfowl including Goldeneye and Goosander and is a reasonably regular spot for spring Black Tern. Stanton Low also has winter wildfowl, but generally attracts rather more passage waders.

Winter   Great Crested Grebe, Wigeon, Shoveler, Pochard, Tufted Duck, Goldeneye, Goosander, Water Rail
Summer   Great Crested Grebe, Redshank
Passage   Common Sandpiper, Green Sandpiper, Greenshank, Black Tern

Foxcote   Leave Buckingham northwards on the A413 and turn right in Maids Moreton then left to the dam. The reservoir can be seen as the road rises beyond the dam. There is a hide that can be visited by prior arrangement with Berks., Bucks. and Oxon. NT.
Stanton Low   Leave Newport Pagnall westwards on the A422. Pass under the M1 and stop at the Black Horse Inn alongside the Grand Union Canal. Walk northwards along the east bank. Several pits can be seen from the A422, and cars may be driven along the towpath.

Kennet Valley* OS175

Between Newbury and Reading, where it joins the youthful Thames, the River Kennet winds through a wide valley that has been extensively excavated for gravel. The flooded pits are of various ages and at various stages of exploitation, but all offer something to birds and together form

114

a significant wetland in this part of England. Older pits have reed and willow scrub along their margins while the exploited pits have shingle areas suitable for Little Ringed Plover. With new pits opening year by year the long-term advice is to explore with the aid of the very latest OS map, but the old-established pits at Thatcham and Theale are well worthwhile. Thatcham has good reed beds while Theale has deep water for diving duck.

Summer   Great Crested Grebe, Snipe, Yellow Wagtail, Sedge Warbler, Reed Warbler

Winter   Great Crested Grebe, Canada Goose, Shoveler, Tufted Duck, Pochard

The A4 runs along the northern side of the valley with many subsidiary roads leading southwards between Newbury and Reading. Footpaths run along the banks of the Kennet and Avon Canal and offer good birding for miles. Walk westwards along the northern bank from Thatcham Station for the reed beds. In Theale stop at the second bridge southwards off the A4 and explore along the southern banks of the canal.

Keyhaven**   OS196

This much underrated area is situated at the mouth of the Solent near Hurst Castle and immediately south of the New Forest. Unlike Needs Oar to the east, access is comparatively straightforward. Because of vegetational changes there is much more exposed mud here than formerly, and populations of waders and wildfowl have increased

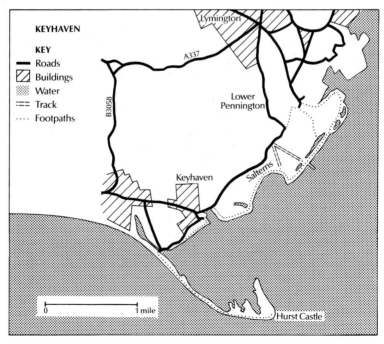

accordingly. Brent Geese have also become established. Most of these birds frequent the inter-tidal area, but behind the seawall there is a series of lagoons and splashy fields that forms a base for good flocks of scarce wintering waders. Spotted Redshank are regular and up to 180 Ruff are a significant percentage of the British total.

Passage birds are also attracted by the lagoons and spring and autumn see regular numbers of Little Stint, Curlew Sandpiper, Wood Sandpiper and terns, including Black. In summer there is a large Black-headed gullery (watch out for Mediterranean) and an important population of Little Terns.

Winter	Brent Goose, Wigeon, Grey Plover, Black-tailed Godwit, Dunlin, Turnstone, Sanderling, Spotted Redshank, Ruff
Summer	Black-headed Gull, Little Tern
Passage	Black-tailed Godwit, Spotted Redshank, Greenshank, Wood Sandpiper, Green Sandpiper, Little Stint, Curlew Sandpiper

Leave the A337 a short distance south of Lymington turning left along Lower Pennington Lane near the White Hart pub. Continue through the village on to a track that turns to the right along the back of the grazing marshes to a rubbish dump with yellow notice prohibiting dumping! Park and walk down a straight track to the seawall. Explore left and right as far as The Salterns and Keyhaven.

Langstone Harbour***** OS197

Though virtually surrounded by urban development, Langstone is one of the very best areas in the country for wildfowl and waders. Its huge mud banks offer rich feeding, and some low-lying islands provide safe high tide refuge. Much of the area forms an RSPB reserve, but one that with a few important sections disappears underwater twice each day. Along with other areas of south-east England Langstone has enjoyed the Brent Goose boom, and up to 8000 have been noted, with regular maxima of over 4000. These flocks are usually very tame at high water and can often be photographed from the main roads. The total represents about 14 per cent of the British population. Shelduck, Teal and Wigeon all reach four figures with smaller numbers of other surface feeders plus Red-breasted Merganser.

Wader numbers are impressive with 20,000 Dunlin quite outstanding. There are also good numbers of Black-tailed Godwit and Grey Plover as well as other species, including wintering Greenshank. In the north-eastern section Black-necked Grebes are regular in winter, and the peak of 45 birds is the largest in the country.

The north-western corner of the harbour is occupied by Farlington Marshes, an area of embanked grazing intersected with drainage dykes and bushes and with several splashy lagoons. This is famous bird-watching territory and a haunt of many passage waders and rarities. It also offers excellent vantage points for seeing most of the birds that use the Harbour.

Winter Black-necked Grebe, Brent Goose, Shelduck, Teal, Wigeon, Gadwall, Pintail, Shoveler, Goldeneye, Red-breasted Merganser, Long-tailed Duck, Oystercatcher, Ringed Plover, Grey Plover, Dunlin, Knot, Redshank, Black-tailed Godwit, Bar-tailed Godwit, Greenshank, gulls

Summer Ringed Plover, Redshank, Common Tern, Little Tern

Passage Ringed Plover, Grey Plover, Dunlin, Little Stint, Curlew Sandpiper, Greenshank, Spotted Redshank, Green Sandpiper, Wood Sandpiper, terns, rarities

Though this is a large area there are several good access points.

Farlington Leave Portsmouth northwards on the A2030 to the intersection with the A27. A narrow track leaves the roundabout eastwards from beneath the A27 flyover. Take this and walk the wall out to the southern tip. The RSPB Warden is at 6 Francis Road, Purbrook, Portsmouth PO7 8WW.

Hayling Take the B2149 southwards on Hayling Island. Turn right into Station Road. Pass the Station, continue into Park Road and turn right into North Shore Road. A fence at the end may be by-passed to give access to the harbour wall.

Havant Park near The Ship Inn on the A3023 north of Langstone Bridge and walk to the bridge for views of Black-necked Grebes. Return to The Ship and take public footpaths east and/or west for viewing.

Harbour Mouth This can be reached on either side and there is a foot ferry across.

Marlborough*   OS173/174

More famous for its school than its birds, the area around Marlborough offers some exciting opportunities for birding in quite delightful surroundings. Nearest is Savernake Forest with its old oaks and beeches immediately south of the A4 (now a very pleasant road once more). Birds include Nightjar, Redstart and Nightingale. To the north west of the town lie Marlborough Downs, typical chalkland with large open fields interrupted by clumps of trees and hedgerows. Typical Hobby country this with Stone-curlew still a possibility in wide open country-side. A similar area to the east is Lambourn Downs, better known for racehorses. Cirl Buntings may still exist here. Below Hungerford the Kennet and its carriers occupy a low-lying reed- and bush-strewn valley with typical marshland warblers.

Coate Water, just outside Swindon, has reed beds, scrub and is an LNR. It holds winter duck, summering warblers and is a regular haunt of Hobby.

Summer Hobby, Sparrowhawk, Stone-curlew, Nightjar, Great Spotted Wood-pecker, Lesser Spotted Woodpecker, Nightingale, Wheatear, Redstart, Wood Warbler, Sedge Warbler, Reed Warbler, Grasshopper Warbler

Savernake Leave Marlborough eastwards on the A4 and turn left on minor roads into the Forest. Explore along various tracks and paths.

Marlborough Downs Leave Marlborough north-westwards on the unclassified road towards Broad Hinton. Stop and explore.

Lambourn Downs Leave the M4 at Exit 14 and take the A338 northwards towards Wantage. Turn left on the B4000 to Lambourn and continue north-wards to the downs on the B4100. Numerous paths and tracks for exploration.

Kennet Leave Hungerford eastwards on the A4 and take the first right to the river. Explore downstream on the southern bank across the open grassland of the Common.

Coate Water Leave the M4 at Exit 15 and stop after 3km (2m) on the Swindon road at SU179821. Open daily, permits to use hides may be obtained from the Warden. *Tel:* (0793) 22837.

Needs Oar Point**   OS196

Needs Oar lies at the mouth of the Beaulieu River and is a reserve of the Hampshire and Isle of Wight NT (HIWNT). Though the river is good for duck, especially Shoveler, Wigeon and Pintail, most of the usual wader species occur near the mouth. The nearby lagoons known as The Gins are famous as a major winter haunt of Spotted Redshank. Passage waders are particularly good here. At the Point itself some 20,000 pairs of Black-headed Gulls breed with among them a pair or two (or hybrids) of Mediterranean Gulls. There are also important colonies of Common, Little and Sandwich Terns.

Winter Brent Goose, Mallard, Teal, Wigeon, Pintail, Shoveler, Goldeneye, Dunlin, Turnstone, Ringed Plover, Grey Plover, Spotted Redshank

Summer Black-headed Gull, Mediterranean Gull, Common Tern, Little Tern, Sandwich Tern

Passage Spotted Redshank, Greenshank, Wood Sandpiper, Little Stint, Curlew Sandpiper, Ruff, Black Tern

Leave Beaulieu westwards on the B3054 and turn left after 300m (330yd) towards Buckler's Hard. Continue south to St Leonard's where the road turns sharp right. A track on the left leads to the reserve. Entry is by permit from HIWNT, and only a limited number are available.

New Forest****   OS195/196

The New Forest lies between Southampton Water and the Hampshire Avon and is one of the largest 'open' areas in southern England. Some parts are private, but huge areas are open to all, and the tens of thousands of acres regularly attract thousands of people in summer. By good fortune and careful management most trippers are concentrated into specific areas where they can park, camp and enjoy themselves leaving the rest to those who walk, ride and watch birds. The main tool in this concentration is parking regulations, so please abide by the rules even though it means parking next to 'grockles'.

Large areas of the forest are covered with heather and grass with invading scrub of birch and other trees. There are good pine coverts and some of the most splendid deciduous woods in the country. The population of breeding birds is very rich, including species that are difficult or even impossible to find elsewhere in southern England. Wood Warbler and Redstart are typical examples. But above all else the Forest is known as the breeding haunt of several really rare birds. This, of course, poses problems, for mad egg-collectors still roam our countryside and, even though they are as well informed as most bird-watchers, it is still impossible to publish the exact whereabouts of several species. Equally unfortunately those who visit the Forest without guidance often find it a difficult (even empty) place.

Specialities include Dartford Warbler (the primary British stronghold), Honey Buzzard, Montagu's Harrier, Hobby, Goshawk, Firecrest and Serin. Fortunately many of these can be seen soaring around from a good vantage point without ever disturbing their breeding sites. They are also outnumbered by Buzzard and Sparrowhawk. Red-backed Shrike and Woodlark have both suffered a serious decline and should be left alone.

Summer Buzzard, Honey Buzzard, Sparrowhawk, Goshawk, Hobby, Montagu's Harrier, Woodcock, Nightjar, Wheatear, Redstart, Stonechat, Nightingale, Wood Warbler, Firecrest, Crossbill, Hawfinch, Redpoll, Serin, Siskin

A really first-rate day can be enjoyed in many different parts of the New Forest by exploring conifer and deciduous enclosures and adjacent areas of heath with birch and gorse. Try:

Beaulieu Road South of the B3058 to the west of the railway where there are heathland and conifer birds and good vantage points.

Beaulieu Heath West of the B3054 between Beaulieu and Dibden.

Rhinefield On the A35 near Rhinefield Lodge and Knightwood Oak.

NB The best advice of all is to visit any one of these areas and watch out for other birders. If you find several with telescopes and tripods ask them where to go. If they have binoculars and dogs you are in the wrong place.

Newtown Marsh, Isle of Wight** OS196

This is probably the best birding spot on the island and a regular haunt of local and holiday watchers. Certainly passage birds can be exciting with waders, terns and the occasional harrier providing interest. In winter it is the best place for wildfowl with Brent, Teal, Wigeon, Shelduck and Pintail in reasonable numbers along with Dunlin and a couple of hundred Black-tailed Godwits.

Winter Brent Goose, Shelduck, Teal, Wigeon, Pintail, Dunlin, Ringed Plover, Grey Plover, Turnstone, Black-tailed Godwit

Passage Greenshank, Wood Sandpiper, Green Sandpiper, Bar-tailed Godwit, Common Tern, Little Tern

Newtown lies north of the A3054 west of Newport. A footpath leads from the village to a seawall that formerly enclosed an area of pasture and which gives access to the best areas. This is an LNR with a nature trail and observation post (permit required).

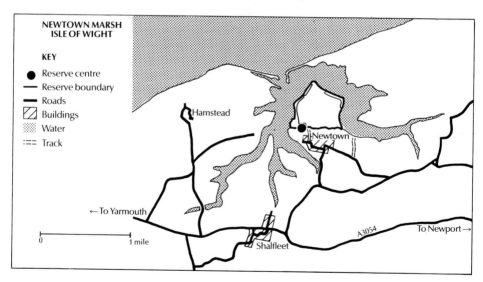

**NEWTOWN MARSH
ISLE OF WIGHT**

KEY
● Reserve centre
— Reserve boundary
■ Roads
▨ Buildings
▦ Water
≡≡ Track

Hamstead

Newtown

← To Yarmouth

0   1 mile

A3054   To Newport →

Shalfleet

Oxford* OS164

Though more famous for its University and car factory, Oxford has good birding within easy reach of the city. The ring road to the west offers views over low-lying meadows with breeding Redshank and

120

Snipe and wintering duck. Wytham Woods has the world's most studied Great Tits as well as a good collection of other breeding birds including Redstart and Wood Warbler. To the south-west lie Farmoor Reservoirs I and II. Both are large, concrete-banked pools and both are used for fishing in the summer. The older pool is also the base of a sailing club. Nevertheless both attract a few waders and terns on passage and hold reasonable numbers of duck and grebes in winter.

Winter   Great Crested Grebe, Teal, Wigeon, Pochard, Tufted Duck

Summer Redshank, Snipe, Great Spotted Woodpecker, Lesser Spotted Woodpecker, Redstart, Wood Warbler

Passage Common Sandpiper, Common Tern, Black Tern

Wytham The woods lie to the north and west of the city between the ring road
Woods   and the A40 westwards. There are several tracks through the woods.
Farmoor Leave Oxford westwards on the A420 and fork right in Botley on the A4141. Turn left at Farmoor on the B4017 and the reservoirs are on the right. Access by permit, ask at gate.

Portsmouth Harbour***   OS196

Though overshadowed by its more famous neighbour Langstone Harbour to the east, Portsmouth is nevertheless an outstanding bird haunt. Industry is slowly eroding its feeding zones, but huge numbers of Dunlin still occur and at over 500 the flock of Knot is the third largest in southern England. Black-tailed Godwit and Ringed Plover both winter in significant numbers. Brent Geese also winter and are increasing. Numbers vary, but over 2500 have been counted. In general, duck are less abundant here than at Langstone and passage waders also find the latter more suitable to their needs.

Winter   Brent Goose, Shelduck, Ringed Plover, Grey Plover, Black-tailed Godwit, Dunlin, Knot, Redshank

Access can be had at several points, though most are unsalubrious. The north-east corner is generally good with the bridge on the A3 south of Cosham and the slip road northwards to the A27 west offering good views. There is a ford to Hornsea Island reached by taking the first right on the southern side of the bridge. The western side is generally less productive.

Selborne*   OS186

Not so much a good birding area as a place of pilgrimage and homage to Gilbert White who was instrumental in getting bird-watching (as against bird-collecting) going. The village lies on the B3006 between Alton and Petersfield, and the Wakes Museum and the beech hangar are well signposted. Take a copy of The Natural History of Selborne and enjoy common birds.

Summer Wood Warbler, Willow Warbler, Chiffchaff, Treecreeper, Nuthatch, Goldcrest

Leave Alton on the B3006 to Selborne. The path to the hangar lies just past the pub.

Southampton Water West**   OS196

Southampton is one of the world's most famous harbours and still the home of the few extant transatlantic liners. Not surprisingly it is heavily industrialized with docks, terminals, jetties and a huge oil refinery. Despite it all, salmon still run up to the Test and Itchen, and birds still congregate on the extensive areas of mud. Most concentrate on the wider western shore and roost at Eling Marsh, Dibden Bay, Fawley and Calshot. The latter with its spit and castle is probably the best with over 5000 Dunlin, up to 2500 Redshank and good numbers of other species. This same area is also good for wildfowl with a small flock of Brent and decent numbers of Teal and Wigeon.

At Fawley, apart from the refinery, there is also a power station with cooling lagoons that often hold good birds. Further north at Dibden a series of large lagoons has been created to hold dredgings from the main channel. Two of these are virtually reclaimed, but the others are still going strong and regularly hold the best passage waders in the area as well as forming an important wader roost. Beyond Eling HIWNT have a reserve on the Lower Test Marshes. This area of reeds and marshes is good at all seasons and regularly holds Bearded Tit and Common Sandpiper in winter. A few waders and the usual warblers breed.

Winter Brent Goose, Shelduck, Teal, Wigeon, Goldeneye, Red-breasted Merganser, Grey Plover, Dunlin, Redshank, Common Sandpiper, Black-tailed Godwit, Bar-tailed Godwit, gulls, Bearded Tit
Passage Black-tailed Godwit, Greenshank, Little Stint, Curlew Sandpiper

Lower Test Leave the M271 at the first exit north of the Totton flyover. Take first exit
Marshes from the roundabout and park by the level crossing in 200m (220yd). Cross railway and take footpath into the reserve.
Eling Leave the A35 southwards immediately west of Totton and park soon after the bridge over Bartley Water in Eling. A footpath just past the church leads to the shore.
Dibden Leave the B3053 at Hythe and proceed to the Pier. Turn left and park where the road turns away from the shore. A footpath continues along the shore to the bay.
Fawley Take the B3053 past the refinery to the village and turn left to Ashlett. A footpath leads along the shore.
Calshott Continue southwards on the B3053 to Calshott and to the shore at Hillhead. Turn left to the spit and castle.

Titchfield Haven*** OS196

This attractive reserve lies on the Solent shore south-east of South-ampton and is a splendid place at all seasons. The shingle beach crosses the mouth of the River Meon creating a freshwater lagoon that attracts a wide variety of species to feed and bathe. It is surrounded by reeds, and these hold the usual species as well as some of the less usual. Duck, especially Teal and Wigeon, are important in winter and Black-tailed Godwit and other waders regularly roost here. Huge numbers of gulls roost on Southampton Water and many come to bathe at Titchfield. In recent years Ring-billed has become almost regular along with Glaucous and the occasional Iceland. In spring and autumn terns may prove interesting and there is a good passage of 'fresh' waders. In summer Sedge and Reed Warblers are numerous.

Winter — Wigeon, Teal, Black-tailed Godwit, Turnstone, Sanderling, Glaucous Gull, gulls

Summer — Sedge Warbler, Reed Warbler

Passage — Green Sandpiper, Wood Sandpiper, Little Stint, Curlew Sandpiper, terns

Leave Fareham westwards on the A27 and turn left on to the B3334 into Titchfield. Continue to Stubbington and turn right on to minor roads to Hill Head. At the shore turn right and watch for the Warden's house on the right at a nasty corner. Access to hides via the Warden, Haven Cottage, Hill Head, Fareham, but views may be obtained from the road in 200m (220yd).

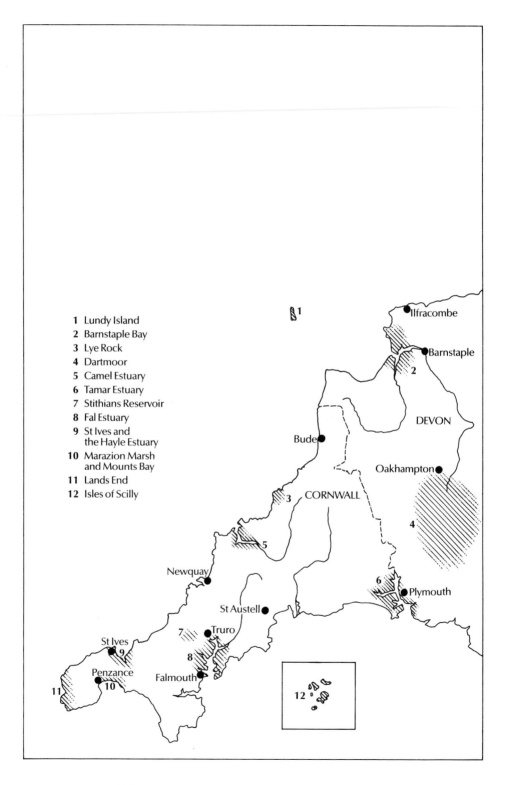

1 Lundy Island
2 Barnstaple Bay
3 Lye Rock
4 Dartmoor
5 Camel Estuary
6 Tamar Estuary
7 Stithians Reservoir
8 Fal Estuary
9 St Ives and
   the Hayle Estuary
10 Marazion Marsh
   and Mounts Bay
11 Lands End
12 Isles of Scilly

Ilfracombe

Barnstaple

2

DEVON

Bude

Oakhampton

CORNWALL

3

4

5

Newquay

Plymouth

6

St Austell

7 Truro

St Ives
9
8

Penzance

Falmouth

11   10

12

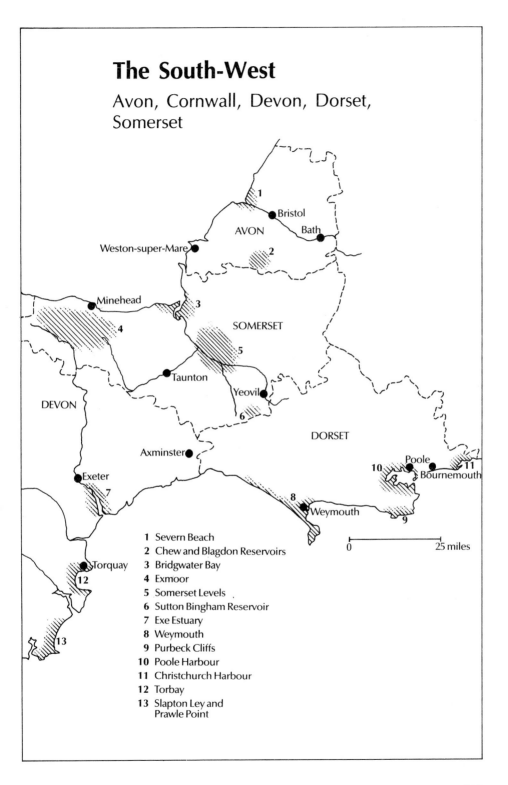

The South-West

Avon, Cornwall, Devon, Dorset, Somerset

AVON

Bristol

Bath

Weston-super-Mare

SOMERSET

Minehead

Taunton

Yeovil

DEVON

Axminster

DORSET

Poole

Exeter

Bournemouth

Weymouth

Torquay

1 Severn Beach
2 Chew and Blagdon Reservoirs
3 Bridgwater Bay
4 Exmoor
5 Somerset Levels
6 Sutton Bingham Reservoir
7 Exe Estuary
8 Weymouth
9 Purbeck Cliffs
10 Poole Harbour
11 Christchurch Harbour
12 Torbay
13 Slapton Ley and
Prawle Point

0   25 miles

Barnstaple Bay***

OS180

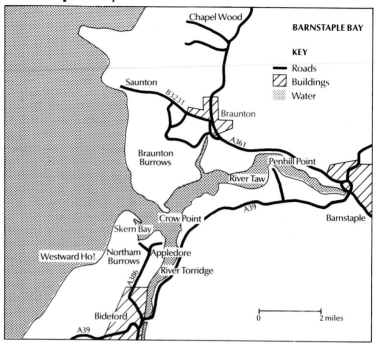

Two rivers enter the sea at the centre of Barnstaple Bay. The Taw is the larger, stretching inland to Barnstaple, while the Torridge extends southwards to and beyond Bideford. At their confluence both estuaries are protected from the sea by large dune systems with the famous Braunton Burrows to the north and Northam Burrows on the southern side. The former are partly an NNR. Both systems provide excellent vantage points for viewing the estuary. Winter brings a variety of waders and wildfowl including Shelduck, Wigeon and small numbers of Brent Geese and Bewick's Swans. Oystercatcher, Ringed Plover, Sanderling and Curlew are significant and there are always a few Ruff, Greenshank, Spotted Redshank, Avocet and Common and Green Sandpipers.

During passsage periods Whimbrel, Sandwich Tern, Little Stint, Curlew Sandpiper and Snow Bunting occur, while a Merlin may arrive in late autumn and stay on to winter.

Chapel Wood near Georgeham is an RSPB woodland reserve that, because of its wide variety of introduced tree species, has an almost park-like appearance. It holds Buzzard and Sparrowhawk as well as Pied Flycatcher and all three woodpeckers.

Winter Slavonian Grebe, Brent Goose, Shelduck, Teal, Wigeon, Shoveler, Eider, Scoter, Buzzard, Peregrine, Merlin, Grey Plover, Bar-tailed Godwit, Green Sandpiper, Common Sandpiper, Greenshank, Spotted Redshank, Sanderling, Turnstone, Purple Sandpiper, Knot, Ruff

Summer Buzzard, Sparrowhawk, Shelduck, Ringed Plover, Oystercatcher, Reed Warbler, Sedge Warbler, Lesser Spotted Woodpecker

Autumn Merlin, Bar-tailed Godwit, Spotted Redshank, Ruff, Greenshank, Snow Bunting

126

Braunton Burrows	Leave Barnstaple westwards on the A361 and turn left in Braunton towards Saunton. After 1½km (1m) turn left to the Burrows. Drive along a track behind the dunes towards the estuary, taking note of NCC maps and signs; car park at Broadsands. Access may be interrupted by the Army and the last part must be walked to Crow Point.
Northam Burrows	Leave Bideford northwards on A386 towards Westward Ho! Head on towards Appledore and turn left (Broad Lane) out towards Skern Bay.
Penhill Point	Reached by small lane off A39 west of Barnstaple for good views over the southern shore of Taw.
Chapel Wood	Entrance near Georgeham between Barnstaple and Ilfracombe at map OS Ref: 483415.

Bridgwater Bay*** OS182

Bridgwater Bay consists of the estuaries of the rivers Parrett and Hunstpill, together with Steart Island and the surrounding inter-tidal shoreline, part of which is an NNR. Much of the area is covered with mud, and there are large areas of saltings. Though known internationally as a moulting ground for up to 3000 Shelduck, the area is rich in other wildfowl and in waders. All the usual species occur, but over 1000 Black-tailed Godwit in autumn represent 20 per cent of the British total, and the 1400 Whimbrel in spring form the largest concentration in the country.

Winter	Shelduck, Wigeon, Teal, Pintail, Shoveler, Dunlin, Redshank, Black-tailed Godwit, Curlew
Spring	Whimbrel
Autumn	Shelduck, Ringed Plover, Grey Plover, Black-tailed Godwit, Greenshank, Redshank, Spotted Redshank, Knot, Turnstone

Leave Bridgwater westwards on the A39 and turn right at Cannington on to unclassified roads past Combwich to Steart. Walk northwards towards Steart Point where there is a lagoon and hide. For the eastern shore take the A38 to West Huntspill and follow the footpath along the river to the beach. Walk northwards. Hides are open on Fenning Island at weekends. Warden, D'Arches, Stolford, Stogunsey, Bridgwater. *Tel*: (0278) 652426.

Camel Estuary* OS200

Formerly a notable haunt of White-fronted Geese at the Walmsley Sanctuary, the Camel still retains interest even though these birds are now only hard-weather visitors. Most bird interest lies at the upper end of the estuary around the Amble Marshes area where wintering waders include Golden Plover and Curlew in good numbers. Teal and Wigeon are also numerous and passage periods produce terns and waders such as Whimbrel, Greenshank, Common Sandpiper and Spotted Redshank. Wintering waders include Greenshank and Little Stint.

Winter	Great Northern Diver, Slavonian Grebe, White-fronted Goose,

Wigeon, Teal, Eider, Grey Plover, Golden Plover, Little Stint, Knot, Sanderling, Ruff, Spotted Redshank, Greenshank, godwits, Curlew

Spring Sandwich Tern, Black Tern, Greenshank, Ruff

Autumn Merlin, Little Stint, Curlew Sandpiper, Spotted Redshank, Greenshank, Whimbrel, Ruff

The mouth can be seen from Padstow and Rock. Higher up leave Wadebridge eastwards on the A39 and turn left after crossing the River Camel on to the B3314 to Trewornan Bridge. On the left a footpath leads to Burniere Point and a hide belonging to the Cornwall Bird-watching and Preservation Society. The Society also have a hide at Tregunna west of Wadebridge. Take the A39 westwards and take right turn signposted Edmunton. Turn right to Tregunna and park near the farm. A lane leads 400m (440yds) to the hide and estuary.

Though keys from the Society are required to use the hides, much can be seen by the casual visitor.

Chew and Blagdon Reservoirs*** OS172

These famous reservoirs lie within a few km of each other on the north side of the Mendip Hills south of Bristol. Chew Valley Lake, to give it its proper name, is 490ha (1210a) and was flooded in 1953. Since then it has gained an enviable reputation for producing good birding at all seasons. The banks are mostly natural, gently shelving, and offer a plentiful supply of food. A large island has encouraged a variety of duck to breed, and their numbers are augmented in winter when the reservoir is ranked among the most important in the country. Wigeon, Shoveler, Pochard and Tufted Duck all form substantial flocks. In summer they are joined by Ruddy Duck and Garganey, and in winter by good numbers of Goldeneye and Goosander.

Waders and terns occur mostly on passage, but are then particularly interesting. Black Terns are regular and Little Gulls are frequently present. Black-tailed Godwit, Greenshank, Wood Sandpiper, Spotted Redshank, Ruff and others are regular, and there is always a good chance of an American wader here. The first European record of Pied-billed Grebe (and the second) was here.

Nearby Blagdon is much deeper than Chew, but regularly holds numbers of duck, especially when birds have been disturbed from Chew. Most bird-watchers work the two at the same time.

Winter Wigeon, Shoveler, Gadwall, Pochard, Tufted Duck, Goldeneye, Goosander, Ruddy Duck, Water Rail, Bearded Tit

Spring Garganey, Black Tern

Summer Shelduck, Gadwall, Shoveler, Garganey, Ruddy Duck, Reed Warbler, Sedge Warbler

Autumn Black-necked Grebe, Little Ringed Plover, Ruff, Greenshank, Spotted Redshank, Green Sandpiper, Wood Sandpiper, Curlew Sandpiper, Little Stint, Black-tailed Godwit, Black Tern, Common Tern, Little Gull

Chew Leave Bristol southwards on the A37 and turn right on to the A368 which crosses the south-eastern corner of the reservoir. Keep taking right turns to circumnavigate the entire lake viewing at Villice Bay, Heron Green, Herriott's Bridge and the dam. At Herriott's Bridge there is an area of reeds and pools with a public hide. Permits to walk the shoreline here and at Blagdon can be obtained from Woodford Lodge, Chew Stoke on the western bank of the reservoir.

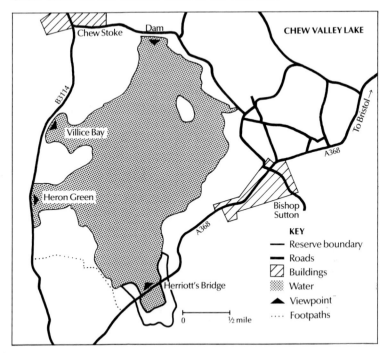

Blagdon Leave Bristol southwards on the A38 and turn left to Blagdon on the A368. Turn left at Blagdon to the dam signposted Butcombe. There is a footpath along the southern shore west of Ubley. Permits from Chew if requested for hide.

Christchurch Harbour* OS195

Although Christchurch Harbour is comparatively small, it does have quite large mudbanks with areas of saltings and shingle. Unfortunately it is disturbed by sailing in summer. Christchurch Borough Council also has a local nature reserve, with an information caravan, at Stanpit Marsh. This offers a variety of habitats – saltings, tidal mud, fresh pools, reed beds and water meadows. During the autumn all the usual waders (26 species have been recorded) can be found here in small numbers and the gorse bushes sometimes attract interesting passerine migrants. But a better venue for these species is Hengistbury Head on the southern side of the Harbour. Seabird movements can be good.

Winter Divers, grebes, Dunlin, Scoter, Snipe
Autumn Little Stint, Curlew Sandpiper, Sanderling skuas, auks, terns, Yellow Wagtail, Sedge Warbler, Reed Warbler

There is a public path on the east side of Town Bridge over the River Avon to Stanpit at Stanpit Lane, Christchurch, which is the best vantage point for viewing. There is also an information centre. Hengistbury is reached by crossing the bridge over the Stour signposted Southbourne and turning left after ½km (¼m).

Dartmoor*   OS191/202

Dartmoor National Park covers an area of nearly 100,000ha (247,000a) and forms the most significant upland area in southern England. It is, of course, thronged by tourists in summer, but the bird-watcher need not be daunted by either size or people. Though the high grass and heather clad moors roll on for mile after mile, and the twinkling rivers rush over shallow bottoms hemmed in by delightful oakwoods in all directions, still the watcher can see the best birds in a comparatively short time. A great deal can be seen from a car, but a certain amount of foot-slogging is required. On a fine day Dartmoor can be a delight, but it is noted for its fogs and the weather can change very rapidly. All walkers should be thoroughly prepared when setting out on a hike and the inexperienced should be accompanied by a seasoned hill walker. The main areas worth exploring are:

1 Burrator Reservoir and Plantations
2 Fernworthy Reservoir and Plantations
3 Okehampton area
4 Yarner Wood area and Hay Tor
5 Soussons Down Plantations and Wistman's Wood

Burrator, like other high-level reservoirs, is not particularly good for wildfowl, though wintering duck regularly include Goosander and Goldeneye. The surrounding plantations hold Crossbill, Redpoll and the regular warblers, while pure deciduous areas have Wood Warbler in summer and Brambling in winter. Buzzard, Sparrowhawk and Lesser Spotted Woodpecker are resident, and Dipper and Grey Wagtails breed along the streams.

Fernworthy is very similar, though even higher. The surrounding woods and fields are best in summer with Redstart quite numerous along with Tree Pipit, all three woodpeckers, Goldcrest and Cuckoo. The access lanes up via Chagford are often alive with birds in summer.

Okehampton is the base for exploring the most desolate and beautiful area of Dartmoor. To the south moors stretch unbroken for miles while the valleys of the East and West Okement Rivers are lined with rich oakwoods. Red Grouse are present high up and Golden Plover breed in small numbers. The valleys have Buzzard and Sparrowhawk plus a variety of warblers including Wood Warbler, plus Redstart.

Hay Tor is one of the typical granite outcrops that attract numerous tourists to Dartmoor and one side is heavily disturbed. A short walk, however, regains solitude and the chance of moorland birds, including Red Grouse and possible Ring Ouzel. Nearby Yarner Wood is an NNR with a wealth of species including Pied Flycatcher, Wood Warbler, Redstart, Tree Pipit and, in more open areas, Nightjar and Grasshopper Warbler.

Near Two Bridges lies Wistman's Wood, an NNR of old oaks that borders some good open moorland. At nearby Postbridge is Soussons Down with extensive plantations that are notable in winter as a haunt of Hen Harrier as well as Merlin, Red Grouse and even the occasional Great Grey Shrike.

Summer   Buzzard, Sparrowhawk, Red Grouse, Dipper, Grey Wagtail, Tree Pipit, Wood Warbler, Blackcap, Garden Warbler, Pied Flycatcher, Spotted Flycatcher, Redstart, Ring Ouzel, Wheatear, Whinchat, Redpoll

Winter   Buzzard, Sparrowhawk, Hen Harrier, Merlin, Great Grey Shrike, Dipper, Crossbill, Siskin, Redpoll, Brambling

Burrator   Take the A386 from Plymouth turning right at Yelverton on to the B3212. A road on the right leads to the reservoir and on to the woods at the north-eastern end.

Fernworthy   Leave Chagford on a maze of lanes to the reservoir and the woods which lie mainly south-west of the information centre.

Okehampton   Okehampton Castle NT has excellent woods and is well signposted south of the town. Woods along the East Okement River are nearby. For moorland species continue southwards towards the Army Camp

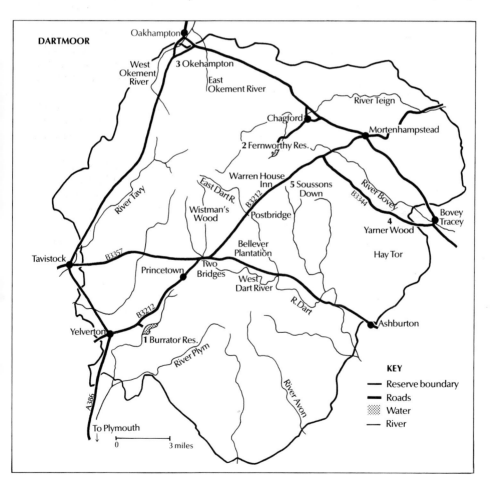

and explore off the road. Access may be restricted by military activities, but there are prominent signs and red flags at such times.

Yarner Wood Leave Bovey Tracey westwards on the B3344 and the NNR is on the left. Hay Tor lies to the south.

Soussons Down Walk northwards up the West Dart River to Wistman's Wood. Return and continue eastwards to Two Bridges and beyond on the B3212. Before Postbridge watch out for the Bellever Planation and the East Dart River. Several footpaths enable exploration. Continue eastwards to a car park opposite Warren House Inn. Walk eastwards through old mining debris and south to Soussons Down.

Exe Estuary****   OS192

The Exe is the most important area in the south-west for wildfowl and waders with several species congregating in internationally important numbers. Basically muddy, the inter-tidal area extends for 10km (6¼m) from Topsham to Exmouth with flats up to 1½km (1m) wide. Unfortunately the estuary is heavily developed, giving few opportunities to breeding birds, though the western shore is protected as a bird sanctuary and Dawlish Warren is a local bird reserve. Outstanding winter residents include up to 700 Black-tailed Godwit (17 per cent of the UK total) along with 1000 Brent, 4500 Wigeon and 3000 Oyster-catchers. There are also Red-breasted Mergansers, Ruff and Green-shank, as well as divers, grebes, seaduck, Peregrine, Avocet and an interesting array of gulls.

Spring sees a good passage of terns, waders and some scarcer birds, while in autumn passage waders are present throughout the period. There are also terns, together with the odd skua, and often Hobby and Osprey stay over for a few days.

The main high-tide roosts are at Dawlish Warren and Powderham Park and these two areas, together with the Exminster Marshes, are the main centres of bird-watching. Indeed, though the estuary can also be viewed from Exmouth and other places on the eastern shore, almost all birders concentrate on the west bank.

Winter Red-throated Diver, Slavonian Grebe, Brent Goose, Shelduck, Wigeon, Pintail, Shoveler, Scoter, Goldeneye, Red-breased Merganser, Peregrine, Ringed Plover, Grey Plover, Turnstone, Knot, Sanderling, Purple Sandpiper, Spotted Redshank, Greenshank, Ruff, Black-tailed Godwit, Bar-tailed Godwit, Avocet, Short-eared Owl

Passage Garganey, Merlin, Hobby, Osprey, Whimbrel, Green Sandpiper, Little Stint, Curlew Sandpiper, Ruff, Greenshank, Spotted Redshank, Common Tern, Black Tern, Arctic Skua, Great Skua

Exminster Marshes Leave Exeter southwards on the A379 to Exminster and turn left to the Swan's Nest Inn. Continue over the railway across splashy fields to the canal bank and walk southwards. This area depends on flooding and should be thoroughly explored.

Powderham Continue southwards on the A379 and turn left to Powderham. At the church a tunnel under the railway gives views of the estuary and a footpath on the left crosses the railway to the seawall. Continue southwards on the road beside the railway to view pools and the Park.

132

Dawlish Continue southwards to rejoin the A379 and follow signs to Dawlish
Warren Warren and the car park. Walk northwards to the golf course and turn
left to look back into the estuary. There is a hide here.

Exmoor* OS180/181

Though known as an area of open moorland, most of Exmoor is
privately owned with only a few commons such as Withypool Common
and Porlock Common as exceptions. Mostly the area consists of rough
grass and heather intersected by deep, well-wooded valleys. Though
known as a southern outpost of the Black Grouse, these birds are very
scarce and are certainly best sought farther north. Red Grouse, too, are
thin on the ground, but a walk across a heather moor may flush one or
two. In fact the bare open areas are rather thin for birds and while
Curlew, Ring Ouzel and Merlin breed, they are all decidedly scarce.
The wooded valleys on the other hand are full of birds with Wood
Warbler, Pied Flycatcher and Redstart abundant. Buzzards too are
numerous and there is a good chance of Hobby and Montagu's Harrier.

Summer Buzzard, Sparrowhawk, Montagu's Harrier, Hobby, Red Grouse,
Curlew, Ring Ouzel, Dipper, Pied Flycatcher, Redstart, Stonechat,
Whinchat, Wood Warbler, Raven

Exploration with the aid of OS maps is recommended with the area
between Porlock and Dulverton as good as any. Take the B3222
westwards from Dulverton and fork right at Five Ways Cross. This leads
down a wooded valley and then beyond up to Hawkridge Ridge.
Alternatively (additionally?), explore to the south over East Anstey
Common. In the west the Molland Common area is good for raptors.

Fal Estuary** OS204

Fal Estuary is really a misnomer, for the centre of this complex is the
deep Carrick Roads channel, and true estuarine conditions are concentrated in smaller areas at the mouths of the rivers Fal-Ruan, Tresillian,
Truro and Restronguet Creek. Here there are significant concentrations
of wildfowl and waders, while the deeper waters hold divers, grebes
and seaduck.
  Black-tailed Godwit winter in important numbers along with Curlew
and a few Spotted Redshank and Greenshank. Mostly these birds gather
on the Ruan Lanihorne mudflats and passage waders are best here too,
though the Tresillian River also has a good population.
  To the north Gerrans Bay has a good concentration of Black-throated
and other divers and grebes. To the south Falmouth Bay is a fine
gull-watching spot with rare species regular in season.

Winter Black-throated Diver, Great Northern Diver, Red-throated Diver,
Slavonian Grebe, Black-necked Grebe, Wigeon, Eider, Scoter, Black-
tailed Godwit, Bar-tailed Godwit, Curlew, Greenshank, Spotted Redshank, Avocet

133

Passage Ringed Plover, Black-tailed Godwit, Little Stint, Curlew Sandpiper, Ruff, Greenshank, Spotted Redshank, Green Sandpiper

Carrick Roads Best watched from Penarrow Point reached on foot from Mylor which lies east of the A39 north of Falmouth.

Tresillian Park at Pencalenick east of Truro on the A39 and follow the riverbank footpath toward St Clements.

Ruan Take the A39 eastwards from Truro and turn right on to the A3078 to
Lanihorne Ruan High Lanes. Take the road to Philleigh and after 200m (220yd) a private road to Trelonk Farm. A generous farmer allows parking and has permitted the erection of a hide. Keys *must* be obtained to visit this area from Mr S. Gay, Lower Farm, Trewithian, Nr Portscatho. Do not visit without permission.

Devoran Creek Leave Falmouth on the A39 which runs beside the Creek. Continue and take the first right to Devoran and alongside the tidal area to Penpoll.

Isles of Scilly*****   OS203

The Scilly (silly?) season is October and at that time some 2000 birders (twitchers?) descend on the islands in search of rarities. Mostly they hope for American birds that have got lost over the Atlantic and find among the isles their first landfall – they are seldom disappointed. The island grapevine works with amazing efficiency, and local boatmen are on stand-by to ferry the hordes to whichever island has produced the newest and rarest birds. Most of the visitors stay on St Mary's where the social life includes regular slide shows, quizzes, sales of photographs and drawings of yesterday's rarities and non-stop bird chat. The chances of anyone finding a rarity for themselves are slim, but some 50–60 really rare birds turn up every year.

At other seasons visiting bird-watchers can have the islands more or less to themselves. Spring is lovely with breeding auks, Manx Shearwaters and terns as well as a good passage of arriving summer visitors plus the occasional overshooting rarity. Summer is rather thin with many mainland species absent. Early autumn passage is good with rarities, including Americans, regularly present. Then comes October with vagrants from all directions including Siberian species (Sibes) as well as transatlantic waifs. At present a new bird is added to the British List almost every year . Late autumn and early winter may produce a rarity that has stayed on or even a late arrival, and November is now receiving much more attention than formerly.

Of the hundred islands only five are inhabited and these form the base for all visiting bird-watchers. St Mary's is the largest, with Hugh Town the only large centre of population. The others are Tresco, St Martin's, Bryher and St Agnes. The latter (formerly boasting a bird observatory) is a little gem that regularly produces rare birds in the loveliest of surroundings. Among the uninhabited islands Annet is a bird reserve with breeding seabirds including Puffin, Manx Shearwater and Storm Petrel. A few pairs of Roseate Terns still breed among the colonies of Common Terns that are scattered among the islands.

Though most parts of most islands are scoured daily in October there are some areas that are always checked first. These include the Porth

Hellick Pool and the St Agnes Pool for waders; the golf course and airfield on St Mary's for Buff-breasted Sandpipers; Porth Hellick on St Mary's and Horse Point on St Agnes for Sooty and Great Shearwaters; Holy Vale and Garrison Hill on St Mary's and the Parsonage on St Agnes for passerines, though these can and do turn up anywhere.

Inter-island boats leave Hugh Town every morning soon after 10.00 with exact times posted outside the shipping office in Main Street.

Winter   Great Northern Diver, Shag, Long-tailed Duck, Turnstone, Sanderling, Chiffchaff, Blackcap

Spring   Hoopoe, Black Redstart

Summer   Fulmar, Manx Shearwater, Storm Petrel, Shag, Common Tern, Roseate Tern, Puffin, Guillemot

Autumn   Sooty Shearwater, Great Shearwater, Pectoral Sandpiper, Buff-breasted Sandpiper, and all manner of rarities and vagrants

St Mary's   This island is reached via MV *Scillonian* from Penzance in 2½ hours, and the crossing is potentially rough. Details: Isles of Scilly Steamship Co., Penzance Quay, Cornwall. There is also a British Airways helicopter service from Eastern Green, Penzance – about 20 minutes. Accommodation mostly on St Mary's, but also on other inhabited islands – booking essential for October.

Note   Birders are now welcome on the Isles of Scilly, but sensible behaviour with regard to private land must be maintained to preserve this relationship.

Land's End**   OS203

Porthgwarra rates second only to the Isles of Scilly in the attention it receives from the autumn rarity hunters, and most Scilly-bound watchers invariably stop over to see what's about. In a way this is somewhat surprising, for Land's End boasts several other areas, such as the attractive Cot Valley near St Just, that could be equally productive. Perhaps it is the cliff-top car park at Porthgwarra that makes access so easy that is the difference. The coastline from St Levan Church to Carn Lês Boel offers a variety of habitats with sufficient cover to hold migrant passerines of a variety of species. Melodious Warbler, Tawny and Richard's Pipits, Ortolan Bunting, Firecrest, Yellow-browed Warbler and Red-breasted Flycatcher are more or less annual and real rarities turn up every year. St Just airfield may produce Dotterel and there is a good chance of a new British bird.

Autumn   Sooty Shearwater, Great Shearwater, Arctic Skua, Great Skua, Dotterel, Tawny Pipit, Richard's Pipit, Melodious Warbler, Barred Warbler, Firecrest

Leave Penzance westwards on the A30 and turn left on the B3283. Continue to the B3315 towards Sennen and turn left at a sharp bend signposted Porthgwarra. Continue to the car park. Paths allow exploration eastwards to St Levan Church and northwards along the cliffs towards Land's End. St Just airfield lies south of St Just on the B3306 with the Nanquido Valley extending westwards.

135

Lundy** OS180

Lundy Island lies in the Bristol Channel and has a history of seabird and migration studies. The bird observatory closed in 1973, and migrants are now searched for on a more casual basis. The seabirds include Manx Shearwater and Storm Petrel, though the large numbers of the former seen offshore probably come from the Pembrokeshire colonies. There are also Puffins, notably at Battery Point.

Migrants concentrate in the Millcombe Valley and other nearby areas of cover in the south-east of the Island.

Summer   Manx Shearwater, Fulmar, Storm Petrel, Shag, Kittiwake, Puffin, Guillemot, Razorbill

Passage   Warblers, chats, flycatchers, vagrants

Regular transport is by the *Polar Bear* supply ship, though during the summer helicopters run from Hartland and pleasure boats from Ilfracombe. For details of services and accommodation at Millcombe Hotel and Cottages contact the Landmark Trust, Shottesbrooke, Maidenhead, Berks SL6 3SW. *Tel*: Littlewick Green 5925.

Lye Rock* OS200

The area east of Tintagel holds the best mainland colonies of cliff-breeding seabirds in the region and is, in any case, a beautiful stretch of coastline.

Summer   Fulmar, Cormorant, Puffin, Razorbill, Guillemot, Kittiwake, Raven

Leave Tintagel northwards on the B3263 and park in Bossiney. A footpath at the north end of the village leads to Bossiney Haven. Walk south to Lye Rock or north to Long Island and Short Island beyond.

Marazion Marsh and Mounts Bay** OS203

The largest reed-bed in Cornwall is on the site of a submerged forest and very handy for Penzance. The adjacent Mounts Bay holds seabirds and the harbours at Penzance and Newlyn should not be ignored. The area is undoubtedly attractive to any transatlantic vagrant that turns up and a wide variety of birds can be seen. Winter brings divers and grebes along with unusual gulls, including Iceland and Glaucous, and a variety of waders among which Turnstone, Sanderling and Purple Sandpiper are regular. Bearded Tit and Bittern may appear.

Spring brings Black-throated Diver, Garganey and a variety of possible overshoots including Spoonbill, Kentish Plover and Hoopoe. In autumn waders include Little Stint, Curlew Sandpiper and at least one American species along with Black Tern, Little Gull and the elusive, but probably regular, Aquatic Warbler. Frankly anything can turn up here and even Spotted Crake is seen regularly.

Winter	Great Northern Diver, Slavonian Grebe, Scoter, Little Gull, Iceland Gull, Glaucous Gull, Mediterranean Gull, Sanderling, Turnstone, Purple Sandpiper, Water Rail
Spring	Black-throated Diver, Garganey, Ruff, Whimbrel, Little Ringed Plover, Sandwich Tern, Common Tern
Summer	Buzzard, Reed Warbler, Sedge Warbler, Stonechat
Autumn	Spotted Crake, Greenshank, Sanderling, Little Stint, Curlew Sandpiper, Little Gull, Black Tern, Aquatic Warbler

Marazion Leave Penzance eastwards on the A30 and bear right on to the A394 when the A30 leaves the coast. Drive along the shore and view the marsh to the left. There is access to the marsh via the car park at the eastern end, but this is seldom necessary.

Mounts Bay Check the gull flocks at Eastern Green opposite the Heliport east of Penzance. Also the sewage outfall beyond the harbour wall at Newlyn.

Poole Harbour***** OS195

Poole Harbour is a huge natural inlet immediately west of the Bournemouth–Poole complex. As a result much of its northern shoreline has been developed and attracts few birds. To the south and west, however, it is bordered by extensive heaths that are a major attraction in their own right. The inter-tidal mud banks hold large numbers of wildfowl and waders including nearly 10 per cent of Britain's wintering Black-tailed Godwit (500) as well as Ruff and Spotted Redshank. Shelduck, Teal and Pintail are significant, as well as good numbers of Red-breasted Mergansers and both Black-necked and Slavonian Grebes. Most wildfowl and waders concentrate at Brands Bay, Newtown Bay and on each side of the Arne reserve. Additionally, Brownsea Island, once a derelict and overgrown 'sanctuary' has been transformed by its owners, the National Trust, and its administrators, the Dorset NT, into a splendid bird reserve with a lagoon that regularly attracts the best of passage waders as well as breeding Sandwich Terns. It has well-positioned hides and 60 breeding species, including a 100+ pairs heronry as well as Nightjar and Dartford Warbler. Golden Pheasant also breed and Avocet winter.

Little Sea, a land-locked lagoon on the seaward side of the Harbour regularly holds duck and has a hide to watch them. Beyond is the sea with its sea-duck and grebes.

The heaths on the south side of Poole Harbour are famed as the stronghold of the Dartford Warbler and are by far the easiest place to see these elusive resident birds. Studland Heath is an NNR and Arne is a reserve of the RSPB. Both have efficient managements and information centres. Heaths also hold Nightjar, while woodland (deciduous and pine) has Buzzard, Sparrowhawk and a good selection of warblers. Reed beds at Arne hold the usual warblers plus Bearded Tit and Cetti's Warbler.

137

There is a lot to the Poole area, and exploration should not be rushed. Insects are noteworthy and all six British reptiles occur.

Winter Black-necked Grebe, Slavonian Grebe, Shelduck, Teal, Pintail, Shoveler, Red-breasted Merganser, Black-tailed Godwit, Bar-tailed Godwit, Spotted Redshank, Ruff

Summer Sparrowhawk, Buzzard, Water Rail, Nightjar, Dartford Warbler, Sedge Warbler, Reed Warbler, Cetti's Warbler, Bearded Tit

Passage Little Stint, Curlew Sandpiper, Black-tailed Godwit, Greenshank, Spotted Redshank, Wood Sandpiper, Green Sandpiper, Black Tern

Arne Leave Wareham southwards on the A351 and turn left after 1km (½m) to Arne. There is a reception area on the right after 3km (2m) a short distance before the village. Walk to the church and thence to Shipstal Point, the best spot for duck and terns. Conducted tours can be arranged with the Warden, Syldata, Arne, Wareham BH20 5BJ.

Studland Take the B3351 from Corfe Castle to Studland and continue northwards to Little Sea where a hide overlooks the lagoon. Continue northwards to the Ferry for views over Poole Harbour. A footpath leads along the shore to Redhorse Quay and beyond.

Brownsea Take the ferry, hourly between 10.00 and 5.00, from Sandbanks or Poole Quay on the northern shore of the Harbour. There is a NT information centre at Town Quay and a Dorset NT centre on the island. The Trust operates guided tours at 2.30 daily through the summer.

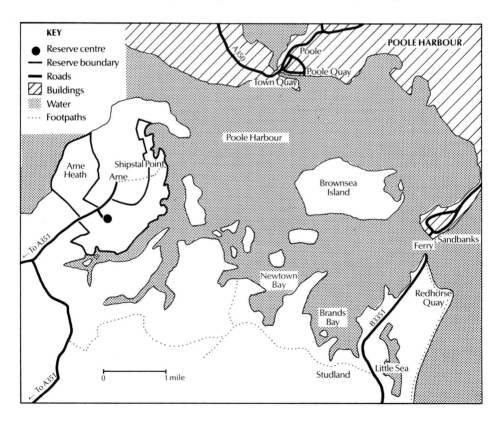

KEY
- ● Reserve centre
- ▬ Reserve boundary
- ▬ Roads
- ▨ Buildings
- ▦ Water
- ···· Footpaths

Prawle Point and Slapton Ley*** OS202

Prawle Point is the southernmost point of Devon and juts out into the Channel in a way that makes it an obvious place for migrant watchers. Dominant birds are migrating seabirds and small migrant passerines, both nocturnal and visible. The general lack of breeding-bird habitat makes it all the easier to spot grounded migrants, though this is the major stronghold of Cirl Bunting in Britain.

As with sea-watching elsewhere, wind strength and direction are all-important. Spring sees passage of gulls, terns, skuas and waders, while in autumn there are Gannets and Shearwaters as well. Passerines occur around the car park and in other bushy areas and regularly include rarities such as Melodious Warbler. American passerines have been noted here.

Behind the shingle at Start Bay lies Slapton Ley, a freshwater lagoon with large areas of reeds. There is a field-study centre here and a ringing station with an enviable record of producing autumn Aquatic Warblers. Open water has good flocks of diving duck including Ruddy Duck, and Great Crested Grebes breed. The Bay holds Great Northern Diver and Eiders in winter. Like Prawle Point, however, Slapton is at its best during migration when a wide variety of birds pass through. These regularly include Marsh Harrier, Black and Sandwich Terns, Garganey, Sooty Shearwater and minor rarities such as Hoopoe. Breeding birds include Cetti's Warbler and Cirl Bunting.

Winter	Great Northern Diver, Slavonian Grebe, Gadwall, Pochard, Tufted Duck, Eider, Scoter, Long-tailed Duck, Goldeneye, Goosander, Turnstone, Sanderling, Chiffchaff, Firecrest
Passage	Sooty Shearwater, Manx Shearwater, Marsh Harrier, Hobby, Mediterranean Gull, Little Gull, Black Tern, Sandwich Tern, Arctic Skua, Great Skua, Pomarine Skua, Aquatic Warbler, warblers, chats, flycatchers, rarities
Summer	Fulmar, Water Rail, Grey Wagtail, Sedge Warbler, Reed Warbler, Grasshopper Warbler, Cetti's Warbler, Cirl Bunting
Prawle	Roads south from the A379 at Frogmore, Chillington and Stokenham lead to Prawle Point via East Prawle. There is a car park at the end with good bushes. From here walk eastwards along a coastal path to the woods around the Point for migrants and Cirl Bunting.
Slapton	The A379 south of Dartmouth separates the Ley from the sea. Stop at many points and scan thoroughly. The field-study centre offers courses and accommodation.

Purbeck Cliffs* OS195

These limestone cliffs, which lie to the south of Poole Harbour, are among the most spectacular on the south coast. Rising to 100m (325ft) within 400m (440yd) of the sea, they provide a home for a variety of breeding seabirds which can be found between St Aldhelm's and

Durlston Heads. Sea-watching can be very good and Black Redstarts are to be seen in winter.

Winter   Black Redstart
Spring   Divers, Scoter, Gannet
Summer   Guillemot, Razorbill, Puffin, Kittiwake, Cormorant, Shag, Raven, Fulmar

Leave Swanage southwards to Durlston Head. Take the cliff path westwards past the lighthouses for a 8km (5m) walk to St Aldhelm's Head. There are several paths and tracks which provide 'escape routes' inland, but St Aldhelm's is almost the best part.

St Ives and Hayle Estuary****   OS203

Best known as a holiday resort and artist colony, St Ives takes on a fresh character when bird-watchers arrive for the autumn passage. The Island, actually only a peninsula, becomes the focal point whenever north-westerly gales drive seabirds into the Bristol Channel and they are forced close inshore as they beat their way back into the open sea. But St Ives Bay is always sheltered and holds seabirds at every season.

Nearby the delightful Hayle Estuary is sufficiently small to allow close views of waders at all times and particularly in autumn when rare birds are regularly present. Carnsew Pool is an embanked 'false estuary' that always holds water, while Copperhouse Creek is an extension of the estuary eastwards on the northern side of the town.

Winter birds include the usual waders and gulls, the latter gathering on the Hayle and at the sewage outfall at St Ives. Inevitably they include rarities with Mediterranean and Glaucous regular. Also fast becoming annual is the Ring-billed Gull that arrives in late winter with the passage of Common Gulls. Divers and grebes winter in St Ives Bay and Bar-tailed Godwits and a few Knot on the Hayle.

Spring and summer may be rather thin, though Black Terns regularly pass through, and it is the autumn that brings in the birds and the watchers. Then up to 30,000 Kittiwakes may be seen from The Island along with a few Sabine's Gulls making this the most regular spot in the country for this species. Terns may be abundant, together with their attendant skuas, and shearwaters and petrels, phalaropes, auks and divers can all be seen in suitable conditions. Like most sea-watch spots St Ives Island needs specific winds to produce the goods, and then the conditions may be dauntingly foul. On a good day there are rare seabirds galore.

Autumn also brings the best of the American waders to the Hayle and Pectoral Sandpipers are often on Copperhouse Creek. White-rumped Sandpiper and dowitchers are possibles along with Wood and Curlew Sandpipers, Little Stint, Ruff and Little Ringed Plover. Terns are regularly present, often including Roseate and Black, and the scarcer grebes often frequent Carnsew Pool.

Winter   Black-throated Diver, Great Northern Diver, Slavonian Grebe, Gadwall, Wigeon, Red-breasted Merganser, Ringed Plover, Grey Plover,

Turnstone, Knot, Greenshank, Common Sandpiper, Bar-tailed Godwit, Mediterranean Gull, Glaucous Gull

Spring Whimbrel, Ruff, Little Ringed Plover, Sandwich Tern, Black Tern

Autumn Sooty Shearwater, Manx (and Balearic) Shearwater, Leach's Petrel, Mediterranean Gull, Sabine's Gull, Little Gull, Roseate Tern, Black Tern, Arctic Skua, Great Skua, Pomarine Skua, Grey Phalarope, Spotted Redshank, Greenshank, Wood Sandpiper, Curlew Sandpiper, Little Stint, Ruff

St Ives Follow signs to the car park on the northern edge of town and take the path up the adjacent headland. The Bay and Harbour are of straighforward access.

Hayle Estuary Park in Hayle and follow roads right round the estuary. There is a pub at the head of the estuary where cars may be parked and where the RSPB has a hide. Carnsew Pool is reached via a footpath along the estuary shore from the south.

Severn Beach* OS172

A small village on the Severn Estuary about 5km (3m) south of the Severn Bridge. At this point a huge area of mud, sand, rock and shingle is exposed providing a home to one of the best concentrations of waders on the southern shore of the estuary – only Bridgwater Bay has more waders. The shoreline extends southwards to Chittening Warth (which is best approached from this area) where many waders gather at high tide.

Winter Ringed Plover, Grey Plover, Turnstone, Purple Sandpiper, Redshank, Bar-tailed Godwit, Curlew, Dunlin, Knot

Leave the M5 at Exit 17 or 18 westwards on to minor roads to Severn Beach off the A403. Walk southwards for Chittening Warth.

Somerset Levels*** OS182

The Somerset Levels, or the 'Moors and Levels' as they are correctly called, are one of the last large areas of lowland floods not totally destroyed by farming interests. In 1983 the political debate over the future of this outstanding area reached television screens and national papers as the NCC, RSPB and other conservation bodies argued their case with local farming interests and the Ministry of Agriculture. Statutory status proved ineffective in protecting these areas of low-lying grazing, and as a result the RSPB purchased 200ha (490a) of West Sedgemoor as a reserve. Though this is probably the best area, it is but a drop in the ocean when compared with the 250 square miles of the whole area. It may well be that in future little will remain of the Somerset Levels except the RSPB reserve.

The Levels are drained by five rivers and a maze of drainage ditches called rhynes. They offer good summer grazing, but are generally too heavily flooded for cattle in winter. At this time some 12,000 duck, including good flocks of Wigeon and Teal, use their splashy pastures to feed along with 100–300 Bewick Swans and numerous Golden Plover, Snipe and Dunlin. In summer Snipe, Curlew and, outstandingly, a small number of Black-tailed Godwits breed. There are also Yellow Wagtails, Whinchats and, on passage, the area is a staging post for Whimbrel which may number several thousand in spring.

Nearby, along the southern edge of West Sedgemoor, there is a well-wooded ridge that has the largest heronry in Somerset as well as Nightingale and Buzzard.

The best areas for birds are:

1 Kingsmoor
2 Moorlinch
3 Tealham-Tadham
4 Wetmoor (now largely improved) and
5 West Sedgemoor

Nearby Shapwick Heath has been mostly destroyed by the commercial extraction of peat despite its status as an NNR. All in all the casual visitor could do no better than visit the RSPB reserve.

Winter Bewick's Swan, Wigeon, Teal, Mallard, Golden Plover, Dunlin
Summer Black-tailed Godwit, Snipe, Redshank, Curlew, Yellow Wagtail

Though the whole area can be explored via roads and footpaths a visit to the RSPB reserve at West Sedgemoor must be arranged with the Warden at Hadleigh, White Street, North Curry, Near Taunton TA3 6HL, as parking and access are difficult.

Stithians Reservoir*   OS204

This is by far the best inland freshwater in the south-west with duck in winter and a good passage of waders, particularly in autumn when water levels are low. It is in any case a shallow-water lake and is preferred by surface feeders such as Teal, Wigeon and Gadwall. Autumn brings all the regular freshwater waders, but often in really good numbers. Green Sandpiper, Greenshank and Ruff are regularly present in double figures and Little Stint and Curlew Sandpipers may be even more numerous. American species include regular Pectoral Sandpiper (once seven together) as well as dowitchers, Lesser Yellow-legs and others. Autumn also brings Garganey, Black Tern, Little Gull and the occasional Peregrine.

Winter Teal, Wigeon, Gadwall, Golden Plover, Ruff, Snipe
Autumn Peregrine, Ringed Plover, Little Ringed Plover, Pectoral Sandpiper, Greenshank, Green Sandpiper, Wood Sandpiper, Little Stint, Curlew Sandpiper, Little Gull, Black Tern

Leave Penryn northwards on the A393 and take left turn signposted Stithians. Follow signs to Carnkie and the reservoir. Surrounding roads give good views especially along the western edge near the Golden

Lion. There are hides at the southern end where the road separates off a small marsh. Keys are available from Cornwall Bird-watching and Protection Society, but are not essential.

Sutton Bingham Reservoir* OS194

Lying on the Dorset border 5km (3m) south of Yeovil, this T-shaped reservoir was flooded in 1956. Large flocks of dabbling duck are attracted by its mainly natural, gently sloping banks, making it the ninth best location in England. There is usually a trickle of waders on passage and Black Terns are regular in autumn. A total of 146 species have been recorded.

Winter   Bewick's Swan, Wigeon, Shoveler, Pintail, Gadwall, Goldeneye, Goosander
Spring   Waders
Autumn   Waders, Black Tern

Leave Yeovil westwards on the A30 and turn left outside the town on to the A37. After 4km (2½m) turn right on to an unclassified road leading to Sutton Bingham. This road provides excellent views over the reservoir, particularly from the causeway before the village. There are numerous vantage points to the south and a public viewing area is open from April to September.

Tamar Estuary**** OS201

This large inter-tidal area, centred on the Devon–Cornwall border at Plymouth, is one of the most important in the south-west for waders and wildfowl, several species of which reach significant numbers. Actually there are several rivers which join the deep Hamoaze channel and Plymouth Sound, but for completeness sake the Plym, Tamar, Tavy and Lynher estuaries plus the so-called St John's and Millbrook Lakes are all jointly treated here.

Plymouth Sound itself holds divers and grebes, mostly Great Northern and Slavonian, but hard weather may bring in other species including Red-necked. Sea-duck are also present, including Long-tailed Duck and Eider. Gull-watchers tend to concentrate on the fish docks and the sewage outfall at The Hoe, where Glaucous, Iceland and Mediterranean are regular in winter along with occasional Ring-billed.

The Plym estuary is rather thin, but still holds Shelduck, Black-tailed Godwit and the occasional wintering Greenshank. Here, too, gulls are a feature. At low tide several thousand may include Glaucous and Mediterranean, and this is one of the best spots for Ring-billed.

The Tavy is also less full of birds than the western side of the complex, but duck are regularly present including Goldeneye, and Slavonian Grebes can often be seen. Wintering waders include Spotted Redshank, Greenshank and Common Sandpiper and sometimes a few

143

Avocets. The best place for Avocets, however, is the upper Tamar near Cargreen where up to 100 spend the winter. To the south is Kingsmill Lake, where many Tamar waders gather at high tide and where some marshy fields regularly hold Greenshank and Little Stint in winter as well as good passage waders in autumn. Peregrine often winter here, as well as on the Tavy below Bere Ferrers, and the occasional Osprey may pause in autumn.

The Lynher estuary is best known for its winter wildfowl, including large numbers of Wigeon, that frequently flight off to St John's Lake, and Pintail which concentrate on the northern shore of the upper estuary. Spotted Redshank and Greenshank both winter along with Green and Common Sandpipers. St John's Lake may have huge flocks of Wigeon, and there are always a few sea-duck or divers and grebes to be seen. At the mouth, near the car ferry at Torpoint, Black-tailed and Bar-tailed Godwits winter, and there are good numbers of other waders.

Taking the whole Tamar complex the area supports nearly 10 per cent of the country's wintering Black-tailed Godwits, 2 per cent of Wigeon and over 1 per cent of our Golden Plover, Dunlin and Redshank. It also has over 75 per cent of Britain's wintering Avocets.

To the south-east of Plymouth lies the intimate Yealm estuary with the attractive Wembury area just along the coast. Fulmars haunt the cliffs, but the inter-tidal rocks are a regular spot for Purple Sandpiper, while Turnstones can be found throughout the year. This is also a good place for Cirl Bunting among the fields. The Yealm has a few wildfowl and waders, but regularly holds wintering Greenshank.

Winter   Great Northern Diver, Slavonian Grebe, Wigeon, Teal, Pintail, Shelduck, Goldeneye, Long-tailed Duck, Scoter, Eider, Peregrine, Avocet, Spotted Redshank, Greenshank, Common Sandpiper, Green Sandpiper, Knot, Black-tailed Godwit, Bar-tailed Godwit, Glaucous Gull, Iceland Gull, Mediterranean Gull, Little Gull

Autumn   Little Stint, Curlew Sandpiper, Green Sandpiper, Wood Sandpiper, Spotted Redshank, Greenshank, Sandwich Tern, Common Tern

Plymouth Sound   Gulls gather at The Hoe at Barbican Docks and Millbank Docks, especially at the sewage outfall at the western end. Also check Jennycliff Bay by crossing Laina Bridge and following signs to Hooe. The bay car park is a good starting point.

Plym   An embanked road extends along the northern shore offering car birding, but by crossing Laina Bridge and following signs to Saltram on foot there is birding in quieter surroundings.

Tavy   Leave the A38 northwards on the eastern side of the Tamar Bridge and follow signs to Budshead. Footpaths lead to Warren Point.

Tamar   Cross the Tamar Bridge and turn off at Carkeel to Botus Fleming where turn right to Cargreen. Thereafter proceed southwards to Landulph Church. Walk along the road to a public footpath with a splashy marsh and continue to Kingsmill Lake. Walk along the shore to watch over the high-tide roost and adjacent fresh marsh area.

Lynher   Cross the Ferry (watch out for divers and grebes) to Torpoint and continue on the A374 to 2km (1¼m) past Antony to a picnic site. Good views over the best part of the estuary.

St John's Lake   Roads lead along the shoreline from Torpoint.

Millbrook Lake Continue from St John's on the B3247.

Wembury Leave the A379 east of Plymouth southwards at Elburton on to a maze of unclassified roads to Wembury Point. Walk down the hill, turning left down a steep footpath roughly opposite the entrance to *HMS Cambridge*.

Torbay*
OS202

Centre of the south Devon tourist industry with Torquay as its heart, this area still offers good birding with breeding seabirds and good seawatching in season. Hope's Nose lies immediately east of Torquay and boasts a good Kittiwake colony at Ore Stone which also holds Guillemots and even a few Razorbills. Sea-watching brings spring terns, skuas and the gulls that often gather at the sewage outfall.

Torbay, especially the southern part, is good for divers and grebes in winter, particularly for Slavonian and Black-necked off Preston. There are also Turnstones and Purple Sandpipers here. Berry Head to the south has a strong colony of Guillemots with Fulmar, Kittiwake and the odd pair of Razorbills.

Winter Great Northern Diver, Red-throated Diver, Slavonian Grebe, Black-necked Grebe, Eider, Scoter, Turnstone, Purple Sandpiper

Summer Fulmar, Shag, Kittiwake, Guillemot, Razorbill

All three sites are easily accessible from the holiday resort at Torquay, though Hope's Nose requires a walk from the highest point of Marine Drive.

Weymouth*****
OS194

The area around the seaside resort of Weymouth offers a variety of bird-rich habitats that have been popular with bird-watchers for generations. Recently the RSPB has acquired Lodmoor to add to its interest in the delightful Radipole Lake, surely one of the finest bird reserves in the country and uniquely situated within the town boundaries. The yacht basin in the town is a noted gull haunt, Portland Harbour holds interesting seabirds, and the Isle of Portland has one of the country's most famous bird observatories. As if this were not enough the Ferrybridge between Portland and the mainland is a noted haunt of rare waders and terns and Abbotsbury has the famous Swannery.

Radipole is, however, the gem of this collection. It consists of the old estuary of the River Wey and is predominantly reeds with scrub along the paths and areas of open water and adjacent mud banks. Bearded Tit and Cetti's Warbler breed along with a strong population of regular warblers. During passage periods good numbers of waders appear including Ruff, Greenshank, Curlew Sandpiper, Little Stint, Spotted Redshank and the occasional American species. Black Terns pass through and there is a strong gathering of Little Gulls. Other gulls often include a rarity or two, sometimes Ring-billed. Garganey are also regular.

Nearby Lodmoor is an area of damp rough grazing that has always taken second place to Radipole, but which has always deserved more than a second look. Doubtless the RSPB has plans to improve its attractions.

Portland Harbour is good for sea-duck with Red-breasted Merganser as well as Slavonian Grebe. Nearby Ferrybridge is an important wintering site for Ringed Plover and a haunt of passage waders and rare gulls and terns.

Portland Bird Observatory is based at the old lighthouse and offers comfortable accommodation to migration students. The passage of seabirds is often very good with Manx (Balearic) Shearwaters as well as Sooty and Cory's regular along with skuas, including Pomarine, in early May. Autumn brings a variety of birds to the small walled fields and rarities turn up every autumn. Corn Bunting resident.

Abbotsbury is generally regarded as rather 'dude', but the Swannery holds several hundred pairs of Mute Swans and is visited by several thousand Wigeon and a good flock of Red-breasted Mergansers in winter.

All in all Weymouth is an outstanding bird area at all seasons.

Winter	Slavonian Grebe, Wigeon, Red-breasted Merganser, Water Rail
Spring	Garganey, Greenshank, Spotted Redshank, Ruff, Black Tern, Pomarine Skua, Arctic Skua, gulls, Hoopoe
Summer	Bearded Tit, Cetti's Warbler, Grasshopper Warbler, Sedge Warbler, Reed Warbler, Corn Bunting
Autumn	Manx (Balearic) Shearwater, Sooty Shearwater, Curlew Sandpiper, Little Stint, Spotted Redshank, Greenshank, Ruff, Wood Sandpiper, Green Sandpiper, Black Tern, Common Tern, Arctic Skua, Mediterranean Gull, warblers, chats, flycatchers, rarities

Radipole	Find the Swannery car park (well signposted) in central Weymouth with the RSPB information centre. Explore by following the nature trail (suitable for the disabled) with hides and listening posts.
Lodmoor	Obtain current information from RSPB at Radipole and/or watch from the coastal A353 out of Weymouth.
Yacht Basin	Easily found in central Weymouth, south of Radipole. There is a road along the western shore.
Ferrybridge and Portland Harbour	Follow signs on the A354 from Weymouth to Portland. Park on the northern side and explore to east and west.
Portland Bird Observatory	Contact the Warden, Old Lower Light, Portland, Dorset.
Abbotsbury	Leave the A35 southwards at the western end of Martintown 5km (3m) west of Dorchester. Follow Abbotsbury signposts.

North-East Scotland

Grampian and Highland (part)

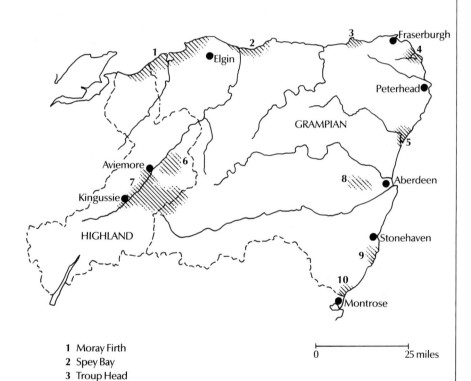

1 Moray Firth
2 Spey Bay
3 Troup Head
4 Loch of Strathbeg
5 Ythan Estuary
6 Loch Garten and Abernethy
7 Speyside
8 Loch of Skene
9 Foulsheugh
10 St Cyrus

0   25 miles

147

Abernethy and Loch Garten**** OS36

The forest at Abernethy was famed for its birds long before the Osprey returned to breed. Then it was a matter of long, lonely walks through the forests and plantations, along the streams, over the moors and bogs and around the lochs. Today thousands of trippers make the trek to see 'The Ospreys', signposted for miles around, at this RSPB reserve. Yet get away from the observation post (which is not a hide so much as a shop with viewing slits) and the birder can explore almost as before. All the Caledonian specialities occur, including Crested Tit, Scottish Crossbill, Black Grouse and Capercaillie. The largest lek of this latter species in the country is in Abernethy.

In autumn Pinkfeet use the area as a stop-over, and 1000 stay on to winter. Ospreys also stay on late and can be seen fishing Loch Garten. In spring many wildfowl pass through and several species may stay late.

Summer Peregrine, Merlin, Osprey, Golden Eagle, Teal, Tufted Duck, Wigeon, Goosander, Black Grouse, Capercaillie, Woodcock, Golden Plover, Greenshank, Common Sandpiper, Long-eared Owl, Crested Tit, Redstart, Siskin, Scottish Crossbill

Passage Pink-footed Goose, Wigeon, Teal, Goldeneye

Winter Whooper Swan, Pink-footed Goose, Hen Harrier, Rough-legged Buzzard, Short-eared Owl, Great Grey Shrike

Leave the A95 eastwards to Boat of Garten on B970. Follow signs to Nethybridge and turn right signposted 'To The Ospreys'. A footpath runs along the west side of Loch Garten to Loch Mallachie. The observation post is further east. There are tracks into the forest and hills off the road to the east that permit full exploration.

Fowlsheugh** OS45

A cliff-breeding seabird reserve of the RSPB some 32km (20m) south of Aberdeen. Truly huge numbers of birds breed here including 30,000 pairs each of Guillemot and Kittiwake, together with 5000 pairs of Razorbill and lesser numbers of Puffin.

Summer Fulmar, Shag, Eider, Kittiwake, Guillemot, Razorbill, Puffin

Leave Stonehaven southwards on the A92 and turn left after 5km (3m) to Crawton where there is a car park. Walk northwards on the cliff top footpath for 1km (½m). Easy viewing.

Moray Firth*** OS27

The southern shore of the Moray Firth between Nairn and Elgin has several outstanding bird areas, including Culbin Bar and its adjacent forests and Findhorn and Burghead Bays. The number of sea-duck here is difficult to estimate, but there are plenty of Common and Velvet

Scoter and up to 10,000 Long-tailed Duck often gather to roost in Burghead Bay. Waders prefer Culbin Bar and Findhorn Bay and include Knot and Bar-tailed Godwit. Winter sees good numbers of divers including Great Northern.

In summer Culbin Bar has large terneries while the nearby forest has Crested Tit, Crossbill, Siskin and Capercaillie. Passage periods bring a variety of species including terns, skuas and waders.

Winter	Great Northern Diver, Black-throated Diver, Red-throated Diver, Whooper Swan, Greylag Goose, Wigeon, Goldeneye, Long-tailed Duck, Scoter, Velvet Scoter, Knot, Curlew
Summer	Capercaillie, Arctic Tern, Common Tern, Little Tern, Crested Tit, Siskin, Crossbill
Autumn	Whimbrel, Greenshank, Little Stint

Culbin Bar	Leave Forres westwards on the A96 and fork right on minor roads to Kintessack village after crossing the Findhorn. Continue to Welhill gate and thence on foot.
Findhorn Bay	Leave Forres eastwards on the A96 and fork left on the B9011. At Kinloss turn left to Findhorn. This road runs alongside the Bay.
Burghead Bay	Leave Forres eastwards on the A96 and fork left on to the B9011. Continue to Burghead Harbour.

Orkney Islands**** OS5/6/7

The Orkneys are separated from Caithness by the Pentland Firth which, at one point, is no more than 10km (6¼m) wide. There are 29 inhabited isles, 38 holmes, and a vast number of skerries. The landscape is gentle and rolling with large areas of agriculture as well as some rolling moorland. In the west there are some fine high cliffs and the best (in terms of species numbers) seabird colonies in Britain.

Orkney is a holiday venue and most visitors will wish to explore all the major bird islands. Mainland, with its capital, Kirkwall, offers a variety of different habitats including freshwater lochs with winter wildfowl. The best of these are the adjacent Lochs of Harray and Stenness, with sea-duck on the latter and other duck on the former. By far the best area for wildfowl, however, is Scapa Flow to the south where up to 2400 Long-tailed Duck regularly winter along with 2000 Eider and 300 Merganser, plus 200 Great Northern Diver and 60 Slavonian Grebe. Waders also winter in good numbers as do gulls, including northern birds such as Glaucous and Iceland Gulls.

But it is in the summer that most visitors make the trip to Orkney. At that time Mainland has two major areas worthy of anyone's attention. Marwick Head, an RSPB reserve, is a magnificent seabird cliff teeming with birds. Fulmar, Kittiwake, Guillemot, Razorbill and Puffin all nest in numbers. Peregrine, Raven and Twite may all be seen as well as visiting Great and Arctic Skuas. The other important Mainland areas are also RSPB reserves – the moors at Hobbister, Birsay and Cottasgarth. These are best known as the stronghold of Hen Harrier. At one time Orkney was their only breeding place in Britain, and it was as a result of protection here that they were able to increase and spread back to the

British mainland. Hobbister also has Merlin, Short-eared Owl, Curlew, Snipe, Redshank and Red Grouse. Loch Kirbister has Red-throated Diver.

Birsay Moors and Cottasgarth are moors of grass and heather with a small reed bed at Dee of Dirkdale where Sedge Warblers breed — something of a local speciality. Here, too, there are Hen Harrier and Merlin, Short-eared Owl, eight species of wader and Red-throated Diver. The RSPB also has a further reserve at The Loons, a marshy area in the north-west of Mainland, that is a breeding ground of wildfowl and waders and a noted Corncrake site.

Hoy is the second largest island and its tall cliffs are noted for breeding seabirds including Black Guillemot, Puffin, Guillemot, Razorbill and masses of Kittiwakes. The highest point is Ward Hill with both skuas and possible Peregrine and Golden Eagle. The RSPB owns a large reserve on Hoy that includes the cliffs of St John's Head with the usual seabirds and a colony of Manx Shearwaters.

The northern islands of Westray and Papa Westray are fortunately well populated by man (and birds) making them surprisingly accessible for small islands. Noup Cliffs on Westray are quite breathtaking with 40,000 Guillemot, 25,000 Kittiwake plus smaller numbers of the other usual cliff-nesting species, including genuine Rock Doves. Kelda Bar is a good view point. North Hill, on the even smaller Papa Westray, is also spectacular with Fowl Craig holding cliff-nesters, and the lower areas a colony of 6000 pairs of Arctic Tern and 100 Arctic Skua. The last Orkney Great Auk was shot here in 1813, but Corncrakes can still be heard and occasionally seen. Between them Westray and Papa Westray support 19 species of seabird — more than any other site in Britain.

One further site deserves a mention. Copinsay was purchased as a memorial to James Fisher and is run by the RSPB. James will be remembered in a variety of ways, but primarily as a serious ornithologist with an encyclopedic knowledge of seabirds and as a professional bird publicist. Copinsay with its 15,000 Guillemots and other seabirds, is a fitting tribute.

Summer Red throated Diver, Fulmar, Shag, Hen Harrier, Peregrine, Merlin, Golden Eagle, Wigeon, Teal, Pintail, Corncrake, Red Grouse, Snipe, Redshank, Curlew, Common Gull, Kittiwake, Arctic Tern, Great Skua, Arctic Skua, Guillemot, Razorbill, Puffin, Black Guillemot

Winter Red-throated Diver, Great Northern Diver, Slavonian Grebe, Black-necked Grebe, Long-tailed Duck, Goldeneye, Velvet Scoter, Scaup, Glaucous Gull, Iceland Gull

Orkney is reached by air to Kirkwall and by boat to Kirkwall and Stromness. The islands are served by many ferries and by Loganair – a beautiful way to fly. Details of transport and accommodation from Orkney Tourist Information Office, Broad Street, Kirkwall, Orkney KW15 1DH.

Marwick Head Leave the A967 westwards, ½km (¼m) north of its junction with A986. On the B9056 watch for the Kitchener Memorial on the right. Park and walk along the track to the cliff tops. The number 129 painted on a rock is one of many good viewpoints.

The Loons Lies in the north-west of the island 18km (11m) north of Stromness immediately north of Loch of Isbister. OS Ref: HY253243. View from the road.

Birsay and Cottasgarth Lie 9km (5½m) north of Finstown at OS Ref: HY368197. Cars may be parked at Lower Cottasgarth Farm. Access unrestricted.

Hobbister Some 9km (5½m) south-west of Kirkwall on the A964 on the east side of Waulkmill Bay. Access unrestricted between A964 and the sea.

Scapa Flow The A961 connects the south-eastern islands giving good views from the barrages.

Noup Cliffs, Westray Via Noup Farm to the lighthouse. No restrictions, but close gates after passing.

Hoy Daily service from Stromness to Moness Pier. RSPB reserve.

Papa Westray A two-minute flight from Westray and walk to North Hill.

Copinsay Access by boat from Newark Bay or Skaill. There is an information centre, and spartan accommodation may be available.

ORKNEY ISLANDS

St Cyrus* OS45

St Cyrus lies at the mouth of the River North Esk and has extensive sand and shingle spits. It holds good numbers of waders and significant spring and autumn concentrations of Goosander, Merganser and Eider. Breeding birds should not be ignored and include both Sedge and Grasshopper Warbler and a good colony of Little Terns. To the north the rocky coastline toward Johnshaven is a wintering ground of Purple Sandpiper and the summer moulting ground of Eider.

Winter Divers, Purple Sandpiper, Turnstone, Redshank
Spring Goosander, Red-breasted Merganser, Eider
Autumn Goosander, Red-breasted Merganser, Arctic Skua, Great Skua, Kittiwake

Leave Montrose northwards on the A92 turning right to St Cyrus. Walk southwards to the river mouth. Access at OS Ref: NO752646 or better at NO743635. Advice and information from the Warden, Rose Cottage, Lannonfauld Road, Hillside, Montrose. *Tel:* (067 483) 615.

Shetland Isles***** OS1/2/3/4

The Shetland Isles lie in latitude 60° north, which is the same as Cape Farewell in Greenland and only 6° south of the Arctic Circle. They are nearer Bergen in Norway than Aberdeen in Scotland and the Shetlanders are proud of their Norse origins and do not think of themselves as Scots. The islands extend for 115km (71½m) from north to south and 60km (37¼m) from east to west. Mainland dominates the area, but its coastline is so indented that nowhere is more than 5km (3m) from the sea. Only 19 of the 100 odd islands are inhabited and over half of the population lives on Mainland. Every one of the islands is good for birds and choice is limited by time and ease of access. The discovery and development of North Sea oil has changed the character of the islands radically. While transport services have improved, hotels are generally full and require early booking. There are various oil terminals, and the once quiet town of Lerwick buzzes to the talk of oilworkers and executives rather than fishermen. Nevertheless, Shetland has much to offer the birder at all seasons.

Most people visit during the breeding season when the seabird colonies of the north and west are among the most dramatic in the world. There are thriving gannetries at Hermaness and Noss, plus a new one beginning to become established on Fair Isle. All three of these sites support splendid colonies of other seabirds including the usual auks, gulls and both skuas. Fetlar and Foula also have good seabird colonies.

Other northern specialities are more elusive, but breeding waders include Whimbrel, Greenshank and at two sites the decidedly rare Red-necked Phalarope. Red-throated Divers are widespread and Great Northerns regularly stay very late in spring. Scoter breed here and there are Manx Shearwater and Storm Petrel on Fetlar. The endemic Shetland Wren (sub-species) is a widespread breeder, while Fair Isle has its own sub-species.

Unlike so many other British and Irish islands, birding is not confined to the summer months. Fair Isle is the site of Britain's number one bird observatory with an incredible list of rare birds to its credit. Indeed until the full possibilities of the Isles of Scilly were discovered, Fair Isle was *the* place to go to add a new bird to the British list. Even now it remains a very good bet and produces exceptional rarities every autumn. Not, of course, that rare birds cannot be found elsewhere in Shetland. The Out Skerries are a favourite with several watchers who prefer to find their own rarities, while there are other areas that would definitely repay an autumn trip. One such is the north-eastern corner of Unst at Skaw.

Winter here has its own attractions with a variety of waders that includes 3500 Purple Sandpiper and twice that number of Turnstone. Wildfowl include 10,000 Eider, 2000 Long-tailed Duck as well as 400 Great Northern Diver and 100 Slavonian Grebe. However, this is northern gull territory *par excellence* and Glaucous and Iceland are regular, while Ivory and Ross's are decidedly frequent. Lerwick Harbour is as good a place as any.

Summer   Red-throated Diver, Great Northern Diver, Fulmar, Manx Shearwater,

Storm Petrel, Gannet, Shag, Wigeon, Eider, Scoter, Red-breasted Merganser, Dunlin, Golden Plover, Black-tailed Godwit, Common Sandpiper, Greenshank, Curlew, Whimbrel, Red-necked Phalarope, Arctic Tern, Arctic Skua, Kittiwake, Common Gull, Guillemot, Razorbill, Puffin, Black Guillemot, Raven, Twite

Winter   Great Northern Diver, Slavonian Grebe, Whooper Swan, Wigeon, Long-tailed Duck, Eider, Velvet Scoter, Purple Sandpiper, Turnstone, Snipe, Redshank, Curlew, Glaucous Gull, Iceland Gull, rare gulls and wildfowl

Mainland   Loch of Spiggie is a shallow, lowland lake in the southern part of the island that is an RSPB reserve, but which can be explored via the surrounding lanes. Red-necked Phalarope breed (sometimes) and Whooper Swan winter along with duck. Long-tailed Duck moult here in spring. Ronas Hill NNR lies on the north-western side of Mainland and extends along 20km (12½m) of coast including some fearsome cliffs with seabird colonies. It is also a stronghold of both skuas. Leave Lerwick northwards on the A970 almost to the northernmost point of the island.

Noss NNR   This is an island on the east coast very near Lerwick. It is best known as a major gannetry. The RSPB has a warden resident in summer. Regular boats cross Noss Sound in summer. Details from the Information Office in Lerwick. Much easier is to take one of the regular boat trips advertised from Lerwick Harbour and see the spectacle from the sea.

Yell Sound
Islands   These lie between Mainland and Yell and are home to a variety of species that can be seen elsewhere in Shetland, including the elusive Leach's Petrel and good colonies of other seabirds. They are a reserve of the RSPB with no visiting arrangements.

Lumbister   Another RSPB reserve some 2km (1¼m) north-west of Mid Yell to the north and west of the A968. It is typical of the area with lochs, streams and moors offering a home to typical birds of Yell.

Fetlar   Home of the famous Snowy Owls (no longer breeding for lack of an adult male) as well as of special Shetland birds such as Whimbrel, and Red-necked Phalarope at Loch Funzie in the east. The northern part of the island is an RSPB reserve (with a summer warden), and this includes seabird cliffs alive with the usual auks and gulls. Storm

SHETLAND ISLANDS

Yell   Unst

Fetlar

Papa Stour   Whalsay

Mainland

Foula   Lerwick   Bressay

Fair Isle

Petrel and Manx Shearwater breed (at Lambhoga), as do both skuas and Red-throated Diver. Loganair fly to Fetlar, and there are car ferry services from Gutcher on Yell. Cottage accommodation is available. Not a place to be done in a day. Contact the Warden, Bealanie Bothy, Fetlar. *Tel:* (095783) 246.

Unst Hermaness NNR is the northernmost point of Britain and one of the most spectacular, if inaccessible, seabird colonies. Huge gannetry plus thousands of auks, Fulmar and Kittiwake. Both skuas have their headquarters here, and since 1972 a lone Black-browed Albatross has summered at the point of Saito. Unst also has Whimbrel, and Snowy Owl is probably more regular here than on Fetlar. Leave Baltasound (accommodation and ferry) northwards on the A968 to Haroldswick and Burrafirth. Watch for skuas and gulls bathing at Loch of Cliff and continue to the end of the road along Burra Firth. Walk over well-worn path in the footsteps of every famous British ornithologist to Hermaness with fabulous views out to Muckle Flugga. The inter-island car ferry lands at Belmont in the south of Unst.

Out Skerries Cottage accommodation, transportation via Whalsay. Spring and especially autumn rarities and vagrants.

Fair Isle Accommodation, in modern, purpose-built observatory with all meals provided, and transportation arranged through the Warden, Fair Isle Bird Observatory, by Lerwick, Shetland. Good seabird colonies, but best for autumn vagrants in September and October.

Lerwick Reached by boat from Aberdeen or Wick and Sumburgh by regular air services. There is an excellent car-ferry service between the major islands and all are served by Loganair.

Loch of Skene*   OS38

A large attractive loch west of Aberdeen best known for its geese and in particular for the 1500 Greylags that roost there. Wigeon are often very numerous.

Winter Greylag Goose, Wigeon, Goldeneye, Tufted Duck, Pochard

Leave Aberdeen westwards on the A944 and view the loch southwards from the road after 18km (11m).

Spey Bay**   OS28

Although there are a few waders at the mouths of the River Spey and Lossie and a good concentration of Purple Sandpipers east of Portgorden, the real importance of this area lies in its sea-duck. They include up to 5000 Scoter, 2000 Velvet Scoter, 1500 Long-tailed Duck as well as Scaup and Eider. Rarities noted include 10 Surf Scoter and 2 King Eider.

Winter Long-tailed Duck, Scoter, Velvet Scoter, rare sea-duck, Purple Sandpiper, Turnstone

The duck tend to roam around the Bay, but can usually be seen from Kingston, Portgordon or Buckie, all reached northwards from the A98.

Speyside*****   OS35/36

The area centred on the Spey Valley has long been a happy hunting ground for those in search of birds. Traditionally Aviemore was the centre, but over the past 25 years this sleepy little town has mushroomed into a fully-fledged holiday resort full of skiers in winter and tourists in summer. For the best of the weather and least number of visitors May and June are best and most birders now stay outside Aviemore and its dreadful hotel and shop complex.

Birders come to the Spey for specialities including, of course, the Ospreys to the north at Loch Garten, which is treated separately (see Abernethy). The present area has Golden Eagle, Dotterel, Snow Bunting, Crested Tit, Scottish Crossbill, Capercaillie, Black Grouse, Greenshank and Goshawk among others. But these birds are spread about the area, and a good week's holiday is required to get the best from it. The main areas to explore are the Cairngorms, the highest massif in Britain and, with the ski-lift, one of the easiest from which to see high-mountain species; Glen More with its forest plantations and nearby Rothiemurchus with the remnants of the Old Caledonian pine woods; Loch an Eilean with its beautiful lake and former Osprey nest site; the Insh Marshes; and Craigellachie birch woods.

The Cairngorms have Dotterel, Snow Bunting, Golden Eagle and various breeding waders. The Glenmore Forest has Loch Morlich, with its camp sites and water sports, but the old pines on the road up to the loch have Crested Tit and Crossbill and more or less merge with Rothiemurchus to the south-west. Queen's forest has Capercaillie and Black Grouse. Loch an Eilean has Crested Tit and Crossbill and is a good place from which to set out to climb the Lairig Ghru, the high pass that is the traditional Cairngorm route. Craigellachie lies just west of Aviemore and is alive with Willow Warblers. Indeed the birches here make Rothiemurchus seem like a birdless desert. Insh marshes are now an RSPB reserve best known for a substantial flock of Whooper Swans. They are, however, also good for wintering duck as well as up to ten Hen Harriers. In summer breeding duck include both sawbills, as well as Spotted Crake, Water Rail, Sedge and Grasshopper Warblers and Common Sandpiper. Outstanding is breeding Wood Sandpiper and the occasional bird may be seen feeding along a marshy edge. In 1968 Bluethroat bred for the first and so far only time in Britain. Raptors are always good and Golden Eagle, Hen Harrier and Goshawk are all good possibilities.

The whole of this vast area should be thoroughly explored.

Summer Teal, Shoveler, Tufted Duck, Goosander, Red-breasted Merganser, Capercaillie, Black Grouse, Spotted Crake, Water Rail, Hen Harrier, Marsh Harrier, Buzzard, Golden Eagle, Goshawk, Sparrowhawk, Merlin, Peregrine, Dotterel, Golden Plover, Common Sandpiper,

Wood Sandpiper, Crested Tit, Scottish Crossbill, Snow Bunting

Winter Whooper Swan, Goldeneye, Hen Harrier

Cairngorms Leave Aviemore eastwards to Coylumbridge and take a minor road off the B970 to Loch Morlich. Continue to the ski-lift and take it to the top. Explore away from the crowds, taking warm and protective clothing, a good map and a compass. Do not be fooled by fine weather in the valley below.

Glenmore As for Cairngorms, but park beyond Loch Morlich and explore around Glenmore Lodge.

Rothiemurchus As for Cairngorms above, but stop and park before Loch Morlich. Cross the outlet stream by a picturesque footbridge (excellent photo of Cairngorm and the Loch) and proceed southwards on tracks into the forest.

Loch an Eilean Leave Aviemore eastwards towards Coylumbridge and turn right on to the B970 toward Feshiebridge. After 2km (1¼m) turn left to the loch. There is a centre and nature trail, and a track leads due east to Rothiemurchus.

Craigellachie Leave Aviemore through the new centre and bear left to the reserve.

Insh Marshes Leave Kingussie southwards on an unclassified road to join the B970. Watch out for the new (confusing) A9. Turn left and within 2km (1¼m)

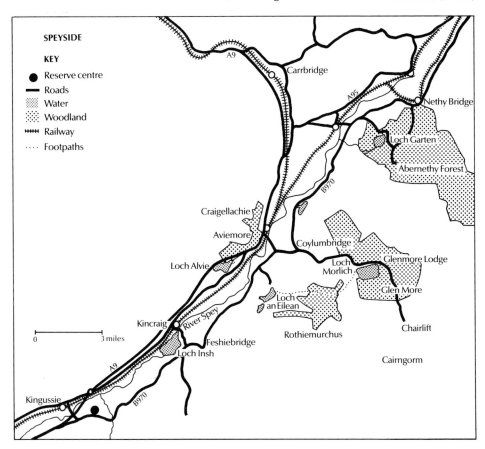

the RSPB reception will be found on the left. Further views may be had by proceeding eastwards on the B970 to Loch Insh and the unclassified road to Kincraig. Advice and information from the Warden, Ivy Cottage, Insh, Nr Kingussie, Highland, PH21 1NT; alternatively contact RSPB headquarters.

Loch of Strathbeg****   OS30

Situated on the north-east coast between Fraserburgh and Peterhead, this is an ideally sited lake that first became an RSPB reserve in 1972. The large loch is the centrepiece, but the reserve includes areas of dune, fresh marsh, damp grazing and woodland that between them attract a wide variety of species. Outstanding are the flocks of up to 5000 each of Pinkfeet and Greylags, but the Whooper Swan flock (250) is among the largest in the country. Duck are numerous with 1000 each of Mallard, Wigeon, Pochard and Tufted. The flock of 500 Goldeneye is the largest in the country (equal with Loch Leven). Bewick's Swan and Goosander are regular as is Smew (not many places for this bird in the country).

In summer there are Water Rail and Sedge Warbler on the marshes along with Eider and other breeding duck.

Passage periods bring a wide variety of species which, because of the geographical position, have included some first-class rarities – Pied-

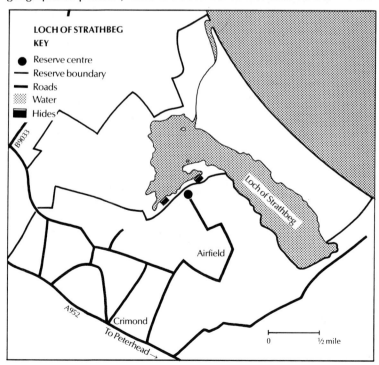

LOCH OF STRATHBEG
KEY
● Reserve centre
— Reserve boundary
▬ Roads
▒ Water
◼ Hides

B9033

Loch of Strathbeg

Airfield

A952
Crimond
To Peterhead →

0   ½ mile

billed Grebe, Little Egret, Great Egret, Red-footed Falcon and Caspian Tern among others.

Winter   Whooper Swan, Bewick's Swan, Pink-footed Goose, Greylag Goose, Barnacle Goose, Shelduck, Mallard, Wigeon, Teal, Pochard, Tufted Duck, Goldeneye, Goosander, Smew, Short-eared Owl

Summer   Eider, Shelduck, Tufted Duck, Water Rail, Sedge Warbler

Passage   Barnacle Goose, Greenshank, Wood Sandpiper, rarities

Leave Fraserburgh southwards on the A92 and turn left on to the A952 towards Peterhead. Past Crimond turn left on to minor roads to the southern side of the loch. There is a reception area and two well-sited hides overlooking newly created lagoons. Access to the reserve is across private land and by advance permit only, on Wednesday and Sunday. Contact RSPB, The Lodge, Sandy, Beds. SG19 20L. *Tel:* (0767) 80551.

Troup Head*   OS29/30

Lies 18km (11m) east of Banff and consists of cliffs 100m (330ft) high and a substantial seabird colony. House Martins also nest. Hell's Lum is a non-birding attraction.

Summer   Fulmar, Kittiwake, Guillemot, Razorbill, Puffin, House Martin

Leave Banff eastwards on the A98 and turn left after 3km (2m) on to the B9031. Turn left 2½km (1½m) past the Gardenstown signpost to Northfield Farm. Walk northwards to the head of a large gully and follow its left bank to the headland.

Ythan Estuary***   OS30/38

Situated on the coast north of Aberdeen, this little estuary has probably the best studied waders and wildfowl in the country. Though 5km (3m) long it is nowhere much more than 400m (440yd) wide, and all the birds can easily be seen. To the east lies the Sands of Forvie NNR with its breeding terns and Eiders while to the north are the splendid seabird cliffs of Bullers of Buchan. Both Pinkfeet, 6500, and Greylags, 2000, use the estuary, though they mostly prefer Meikle Loch to the north. Up to 140 Whooper Swans are regular and the flock of 1500 Eider is of considerable importance. Waders include Redshank, Dunlin and Knot, and there are reasonably regular Goldeneye, Long-tailed Duck and Snow Bunting. A larger variety of waders occurs on passage and the autumn gathering of terns regularly attracts marauding Arctic Skuas.

Winter   Whooper Swan, Greylag Goose, Pink-footed Goose, Wigeon, Goldeneye, Long-tailed Duck, Eider, Common Scoter, Velvet Scoter, Redshank, Knot, Sanderling, Golden Plover, Snow Bunting

Summer   Fulmar, Shag, Eider, Ringed Plover, Arctic Tern, Sandwich Tern, Little Tern, Kittiwake, Guillemot, Razorbill, Puffin

Autumn Grey Plover, Turnstone, Sanderling, Little Stint, Bar-tailed Godwit, Whimbrel, Spotted Redshank, Green Sandpiper, Ruff, Arctic Tern, Arctic Skua

Leave Aberdeen northwards on the A92 and fork right on to the A975 to Newburgh. The road then runs alongside the estuary, crosses it and continues along the eastern shore. The Tarty Burn is a favoured high-tide roost. There is an NCC car park north of Newburgh which gives access to a hide overlooking the ternery. Cotehill Loch and Sand Loch lie off the A975 beside the B9003. Meikle Loch lies further north to the left of the A975 along a short track. Continue northwards to Bullers and take a track on the right to Bullers or Buchan cliffs. For advice and information contact the Warden. *Tel:* (035 881) 330 or 352.

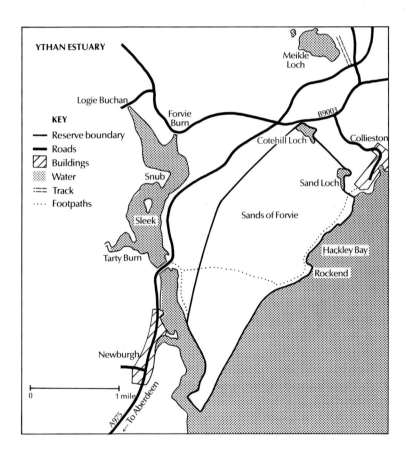

YTHAN ESTUARY

KEY
— Reserve boundary
━ Roads
▨ Buildings
░ Water
≡≡ Track
···· Footpaths

Meikle Loch

Logie Buchan

Forvie Burn

B9003

Cotehill Loch

Collieston

Snub

Sand Loch

Sleek

Sands of Forvie

Tarty Burn

Hackley Bay

Rockend

Newburgh

0   1 mile

A975 ← To Aberdeen

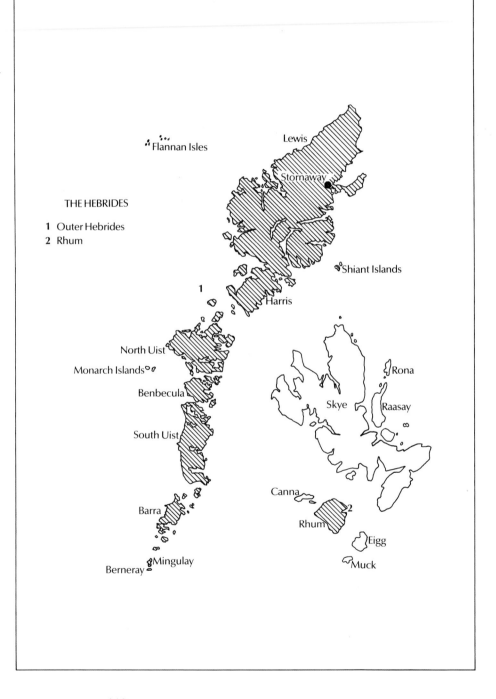

Flannan Isles

Lewis

Stornaway

THE HEBRIDES

1 Outer Hebrides
2 Rhum

Shiant Islands

1

Harris

North Uist

Rona

Monarch Islands

Skye

Raasay

Benbecula

South Uist

Canna

Barra

Rhum

2

Eigg

Mingulay

Muck

Berneray

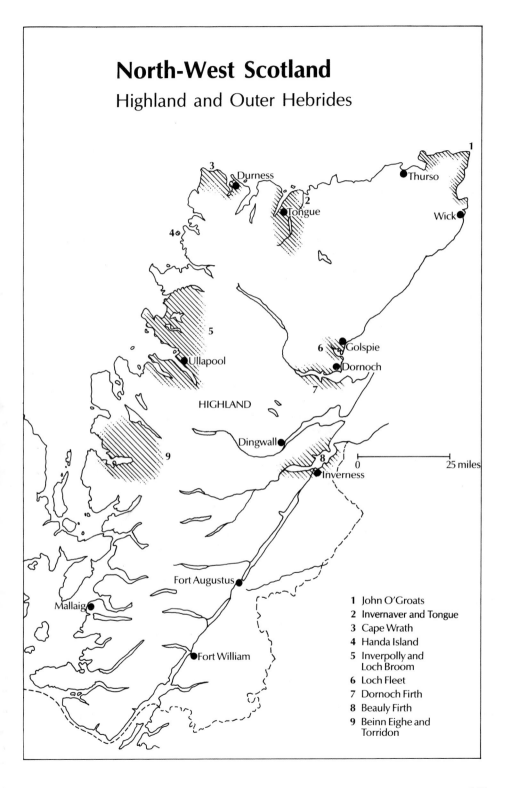

North-West Scotland
Highland and Outer Hebrides

Durness
Thurso
3
2
Tongue
Wick
4
5
Ullapool
6 Golspie
Dornoch
7
HIGHLAND
Dingwall
8
9
Inverness
0   25 miles
Fort Augustus
Mallaig
Fort William

1 John O'Groats
2 Invernaver and Tongue
3 Cape Wrath
4 Handa Island
5 Inverpolly and
  Loch Broom
6 Loch Fleet
7 Dornoch Firth
8 Beauly Firth
9 Beinn Eighe and
  Torridon

Beauly Firth****   OS26/27

This huge estuary includes the Beauly Firth, the Inner Moray Firth and the LNR at Munlochy Bay. Even by covering such a wide area the full sweep of birds may not be included as there is much movement between Moray and its neighbour to the north, Cromarty Firth. Overall there are outstanding populations of wildfowl including 150+ Whooper Swans, 3000 Greylags and 1500 Pinkfeet. The geese can be found on the Beauly Firth and at Munlochy Bay and are particularly obvious during spring passage. There are also large numbers of Shelduck, Wigeon, Teal and Mallard and in late summer Yorkshire Canada Geese migrate here to moult. Sea-duck are particularly noteworthy with up to 6000 Long-tailed Duck representing over half the British total. Some 8000 Scoter are accompanied by 2500 Velvet Scoter – almost three-quarters of the British total of the latter species. Merganser and Goosander both reach 650, the only place where these species gather together in large numbers, and there may be 1000 Goldeneye.

Waders are also numerous with several species reaching 1000+. Bar-tailed Godwit at 2800 are the most significant, though their numbers are swamped by Oystercatcher, Knot and Dunlin. Many 'fresh' waders occur in autumn and at this time there is often a large gathering of sawbills and Kittiwakes.

Winter   Whooper Swan, Pink-footed Goose, Greylag Goose, Shelduck, Wigeon, Teal, Pintail, Eider, Long-tailed Duck, Scoter, Velvet Scoter, Goldeneye, Red-breasted Merganser, Goosander, Oystercatcher, Ringed Plover, Knot, Dunlin, Purple Sandpiper, Sanderling, Bar-tailed Godwit, Black-tailed Godwit, Curlew, Redshank, Turnstone

The area can be worked from a number of places.

Beauly Firth   Southern shore from the A9 westwards out of Inverness. Northern shore by a minor road, leaving the A832 3km (2m) east of Muir of Ord, to North Kessock.

Inner Moray   South shore from the A96 eastwards out of Inverness and the B9039
Firth   which leaves the A96 signposted Ardersier.
Munlochy Bay   May be seen from the car park at OS Ref: NH657537 on the A832 out of Munlochy. Open days are advertised locally.

Beinn Eighe**   OS19,24,25

Britain's first NNR, this huge massif lies between Loch Maree and Loch Torridon. The reserve contains over 120ha (300a) of old Scot's pine as well as extensive birch forests at Coille na Glas Leitire (wood of the Grey Slopes) along the shores of Loch Maree. The high tops hold Golden Eagle, Peregrine, Raven, Dotterel, Ptarmigan and Snow Bunting. The woods are full of Willow Warblers, but they also have Crossbill, Siskin, Black Grouse, Long-eared Owl and the occasional Redwing. Lakes and marshes hold Greenshank, Dunlin, divers and feral Greylags.

Summer   Red-throated Diver, Black-throated Diver, Greylag Goose, Golden

Eagle, Buzzard, Peregrine, Merlin, Black Grouse, Ptarmigan, Green-shank, Dunlin, Dotterel, Long-eared Owl, Redstart, Tree Pipit, Scottish Crossbill, Siskin, Snow Bunting

The reserve lies between the A832 and A896 to the west of Kin-lochewe. The headquarters are at Anancaun Field Station whence a pony track leads into the heart of the area. There is a simple overnight camp site at Taagon Farm close to the main road at Loch Maree. Also at Loch Maree there is a car park and picnic site at the start of Glas Leitire Nature Trail. This produces woodland birds as well as a chance of raptors for those who prefer their hill walking short and easy.

To the west the National Trust for Scotland controls a huge area of Torridon including some high peaks and huge areas of upland. This abuts the NNR. The Trust publishes an excellent guide called *Torridon* which details several walks through and over the mountains – all visitors should obtain a copy in advance or from the NTS visitors' centre on the A896 near the Alligan turn off.

This is a tough country and visitors should be prepared for all eventualities when walking these mountains.

Permits are required in late summer and autumn during the stalking season.

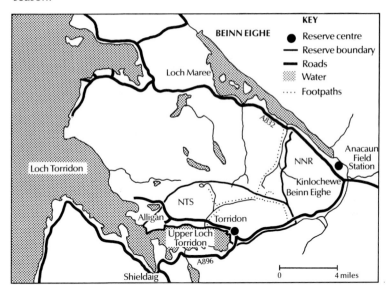

KEY

● Reserve centre
— Reserve boundary
▬ Roads
░ Water
⋯ Footpaths

Dornoch Firth***   OS21

Though smaller than the other firths to the south, Dornoch is certainly the most attractive scenically. It is also rather more manageable than some of its neighbours. Though rich in wildfowl, the most important species are sea-duck with over 7000 each of Long-tailed and Scoter. These haunt the area of the mouth and may be found off Dornoch itself or as far north as Embo, or south to Portmahomack. Other wildfowl are more considerate with Whooper Swan (50) and Teal in the handy Skibo Inlet, Scaup and Wigeon on the Tain and Edderton Sands, and the waders at Dornoch, Edderton and Whiteness Sands. The latter include Bar-tailed Godwit, Knot, Redshank, Dunlin, Grey Plover and Purple Sandpiper.

To the south the large, but shallow, Loch Eye holds 250 Whoopers and up to 2500 Greylags. Morrich More to the north is a firing range, but is good for breeding birds and Tarbat Ness is a fine seawatch site.

Winter   Whooper Swan, Greylag Goose, Shelduck, Mallard, Teal, Wigeon, Pintail, Goldeneye, Scaup, Long-tailed Duck, Eider, Scoter, Velvet Scoter, Red-breasted Merganser, Oystercatcher, Dunlin, Knot, Grey Plover, Redshank, Purple Sandpiper

Tarbat Ness   Leave the A9 5km (3m) south of Tain on the B9165.
Tain   There is a bridge over the railway west of the station.
Edderton Sands   Leave the A9 5km (3m) west of Tain northwards to Ferry Point.
Skibo Inlet   Leave the A9 southwards at Clashmore and turn right at the T-junction to Ferrytown.
Loch Eye   Leave Tain eastwards on the airfield road. Turn right opposite the main runway and right again at a crossroads.

Loch Fleet**   OS21

Lying on the east coast, at low tide the loch is almost totally dry, providing a fine habitat for waders and wildfowl. In 1815 attempts were made to reclaim the upper estuary by building an embankment called The Mound, with limited success. A dense alder swamp above the Mound offers shelter to a variety of breeding birds and the fresh water pool is a favourite haunt of many species. Mergansers arrive in the greatest numbers in autumn, while waders are plentiful in winter, their numbers swelled by the usual array on passage. Eiders are particularly numerous at the mouth of the loch and now breed among the dunes in Ferry Links. Both Scoter and Velvet Scoter winter off Embo in rafts of up to 1000. Long-tailed Duck gather at Littleferry and reach nearly 1500 in May.

Winter   Wigeon, Teal, Goldeneye, Scoter, Velvet Scoter, Eider, Long-tailed Duck, Red-headed Merganser, Knot, Oystercatcher, Curlew
Spring   Shelduck, Long-tailed Duck
Summer   Eider, Capercaillie, Siskin, Crossbill
Autumn   Knot, Greenshank, Turnstone, Merganser, Eider

Leave Dornoch westwards on the B9168, forking right outside the town. Join the A9 and immediately fork right on to the unclassified road to Skelbo. Continue over the railway to the pier. Leave Skelbo westwards along the southern shore, join the A9 and cross The Mound from OS Ref: NH775983. This is a Scottish WT reserve and members and their guests may explore most of the reserve, though not without a permit for Ferry Links Wood on the northern shore.

Handa*** OS9

Lying off the west coast of Sutherland, some 5km (3m) north-west of Scourie, this RSPB island reserve is a major seabird colony. Its cliffs provide a home for some 100,000 breeding birds including 25,000 pair of Guillemot, 10,000 of Kittiwake, 9000 of Razorbill, 3500 Fulmar, 350 Puffin, 300 Shag and a small population of Black Guillemot. Both Great and Arctic Skuas breed here and there are genuine Rock Doves and a few pairs of Red-throated Divers.

Summer   Red-throated Diver, Fulmar, Shag, Kittiwake, Guillemot, Razorbill, Puffin, Black Guillemot, Arctic Skua, Great Skua, Rock Dove

Leave the A894 at Tarbet and find your way to the harbour. Local fishermen run day trips as and when required, but not on Sundays. Volunteer assistants can help the Warden for a week at a time and stay on the reserve: contact the RSPB.

Invernaver and Tongue*** OS10

This area on the north-central coast of Sutherland is wild and rich in birds. It has seabird cliffs and islands, deep sea lochs, deep valleys with large inland lochs, high mountains and moors and some fine woods. Its list of species is impressive with most of the northern specialities.

Roan Island has Fulmar, Shag, Storm Petrel, Black Guillemot, occasional Puffin, Eider, Buzzard, Peregrine and a few Great Skuas. It is also a winter resort of Barnacle Goose. The Kyle of Tongue has some waders on passage, while the village has the most northerly rookery in Britain.

To the south Loch Loyal has Greylags, while the nearby Ben Loyal has Ptarmigan and Golden Eagle. Further south Strath Naver has Hen Harrier among the plantations as well as Scottish Crossbill, Black Grouse and Short-eared Owl.

Invernaver itself lies near Bettyhill to the east and contains a wide variety of habitats within a comparatively small area. Birds include both divers, Greenshank, Ring Ouzel and Twite.

Summer   Red-throated Diver, Black-throated Diver, Fulmar, Storm Petrel, Shag, Eider, Goosander, Peregrine, Golden Eagle, Buzzard, Ptarmigan, Black Grouse, Greenshank, Black Guillemot, Puffin, Arctic Tern, Great Skua, Short-eared Owl, Rook, Ring Ouzel, Twite, Scottish Crossbill

Tongue is a good base. It has a Youth Hostel and private houses may take in guests. Leave southwards on the A836 to Loch Loyal and Ben Loyal. Continue to Invernaver and Bettyhill. Return along the A836 to Tongue.

For Roan Island charter a boat at Tongue.

Inverpolly and Loch Broom*** OS15

Some of the wildest and most remote country in Britain makes up the NNR of Inverpolly and some of the country's best breeding birds can be found there. Though not as high as Beinn Eighe to the south, there are still several significant massifs, and the whole area is a maze of lakes, rivers and streams with stretches of coast to the north and south. The basis of this landscape is the underlying Lewisian gneiss, some of the oldest rocks in the world. Around Knockan limestone creates an area of green and peace in an otherwise extremely tough region.

To the south lies Loch Broom with the famous seabird site of the Summer Isles. While higher up the Loch is Isle Martin, an RSPB reserve. Further south is Little Loch Broom with Gruinard and Dundonnell Forests beyond. The whole of this area is good for birds including many species that are scarce or elusive.

At the north of Inverpolly lies Loch Sionascaig with its deeply indented coastline and numerous bays and islands. The many surrounding lochs and lochans hold Red-throated and Black-throated Divers, Greenshank, Greylag, Dunlin, Golden Plover and others. The hills hold Golden Eagle, Peregrine, Merlin and Buzzard as well as Ptarmigan at Coigach and Col More. In the south Snow Bunting (irregular in Inverpolly), as well as more Ptarmigan, may be found in the Dundonnell Forest area. The Coigach area is a reserve of the RSNC and holds both divers, Golden Eagle, Peregrine, Greenshank and Black Grouse. There are woods at Doire-na-Airbhe, along the river Kirkcaig, and around Loch Sionascaig that hold Black Grouse, Woodcock, Wood and Willow Warblers, Redwing, Redpoll and Scottish Crossbill.

The Summer Isles have Greylags (they moult on Glas Leac Beag), Red-throated Diver, Arctic Tern and Buzzard. Priest Island has Storm Petrel, and Tanera More has Eider and Black Guillemot. In winter there is a good flock of Barnacle Goose.

Isle Martin has some cliffs that hold Fulmar, Shag and Black Guillemot, with a good colony of Arctic Tern and a few Eider in the lower parts.

Summer Black-throated Diver, Red-throated Diver, Storm Petrel, Fulmar, Shag, Grey Heron, Greylag Goose, Eider, Red-breasted Merganser, Golden Eagle, Buzzard, Peregrine, Merlin, Red Grouse, Black Grouse, Ptarmigan, Golden Plover, Common Sandpiper, Dunlin, Greenshank, Woodcock, Black Guillemot, Arctic Tern, Raven, Redwing, Ring Ouzel, Wheatear, Stonechat, Wood Warbler, Pied Flycatcher, Redpoll, Scottish Crossbill, Snow Bunting

The whole area is served by the A832 along the southern shore of Little Loch Broom (woods at Dundonnell Lodge have Pied Flycatcher) which enables the hills to the south (Dundonnell Forest) to be explored. This joins the A835, and a left turn leads to Ullapool. From here boats ply regularly to the Summer Isles and may be chartered for extended trips. They also sail around Isle Martin – the best way to see the birds.

Continuing northwards on the A835 to Elphin, one can find a warden living at Knochan Cottage (*Tel:* Elphin 234). Here is the Knochan Cliff Nature Trail giving excellent views over the three high peaks towards

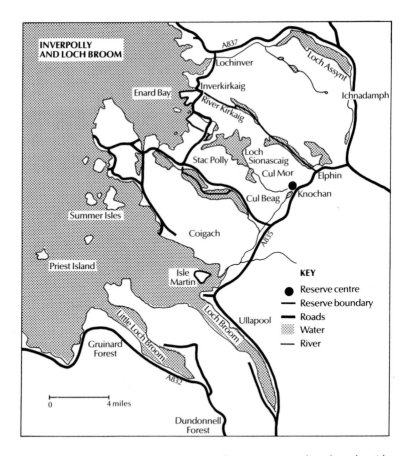

the sea. Further north turn left on to the A837 to Inchnadamph with another NNR (rich in flowers) and a splendid fishing hotel. The A837 then runs along the edge of Loch Assynt to Lochinver. Southwards a minor road runs along the coast, weaving its way in and out of valleys, crossing streams and skirting lakes. Stop and explore as fully as possible especially along the bank of the River Kirkaig. Continue southwards and turn right towards the Summer Isles and the coast. Return to that turning and continue back to the A836 south of Elphin.

This is wild country and worthy of serious exploration – so take it seriously with warm clothing, maps, compass and food.

John o'Groats**   OS12

Though Dunnet Head to the west is the northernmost point of the British mainland, John o'Groats is traditionally regarded as the 'land's end' of Scotland. It is, in many ways, similar, with hosts of tourists and all the trappings. However, a short drive to the east leads to Duncansby Head where cliff-nesting seabirds can be seen from the lighthouse. To the south the main road skirts the sea with seabirds all the way on

167

relatively low cliffs. Guillemot, Puffin, Gannet (not breeding) and both skuas are regular, and the sea is alive with birds. Further south still, just north of Wick, is Noss Head, another seabird station with all the usual cliff-nesters including Puffin.

To the west of John o'Groats is Dunnet Head with yet more cliff-nesting birds of all the usual species including Great and Arctic Skuas. While just outside Dunnet, St John's Loch is good for winter wildfowl.

Inland the moors of this essentially green and fertile area hold skuas, Hen Harrier, Short-eared Owl and much more besides.

Summer	Fulmar, Shag, Gannet, Peregrine, Hen Harrier, Curlew, Kittiwake, Great Skua, Arctic Skua, Guillemot, Razorbill, Puffin, Black Guillemot, Rock Dove, Short-eared Owl
Dunnet Head	Leave John o'Groats westwards on the A836 to Dunnet and turn right to the Head past St John's Loch.
Duncansby Head	Signposted left just after leaving John o'Groats.
Caithness Cliffs	The coastal A9 southwards from John o'Groats passes at varying distances from the cliffs. Near Brough Head is a good place to stop and walk to the cliff tops, but there are many other good stopping places.
Noss Head	Leave Wick on a minor road to the airport. Cross the runway (carefully) and proceed to the Head.

Outer Hebrides*****   OS8/13/14/18/22/31

The Western Isles, as they are often called, are simply splendid for birds with a range of scarce breeding species, some spectacular seabird colonies and an array of regular winter visitors that are worthy of attention in their own right. Additionally, their geographical position at the extreme north-western corner of Europe makes these beautiful islands ideal for migrants including rarities.

They extend some 200km (124m) from Berneray in the south to the Butt of Lewis in the north. The coastline is broken by deep sea lochs that extend well inland, and the islands are divided by shallow, sandy straits that are noted for their dangerous passage. The geology of the Hebrides is of paramount importance to bird and human distribution. The western side of the group faces the open Atlantic and has received large deposits of fine shell sand creating huge beaches. The dunes have created a soil rich in lime, giving rise to the characteristic sweet grass machair (pronounced 'macker'). This fertile strip is in sharp contrast to the central and eastern peat-ridden sections of the islands. While the western side has farms, the eastern side has a mass of acidic lochs and is mainly rocky and barren.

Woodland is decidedly scarce and only the grounds of Stornoway Castle can offer anything like a normal woodland fauna. Here Rook, Blue, Great and Coal Tits, Treecreeper, Robin and so on are the abnormal, worth travelling for, birds.

Seabird cliffs are spectacular, though unlike those of the northern isles, they are far from numerous and all of the best are situated on offshore islands and stacks. It is thus possible to spend a holiday in the Outer Hebrides without ever seeing a cliff full of birds.

Summer Black-throated Diver, Red-throated Diver, Fulmar, Manx Shearwater, Storm Petrel, Leach's Petrel, Gannet, Eider, Red-breasted Merganser, Greylag Goose, Golden Eagle, Buzzard, Hen Harrier, Peregrine, Merlin, Corncrake, Golden Plover, Whimbrel, Greenshank, Dunlin, Red-necked Phalarope, Arctic Skua, Great Skua, Arctic Tern, Little Tern, Razorbill, Guillemot, Puffin, Short-eared Owl, Hebridean Wren/ St Kilda Wren

Winter Great Northern Diver, Whooper Swan, Barnacle Goose, Greenland White-fronted Goose, Glaucous Gull, Iceland Gull, Ivory Gull

Berneray and Mingulay These are the southernmost of the islands and are inhabited only by lighthouse keepers and masses of auks, Kittiwake and Fulmar. The best cliffs are on the western side of Mingulay. Charter or regular weekend cruises from Castlebay, Barra.

Monarch Islands Lie some 9km (5½m) west of North Uist and are best known, not as a resort of seabirds, but of up to 2000 Barnacles plus lesser numbers of Greenland White-fronts in winter. Charter access.

St Kilda Of all the seabird islands none can compare with St Kilda. This remote and precipitous group lies some 70km (45m) west of Griminish Point, North Uist. There are seven islands and stacks, with the Ard Uach-darachd of Conachair the highest seacliff in Britain. Since 1957 the islands have been the base of an Army radar station and an NNR.

St Kilda holds the world's largest gannetry (59,000 pairs), plus huge colonies of Fulmar, Leach's and Storm Petrels, Manx Shearwater, Puffin and the other auks. About 100 pair of the unique St Kilda Wren breed on Hirta, the main island. Visited by charter, or by joining one of the National Trust for Scotland's island cruises. Details from 5 Charlotte Square, Edinburgh EH2 4DU. *Tel:* (031 226) 5922.

Flannan Isles These lie north-west of Gallan Head on the west side of Lewis. They are cliff bound, inhabited only by lighthouse keepers and have numerous Leach's Petrels as well as the usual cliff-nesting auks and gulls. Charter access only.

Shiant Islands These lie south-east of Lewis and have breeding auks, Kittiwake and Fulmar. They are favoured by Barnacles in winter. Access by charter only.

Sula Sgeir This isolated rock has 9000 pairs of Gannet as well as Guillemot, Puffin and Leach's Petrel. Charter access, and very difficult to land, from Ness in northern Lewis.

North Rona A splendid, well-studied island, with auks, both skuas, both storm-petrels, Arctic Tern, Peregrine and summering Turnstone. Access by charter only.

Sule Stack This is another tiny island closer to Orkney than the Hebrides. It has a large gannetry plus small numbers of Guillemot and Kittiwake. Access by charter, difficult landing.

Sule Skerry Near neighbour of Sule Stack with huge Puffinry, Storm Petrel, Black Guillemot, both skuas and Arctic Tern. Difficult access by charter only.

South Uist, Seabirds apart, most visiting birders concentrate on the area of the
Benbecula and Uists, including Benbecula, that are inter-connected by road. Here
North Uist most of the specialities can be found and there is an RSPB reserve at
Balranald and the NNR at Loch Druidibeg, the stronghold of the native
Greylag Goose. Mostly these 'middle islands' are low lying with huge
beaches along their western coasts. Redshank, Ringed Plover, Arctic
Tern and Red-necked Phalarope breed among the machair lochs with
both divers, Arctic Skua, Dunlin, Whimbrel, Peregrine and Hen Harrier
on the moors. Corncrakes are as regular here as anywhere.

Loganair fly to Benbecula and there are car ferries from Oban and
Mallaig to Lochboisdale (good hotel; ladies enter the back bar at your
peril) and from Uig in Skye to Lochmaddy (hotel). Plenty of guest house
accommodation. Loch Druidibeg is adjacent to the main road in the
north of South Uist.

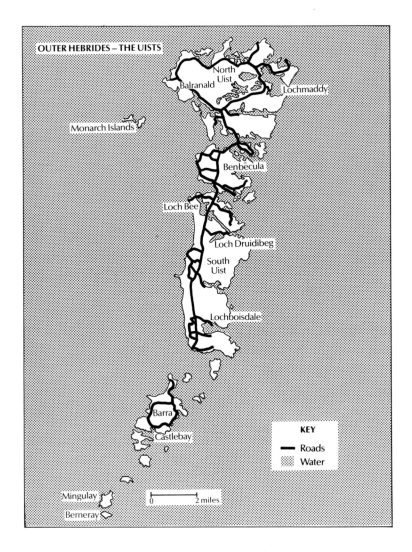

Balranald is reached via the A865 between Tigharry and Paiblesgarry. It is arguably the best area of the machair and is rich in breeding waders, terns and duck. Red-necked Phalarope and Corncrake can both be seen in summer, and there is a splendid passage of Barnacle Geese in spring.

Lewis and Harris The two largest 'islands' are actually two sections of a single island separated by a difference in habitat. Harris, in the south, is mountainous and barren, Lewis is more gentle with agriculture. The Golden Eagle is quite numerous, especially in the south and west, and there are numbers of both divers, both skuas, Peregrine, Merlin, Greylag, Greenshank, Whimbrel, Dunlin, Arctic and Little Terns. Though the whole island is worthy of exploration, the B roads south of Carloway (hotel) around Loch Roag take in some beautiful countryside and excellent low-lying marshy fields. The Butt of Lewis is excellent for sea-watching with arriving and departing geese and good seabirds. There are cliff-nesting birds here, including Black Guillemot. In the central area the mountains around Clisham and to the north and west are good for raptors. In winter Stornoway Harbour is a haunt of northern gulls, and there are 750 Great Northern Divers in the sound of Harris.

General access to the Outer Hebrides is by air to Stornoway, Benbecula, or Barra (land on the cockle strand when the tide is out). There are regular ferries to Stornoway from Ullapool, and from Uig, Skye to Tarbert, Harris, as well as the services noted above for the Uists.

Rhum**   OS39

The island of Rhum rises to over 800m (2659ft) and is one of the wettest places in Britain, lying west of Mallaig and immediately south-west of Skye. For a long time access was restricted, but it has been an NNR since 1957. The island is grass covered, with patches of heather, mountain lichens and mosses, and areas of trees around Loch Scresort and Papadil Lodge. Now used as an outdoor laboratory, research includes an intensive study of the population of red deer and a long-term re-introduction programme of the White-tailed Eagle. This bird first bred here in 1985 and now Rhum is the only place in the country where its presence can be guaranteed.

Other birds include an interesting colony of 100,000 pairs of Manx Shearwaters, near the top of Askival, as well as cliff-breeding seabirds. Two or three pairs of Golden Eagles and Peregrines breed annually.

Summer Red-throated Diver, Manx Shearwater, Fulmar, Red-breasted Merganser, Eider, Golden Eagle, White-tailed Eagle, Peregrine, Merlin, Common Gull, Kittiwake, Arctic Tern, Guillemot, Razorbill, Puffin, Black Guillemot, Golden Plover, Corncrake, Rock Dove, Goldcrest, Twite

Day visitors are free to land at Loch Scresort and explore the area on the south side of the loch. Permission to go beyond this must be sought from the Warden at White House, Kinloch, Isle of Rhum. *Tel:* (0867)

2026. Visitors can stay at Kinloch Castle by arrangement with Hebridean Holidays Ltd. *Tel:* (0687) 2026. Bird-watchers, and other naturalists, wishing to study any particular feature of the island's natural history should write to the NCC West Region, 12 Hope Terrace, Edinburgh EH9 2AS, *Tel:* (031447) 4784, as far in advance as possible. Every effort will be made to provide facilities for research.

MacBraynes' steamers leave Mallaig four times a week for Rhum. The crossing takes 3–3½ hours. Additionally there are day excursions during the summer that allow sufficient time for exploration. There are two nature trails and an informative guide that is available at the jetty.

Cape Wrath**   OS9

Though the main attraction here is the continuous stream of Gannets passing offshore, there are also many other seabirds including, in season, Sooty and Great Shearwaters. To the east are the cliffs of Clo Mor, the highest on the British mainland, with 25,000 pairs of Guillemot and thousands of Razorbill, Puffin, Black Guillemot, Kittiwake and Shag. There are Peregrines here and the nearby moors hold Golden Eagle and Ptarmigan.

To the east of the Kyle of Durness, Faraid Head has further good seabird cliffs and the stacks of Clach Mhor and Clach Bheag na Fharaid. This is a handy area for those who do not wish to spend the day across the Kyle.

Summer Fulmar, Shag, Golden Eagle, Peregrine, Ptarmigan, Corncrake, Curlew, Kittiwake, Guillemot, Razorbill, Puffin, Black Guillemot, Rock Dove

Leave the A838 alongside the Kyle of Durness to Keoldale. There is a ferry across the Kyle with a minibus service to Cape Wrath. For Faraid Head leave Durness northwards to Balnakeil and walk out to the Head.

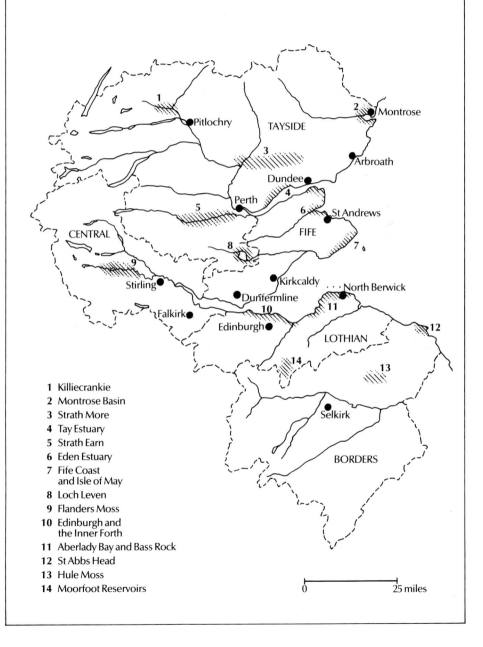

South-East Scotland

Borders, Central, Fife,
Lothian and Tayside

1 Killiecrankie
2 Montrose Basin
3 Strath More
4 Tay Estuary
5 Strath Earn
6 Eden Estuary
7 Fife Coast
 and Isle of May
8 Loch Leven
9 Flanders Moss
10 Edinburgh and
 the Inner Forth
11 Aberlady Bay and Bass Rock
12 St Abbs Head
13 Hule Moss
14 Moorfoot Reservoirs

0   25 miles

Aberlady Bay and Bass Rock**** OS66/67

On the southern shore at the mouth of the Firth of Forth is a group of quite outstanding bird habitats near the town of North Berwick. Starting in the west is Aberlady Bay, an LNR covering some excellent inter-tidal areas and dunes that attract a wide variety of species. In winter up to 4400 Pinkfeet can be found along with Whooper Swan, Wigeon, Eider and Scoter. Aberlady also attracts large numbers of waders and has one of the most important roosts on the Forth. Autumn brings a variety of species including good passage waders, terns, skuas and passerines. Terns sometimes breed in quite good numbers.

To the east lies Gullane Bay, often overshadowed by its westerly neighbour, but good for seaduck, especially Eider, Scoter and Velvet Scoter. Offshore lie the three small rocky islets of Fidra, Eyebroughty and The Lamb. Fidra is the largest and has good (though erratic) tern colonies that include Roseate. There are also Fulmar, Shag, Kittiwake and sometimes auks.

The Lamb has the only colony of Cormorants in the Forth, and Eyebroughty is a noted moulting ground for Eider and a breeding site for gulls.

Further east lies the Bass Rock, a huge lump that sticks out of the sea and is home to 11,000 pairs of Gannets. These birds may be seen from the mainland, but visits are relatively straightforward, making this one of the most accessible of the great gannetries. Just a few km to the east lies the Tyninghame Estuary with a good collection of waders and wildfowl that regularly includes Pinkfeet and both sawbills.

Winter	Red-throated Diver, Red-necked Grebe, Slavonian Grebe, Whooper Swan, Pink-footed Goose, Shelduck, Wigeon, Teal, Goldeneye, Eider, Scoter, Velvet Scoter, Long-tailed Duck, Red-breasted Merganser, Goosander, Oystercatcher, Knot, Purple Sandpiper, Dunlin, Ruff, Redshank, Turnstone, Glaucous Gull, Iceland Gull, Shore Lark, Lapland Bunting, Snow Bunting
Summer	Fulmar, Gannet, Cormorant, Shag, Eider, Common Tern, Arctic Tern, Sandwich Tern, Roseate Tern, Guillemot, Razorbill, Puffin
Passage	Grey Plover, Whimbrel, Greenshank, Wood Sandpiper, Green Sandpiper, Curlew Sandpiper, Black-tailed Godwit, Little Stint, Ruff, terns, Arctic Skua

Aberlady Bay	Leave Edinburgh eastwards on the A1 and take a left on to the A198 beyond Musselburgh. Continue to Aberlady. Continue and stop at the head of the bay (car park for permit holders only, OS Ref: NT472806) where a small bridge crosses the stream. Warden: Tel: (08757) 588. There are no limitations on access except to a small area in summer.
Gullane Bay	Walk along the eastern shore of Aberlady to Gullane Point and turn eastwards into the Bay. Continue to Gullane, walk back along the A198, cutting back to Aberlady across Luffness Links. OS Ref: NT465831.
Fidra, Eyebroughty, The Lamb	Visiting arrangements via the RSPB Scottish Office. Much can be seen by leaving the A198 northwards at Dirleton to Yellowcraig car park and walking westwards along the shore. Roseates (if present) can be seen along here.
Bass Rock	Boats from North Berwick make the trip providing the weather is

suitable. For landing contact the SOC, 21 Regent Terrace, Edinburgh EH7 5BT. *Tel:* (031 556). They usually organize several trips during the summer. Alternatively, contact the boatman, Fred Marr. *Tel:* (0620) 2838.

Tyninghame Estuary Leave Dunbar westwards to West Barns. Turn right and a footpath leads out to Belhaven Bay. Cross the river and continue along the shoreline to the mouth of the estuary. For the inner estuary continue on the A1087, join the A1, turn right on to the A198 and stop at a track on the right after 1km (½m). Walk to the shore.

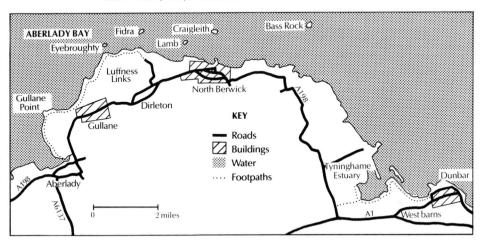

Eden Estuary***   OS59

Best known for the links that guard its mouth north of St Andrews, the Eden has a lot more to offer than a great golf course. Its outer part is mainly sandy, while the inner estuary has some mud banks near Guardbridge. A large area is part of an LNR. Unlike so many of the great firths of the east coast, the Eden is a manageable estuary no more than 2km (1¼m) across even at its widest point. Mostly it is a good deal less. The mouth holds good numbers of sea-duck, especially Scoter and Eider. At the end of the breeding season most of the birds that breed among the Tentsmuir dunes to the north bring their families to the Eden. In bad weather both species come in to shelter near Shelly Point. This shingle spit is a major wader roost (the other is on the saltings at Guardbridge) as well as a good spot for passage waders. Bar-tailed Godwit number over 1500 and up to 100 Black-tailed (rare in Scotland) also winter.

Unfortunately, leisure activities have reduced the tern colonies that formerly existed, though these birds are regularly present throughout the summer.

To the south lies Cameron Reservoir, ideally situated between the Firths of Forth and Tay. It is a splendid wildfowl haunt in winter with up to 2500 Pinkfeet and 250 Greylags. Whoopers plus a wide variety of duck can be found including Gadwall and Goosander.

Winter Pink-footed Goose, Shelduck, Wigeon, Teal, Pintail Goldeneye, Eider, Scoter, Velvet Scoter, Oystercatcher, Grey Plover, Knot, Dunlin, Black-tailed Godwit, Bar-tailed Godwit, Redshank, Turnstone, Sanderling

Summer Eider, Ringed Plover

Autumn Black-tailed Godwit, Whimbrel, Spotted Redshank, Ruff, Common Tern, Arctic Tern

Eden Mouth There is a road along the eastern side of the golf links to Out Head and Shelly Point from the outskirts of St Andrews.

Guardbirdge View from the town. Also try Cable Shore 2km (1¼m) eastwards off the A91.

Cameron Reservoir Leave St Andrews southwards on the A915 and watch for a signpost on the right after 5km (3m). Ask permission at the 'keeper's' cottage.

Edinburgh and the Inner Forth****   OS65/66

The huge estuary of the Forth, on which Edinburgh stands, is a truly magnificent area with outstanding birds at all seasons. There are wonderful inter-tidal areas supporting important concentrations of waders and wildfowl, some splendid seabird islands, and some of the best sea-duck sites in Britain. In this section the whole of the inner Forth from Musselburgh to Alloa is covered. The outer estuary is divided into the northern shore (Isle of May and Fife Coast) and the southern shore (Aberlady bay and Bass Rock).

The area around Alloa and down to Kincardine Bridge is one of the best areas for waders with Oystercatcher, Knot and Dunlin all present in good numbers. Shelduck are also numerous and Mallard, Teal, Wigeon and Goldeneye are all present, and there are also regular Whooper Swan and Merganser. To the north-east lies Gartmorn Dam with Greylags, Whoopers, divers and duck, and Peppermill Dam for passage waders.

Next downstream comes the Grangemouth area, which is heavily industrialized, but which is arguably the best of the lot for waders and wildfowl. The Skinflats area is an RSPB reserve. Wildfowl are similar to the Alloa area, though mostly more numerous, whereas the waders really come into their own on the rich mud-bank feeding. Knot 10,000 and Dunlin 5000 once more dominate, but there are good concentrations of Bar-tailed Godwit and Redshank, while passage brings Greenshank, Whimbrel, Curlew Sandpiper and other 'fresh' waders. Culross, on the northern shore, has similar species.

Between Leith and Musselburgh there are huge mussel beds, as well as a sewage outfall that attracts the best congregation of sea-duck in Britain. Scaup, declining from a peak of 25,000, still represent one of the largest flocks in the country and a significant proportion of the total. However, these numbers may be a thing of the past, perhaps as a result of the building of a sewage treatment works. These birds are joined by 10,000 Eider, 5000 Goldeneye, 1000 Scoter, plus lesser numbers of Velvet Scoter and Long-tailed Duck. Divers and grebes, including Red-necked (up to 50) and Slavonian are regular.

Of all the Firth islands Inchmickery is the best. It is an RSPB reserve featuring good colonies of Sandwich and Common Terns and a small number of Roseate.

Winter	Red-throated Diver, Black throated Diver, Red-necked Grebe, Slavonian Grebe, Great Crested Grebe, Whooper Swan, Shelduck, Mallard, Teal, Wigeon, Pintail, Scaup, Goldeneye, Scoter, Velvet Scoter, Long-tailed Duck, Eider, Red-breasted Merganser, Knot, Dunlin, Oyster-catcher, Redshank, Bar-tailed Godwit
Summer	Sandwich Tern, Common Tern, Roseate Tern, Arctic Skua
Passage	Waders, terns
Alloa	View from the south at Mains of Throsk on the A905 and, to the east, from South Alloa on the B906.
Culross	From Kincardine turn eastwards on minor roads and view before Culross.
Gartmorn Dam	Leave A908 in suburbs of Alloa between Keilarsbrae and New Sauchie on an access road to the east. The LNR has a centre and hides.
Grangemouth and Skinflats	Leave the A905 that skirts Grangemouth, northwards on the B9132. At its junction with the A904 carry straight on to a minor road out along the eastern side of the docks. For Skinflats take the A905 west of Grangemouth and the first right after Skinflats village. Where the road turns sharply left stop and find a way to the seawall.
Leith-Musselburgh	The A901 runs alongside the Forth through the docks and Leith. Continue eastwards to Musselburgh where there are wader lagoons.
Inchmickery	Arrange visits with the RSPB Scottish Office.

Flanders Moss and Lake of Menteith** OS57

This low-lying and decidedly damp area lies at the western end of the Forth Valley between Aberfoyle and Stirling, a noted haunt of Pinkfeet and Greylags. The Loch is the roost of the Greylags that generally feed nearby, while the often impassable Flanders Moss shelters the Pinkfeet that feed further to the east at Kippen and Thornhill. A herd of Whooper Swans is regular and Great Grey Shrike and Hen Harrier also winter. In summer gulls breed along with waders, duck and grouse.

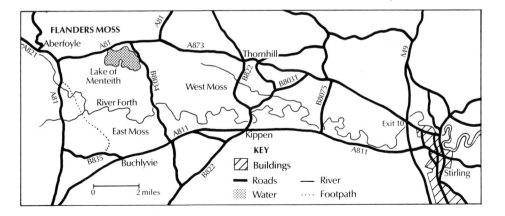

Winter   Whooper Swan, Pink-footed Goose, Greylag Goose, Wigeon, Goldeneye, Hen Harrier, Black Grouse, Short-eared Owl, Great Grey Shrike,
Siskin, Redpoll

Summer   Goosander, Black Grouse, Golden Plover, Woodcock, Lesser Black-
backed Gull

Leave Aberfoyle southwards on the A821 to the A81. Turn right to the
bridge over the river and walk eastwards along the old railway track to
West Moss. Alternatively turn left at the A81 and view the Lake after
4km (2½m). Continue and turn right on the B8034. Continue to the
A811, turn left and turn left again on the B822. At a major bend walk
westwards to East Moss. Other B roads leaving the A811 may give
views of feeding geese.

Hule Moss*   OS74

This loch, with its surrounding bog, lies near the border just north of
Greenlaw and is best known as a Pinkfoot roost with Teal, Pintail and
lesser numbers of other duck. The geese reach a peak in autumn, but
are plentiful enough through the winter.

Winter   Pink-footed Goose, Teal, Pintail, Wigeon, Pochard, Goldeneye

Watch from the A6105 3km (2m) north of Greenlaw as the geese flight
in to roost in the evening.

Isle of May and Fife Coast***   OS59

The northern shore of the Firth of Forth has comparatively few large
inter-tidal areas and holds fewer wildfowl and waders as a result.
Indeed only Largo Bay holds both groups in any numbers, though Fife
Ness also has a wader roost.

Largo Bay, in the west of the area, has good concentrations of
sea-duck including Scoter and a regular double passage of Long-tailed
Duck. To the east Elie Ness is good for Purple Sandpiper and
Turnstone, as well as being a favoured site for sea-watching. Shearwaters, skuas, terns, auks and divers occur in season. To the north lies
the large, but shallow, Kilconquhar Loch with its 1000 Greylags and
fine collection of duck, including 2500 Mallard and up to 250 Gadwall.
Little Gull is numerous here in late summer and may reach several
hundred. These birds are also found at Largo Bay, especially at Lundin
Links east of Leven.

Fife Ness is one of the most prominent headlands along the east coast
of Scotland and is a favoured haunt of migrants and their watchers. The
gardens around the farmhouses and cottages often produce a variety of
passerines and waders and seabirds are often good.

Offshore lies the Isle of May. Known since 1907 as a migration spot,
The May is still the site of a bird observatory and regularly turns up
interesting birds as well as good falls of the commoner species. Its cliffs
hold good numbers of breeding seabirds including the usual auks and

gulls. All in all this is a fine place to watch migrants without the frenetic quality of Scilly.

Winter	Red-throated Diver, Greylag Goose, Mallard, Teal, Gadwall, Wigeon, Shoveler, Pochard, Tufted Duck, Goldeneye, Scoter, Velvet Scoter, Long-tailed Duck, Eider, Turnstone, Purple Sandpiper
Summer	Fulmar, Shag, Kittiwake, Guillemot, Razorbill, Puffin
Autumn	Red-throated Diver, Manx Shearwater, Sooty Shearwater, Turnstone, Whimbrel, Purple Sandpiper, Kittiwake, Little Gull, Great Skua, Arctic Skua, passerines

Largo Bay	Leave Leven on the A915 eastwards. After 2km (1¼m) turn right to Lundin Links and then right again at the disused railway. A bridge under the railway, now a footpath, leads to the shoreline. Also views from Lower Largo 1km (½m) east.
Kilconquhar Loch	Leave Largo on the A915 and keep right on the A921 in 2km (1¼m) turn left on the B941 and view the loch from the north.
Elie Ness	Leave Kilconquhar southwards on the A917 to Elie. Free access to the shoreline.
Fife Ness	Leave Elie eastwards on the A917 to Crail. Continue straight through the town on a minor road to Fife Ness. Park before the golf club.
Isle of May	Boats from Anstruther. For the Observatory and details of accommodation write to NCC, 12 Hope Terrace, Edinburgh 9. For day trips contact the boatman. *Tel:* (03335) 484; or *Tel:* (0333) 310215.

Killiecrankie** OS43

This splendid RSPB reserve offers fine bird-watching in truly beautiful surroundings. From the banks of the River Garry with its Mergansers, Dippers and Grey Wagtails the land rises through woods of oak, birch and ash to open farmland and crag-strewn moorland. This cross-section of habitats offers a fine variety of birds including Redstart, Wood Warbler, Red and Black Grouse, Curlew, Buzzard and occasional Peregrine.

Summer	Red-breasted Merganser, Peregrine, Buzzard, Red Grouse, Black Grouse, Curlew, Woodcock, Common Sandpiper, Dipper, Grey Wagtail, Great Spotted Woodpecker, Redstart, Tree Pipit, Wood Warbler, Garden Warbler, Crossbill

Leave Pitlochry northwards on the A9 and stop after 7km (4¼m). The reserve, which lies to the west, may be visited by prior arrangement with the Warden, Killiecrankie RSPB Reserve, Pitlochry.

Loch Leven*** OS58

One of the richest lakes in the country, best known as the major arrival point of Pink-footed Geese in autumn when up to 10,000 may be seen in the evening or early morning. This large lake, covering some 1600ha (3952a), is an NNR with a distinct wildfowl bias. It holds one of the largest breeding populations of duck (1000 pairs) and is the winter haunt of huge numbers of these birds. As well as Pinkfeet there are up to

179

5000 Greylags, the largest flock of Goldeneye (500) in the country, and the second largest Tufted Duck (2500) flock, and a 1000 or more Mallard, Wigeon and Pochard. Up to 400 Whooper Swans are sometimes to be seen.

Until 1967 Loch Leven was a difficult place to work, with very limited access. Then the RSPB acquired Vane Farm at the south-east corner giving views over one of the best parts of the lake. A lagoon has been created that now attracts many birds of the area.

Woods and dry gorse areas attract a good variety of breeding birds including Redstart, Tree Pipit, Redpoll and others.

Winter Whooper Swan, Pink-footed Goose, Greylag Goose, Mallard, Teal, Wigeon, Gadwall, Pintail, Shoveler, Pochard, Tufted Duck, Golden-eye, Goosander

Summer Mute Swan, Shoveler, Gadwall, Tufted Duck, Red Grouse, Curlew, Common Tern, Cuckoo, Redstart, Spotted Flycatcher, Tree Pipit, Redpoll

Autumn Pink-footed Goose, Greenshank, Ruff

Vane Farm Lies each side of the B9097 off the M90. The nature centre is a converted sheep stead. Excellent hides.

Kirkgate Park Is signposted in Kinross.

Burleigh Sands Some 3km (2m) north-east of Kinross on the A911.

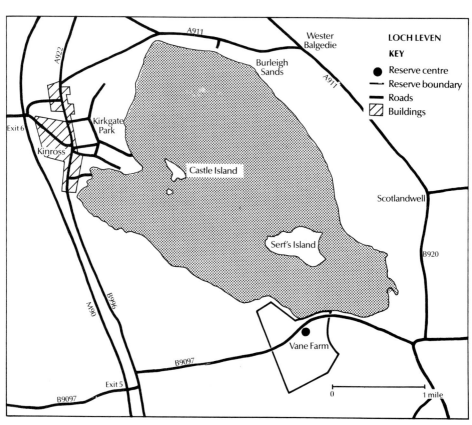

Montrose Basin*** OS54

The estuary of the River South Esk, called the Montrose Basin, is almost completely enclosed by land. At low tide the whole Basin empties out, leaving rich mud flats for feeding wildfowl and waders. Though much shot over in the past, a lot of the area is now a Scottish WT reserve, and it may be that the formerly large flocks of geese will return. Pinkfeet and · Greylags still haunt the area, but mostly less than 500 each. Wigeon are numerous and there are good flocks of Shelduck and Eider. For waders the Basin has never lost its appeal and there are 4000 Knot, 2500 Redshank and nearly 2000 Oystercatcher and Dunlin.

Moulting Eider often gather at Scurdie Ness and at the same time there may be up to 10,000 terns with attendant skuas. Passage waders include the usual species.

Winter   Greylag Goose, Pink-footed Goose, Shelduck, Wigeon, Pintail, Eider, Goldeneye, Oystercatcher, Grey Plover, Ringed Plover, Dunlin, Knot, Redshank, Turnstone, Bar-tailed Godwit, Curlew

Autumn   Grey Plover, Spotted Redshank, Greenshank, Bar-tailed Godwit, Curlew Sandpiper, Common Tern, Arctic Tern, Great Skua, Arctic Skua

The A934 in the south and an unclassified road northwards at Maryton give good views of south and west. The north can be seen from the A953. Scurdie Ness is due east of Ferryden, south of Montrose and a walk south to Mains of Usan may be fruitful for waders. Hides may be used by contacting the Warden, North Tillyside Cottage, Kinnaird Estate, by Brechin, Angus. *Tel:* (03562) 3480.

Moorfoot Reservoirs* OS73

A series of reservoirs in the Moorfoot Hills south of Edinburgh that include Gladhouse and Portmore, both goose roosts. Other wildfowl also use these waters with Goldeneye and Goosander regular. In summer the surrounds hold Black Grouse and Common Sandpiper.

Winter   Greylag Goose, Wigeon, Teal, Goldeneye, Goosander

Summer   Great Crested Grebe, Black Grouse, Common Sandpiper, Whinchat, Tree Pipit, Grasshopper Warbler

Leave Edinburgh southwards on the A7 and turn right on the B6372 just past Gorebridge. Follow this past Rosebery Reservoir, and where the road turns sharp right take the half left up to the fir wood. Turn sharp left and view the reservoir. Do not trespass. Return to the 'main' road and south to Portmore. A track on the left runs to the east side of the loch.

St Abb's Head* OS67

This spectacular and important seabird colony lies on the east coast just north of the border near Berwick-upon-Tweed and is an NTS and Scottish WT reserve. Large numbers of auks and Kittiwake breed,

181

including small numbers of Puffin. Eider and Gannet are regular offshore.

Summer   Fulmar, Gannet, Eider, Guillemot, Razorbill, Puffin, Kittiwake, Rock Pipit, Wheatear

Follow the A1, the A1107 and the B6438 to St Abb's. The reserve car park is ½km (¼m) west of the village. Follow the marked path up the cliffs to the lighthouse and onwards returning along the shore of Mire Loch. The best auks are at the lighthouse and at White Heugh.

Strath Earn**   OS58

Conveniently situated alongside the main A9 between Perth and Dunblane and extending northwards to Methven and Crieff lies one of the country's top goose spots. Pinkfeet are present in their thousands along with lesser numbers of Greylag, Wigeon, Teal and Whooper Swan. They feed in the area south of the A9 between Dupplin Loch and Dunning; near Braco, Greenloaning and Blackford; and north of Kinkell Bridge. The major roosts are on the small nearby lochs with Carsebreck Curling Ponds and Drummond and Dupplin Lochs being favoured.

The area north of the Earn, between Perth and Crieff, is well wooded and a home to Black Grouse and Capercaillie.

Winter   Greylag Goose, Pink-footed Goose, Whooper Swan, Wigeon, Teal
Summer   Great Crested Grebe, Black Grouse, Capercaillie

The whole of Strath Earn can be adequately explored by public roads, and there is no need to trespass on private land.

Dupplin Loch   Lies to the north of the A9 8km (5m) west of Perth. After a further 1km (½m) turn left on the B924 and right on the B934 to Dunning for geese.

Kinkell Bridge   This is reached by turning northwards on the B8062 at Auchterarder for more geese.

Roman Road   For Capercaillie, it lies north-east of Kinkell Bridge on minor roads.

Carsebreck   These can be seen from the A9 between Blackford and Greenloaning.

Curling Ponds   There are geese to south of this road and from the A822 north of Greenloaning.

Drummond Loch   Lies north of Muthill further along the A822.

Strath More***   OS53/54

Strath More is a lowland corridor stretching between Dunkeld and Forfar. In the west the rivers drain into the Tay, while in the east they flow directly into the North Sea. The River South Esk has the Montrose Basin (which *see*) as its estuary. This is a rich farming landscape with several prosperous towns, a fine network of roads, and a number of important lochs and floods. Most of these waters hold duck in winter, and some are used by geese as roosts. The main areas are a group of lochs around Forfar and another group around Blairgowrie, but there are also important sites at Lintrathen, Kirriemuir, and the famous Loch of Lowes near Dunkeld.

The Loch of Lowes is the odd one out, for while it does have winter wildfowl, it is best known as the Scottish WT reserve with breeding Osprey. This is one of only two sites for this species so far made public – the other is at Loch Garten in Speyside. Slavonian Grebe also nest along with Teal, Tufted Duck and Grasshopper Warbler. Goldeneye often summer here and Greylags roost in winter.

Above all, however, Strath More is the major haunt of Greylags and Pinkfeet in Britain with up to 30,000 of each in winter. Around Blairgowrie up to 10,000 Greylags can be found with peak numbers in November. Drumellie and Stormont Lochs are the best, though Loch of Clunie to the west is also good. These birds feed in the valley of the River Isla from Meiklour to Coupar Angus and sometimes further east toward Meigle.

To the east is the Loch of Lintrathen, a deep reservoir with up to 1000 roosting Greylags, 100 Whoopers and one of the largest Mallard flocks (5000) in Scotland. A wide variety of other duck can be found. The Greylags feed to the south and east and may interchange with birds that roost near Kirriemuir at Loch Kinnordy. The latter is a RSPB reserve with a loch surrounded by marshland as a result of former draining activities. It is best known for breeding birds with Redshank, Sedge Warbler, Water Rail, Great Crested Grebe and a large Black-headed Gullery. It was also the first site of breeding Ruddy Duck in Scotland. Woodcock, Sparrowhawk and Long-eared Owl also breed, while in winter there are Teal, Wigeon, Gadwall, Shoveler and Pochard.

The next goose haunt is to the east of Forfar at Lochs Balgavies and Rescobie. Here both Pinkfeet and Greylags roost, the former flighting to feed around Brechin along the South Esk while the Greylags tend to stay near the lochs. Part of Balgavies is a Scottish WT reserve.

Winter	Whooper Swan, Pink-footed Goose, Greylag Goose, Wigeon, Teal, Mallard, Gadwall, Shoveler, Tufted Duck, Pochard, Goldeneye, Goosander
Summer	Slavonian Grebe, Black-necked Grebe, Great Crested Grebe, Capercaillie, Water Rail, Sparrowhawk, Osprey, Mallard, Teal, Shoveler, Gadwall, Tufted Duck, Redshank, Snipe, Woodcock, Black-headed Gull, Green Woodpecker, Dipper, Redstart, Siskin
Passage	Greenshank, Green Sandpiper, Redshank, Whimbrel, Dunlin
Loch of Lowes	Lies immediately east of Dunkeld and is a reserve of the Scottish WT. Access is unrestricted to the south shore. There is a visitors' centre and hide. Tel: (03502) 337.
Blairgowrie Lochs	Lochs of Clunie and Drumellie can be seen from the A923 7km (4¼m) and 3km (2m) west of Blairgowrie. For Stormont Loch leave Blairgowrie southwards on the A923. In 2km (1¼m) cross a level crossing and after ½km (¼m) turn right, cross the railway and view to the south.
Isla Valley	Explore for feeding Greylags eastwards from Meiklour on the A984. Turn right to Coupar Angus and then left on the A94 to Meigle. Minor roads may give closer approaches at certain places.
Loch of Lintrathen	Take the B951 westwards from Kirriemuir and explore around the banks on minor roads. There is a car park at the north-west corner and

a hide at Balnakeilly, the only point of public access. Scottish WT local branch can advise on permits and hide opening times: Contact George Kerr, Frenchies, Glen Isla, by Kirriemuir, Angus.

Loch Kinnordy Off the B951 3km (2m) north-west of Kirriemuir at OS Ref No. 361539. RSPB can supply details of seasonal access and hides, but much can be seen from the road.

Forfar Lochs Leave Forfar eastwards on the B9113 and view Rescobie to the south after 5km (3m). For Balgavies continue eastwards and turn right. Over the railway the loch lies on the right. Continue to the A932, turn left and view on the left-hand side of the road. The Scottish WT have a car park and public hide at the western end of the loch. Contact the Warden, Wielstraw Cottage, Letharn, by Forfar, Angus.

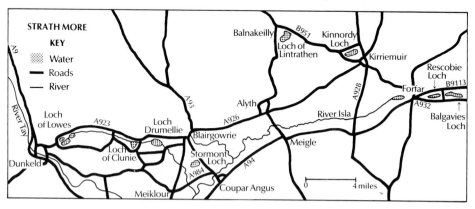

Tay Estuary****   OS53/54

This is a huge estuary by any standards and one that attracts good numbers of both wildfowl and waders. This would make it positively a winter spot were it not for the Tentsmuir area to the south with the exquisite Morton Lochs, much of which is an NNR. Together the estuary and the reserve offer good birding at all seasons. Unfortunately, the estuary proper is much shot over, and the numbers of wildfowl are undoubtedly less than otherwise would be the case. Up to 6000 Pinkfeet roost at the mouth on Abertay Sands and this same area holds up to 16,000 Eider. The latter may, at times, represent nearly a quarter of the UK total.

Greylags prefer the inner estuary and usually some 2000 feed on the Carse of Gowrie and roost at Mugdrum Island. Other duck, notably Goldeneye and Merganser, occur off Newburgh and especially off the coast between Dundee and Monifieth. Just off the latter is Buddon Burn, a haunt of Little Gull from spring to autumn, and one of the major wader areas. Dunlin, Redshank and Bar-tailed Godwit predominate, but a variety of other species occur, especially on passage.

Tentsmuir is a splendid wilderness with dunes and extensive conifer plantations. The Point itself is good for waders and is the best vantage

184

point for the Abertay flocks of geese and Eider. Snow Buntings find a winter home here. Nearby Morton Lochs hold 45 breeding species, including Shoveler, Gadwall, Sedge Warbler and Corn Bunting. Fresh waders are particularly good here, and in autumn include Greenshank, Spotted Redshank and Ruff. Winter brings regular Whooper Swan and duck.

This is a large area, but one that should not prove daunting, even to the casual visitor who picks time and place.

Winter   Whooper Swan, Pink-footed Goose, Greylag Goose, Mallard, Teal, Eider, Goldeneye, Scoter, Long-tailed Duck, Red-breasted Merganser, Oystercatcher, Ringed Plover, Grey Plover, Dunlin, Knot, Sanderling, Redshank, Bar-tailed Godwit, Curlew, Turnstone, Snow Bunting

Spring   Long-tailed Duck, Little Gull

Summer   Shelduck, Eider, Scoter, Shoveler, Gadwall, Tufted Duck, Stonechat, Sedge Warbler, Corn Bunting

Autumn   Eider, Greenshank, Spotted Redshank, Green Sandpiper, Whimbrel, Little Stint, Curlew Sandpiper, Ruff, Little Gull, Common Tern, Arctic Tern

Buddon Burn   Walk eastwards along the shore from Monifieth.

Broughty Ferry   Lies east of Dundee and has a sewage outfall.

North Shore   Leave Dundee westwards on the B958 to Kingoodie for good views over the widest inter-tidal area on a rising tide. To the west, several tracks run down to the shore, notably at Powgarvie. Views are, however, obstructed by large reed beds – watch for Sedge Warblers.

Newburgh   Lies on the southern shore giving good views over Mugdrum Island.

Tentsmuir   Leave Tayport southwards on the B945 and turn left after 3km (2m) to Morton Lochs. Continue to Morton and on to Fetterdale. A maze of forest tracks lead to the Point. There is a public hide at Morton Locks and two that are accessible by permit: contact NCC, 12 Hope Terrace, Edinburgh EH9 2AS. *Tel:* (031447) 4784. There is no access to Abertay Sands at Tentsmuir.

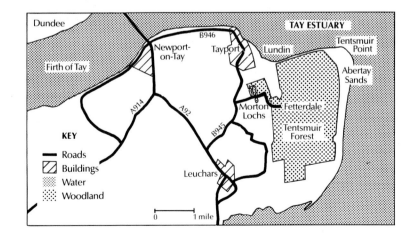

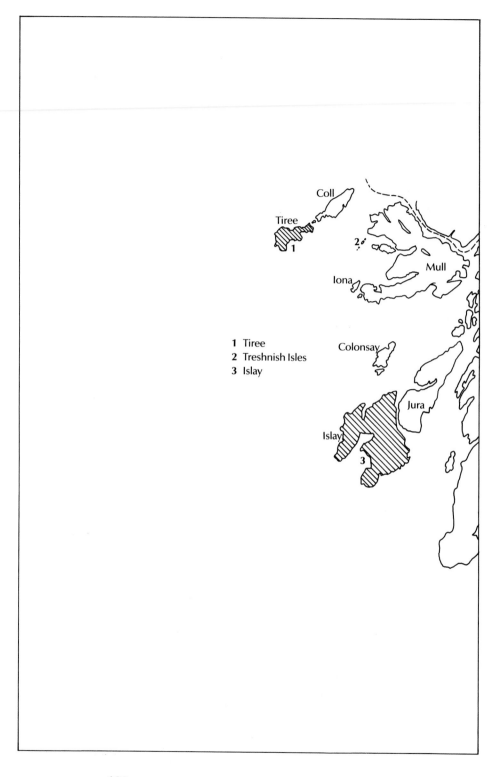

1 Tiree
2 Treshnish Isles
3 Islay

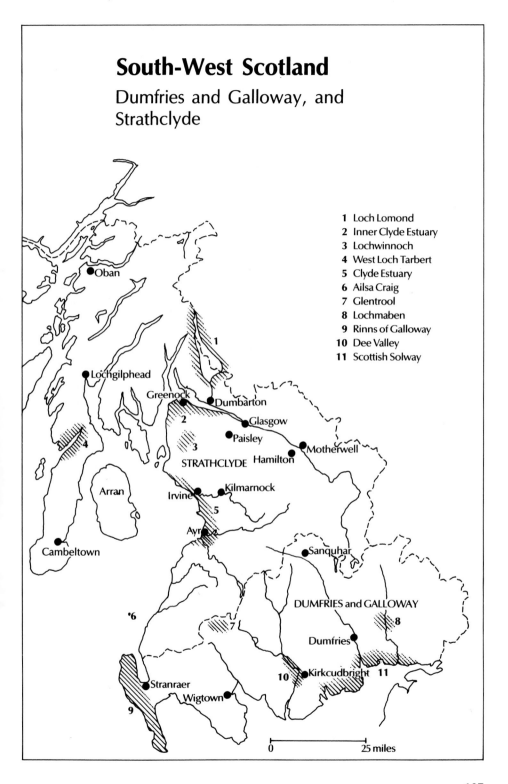

South-West Scotland

Dumfries and Galloway, and
Strathclyde

1 Loch Lomond
2 Inner Clyde Estuary
3 Lochwinnoch
4 West Loch Tarbert
5 Clyde Estuary
6 Ailsa Craig
7 Glentrool
8 Lochmaben
9 Rinns of Galloway
10 Dee Valley
11 Scottish Solway

Oban

Lochgilphead

Greenock

Dumbarton

Glasgow

Paisley

Motherwell

STRATHCLYDE   Hamilton

Arran

Kilmarnock

Irvine

5

Ayr

Cambeltown

Sanquhar

DUMFRIES and GALLOWAY

'6

7

8

Dumfries

10   Kirkcudbright   11

Stranraer

Wigtown

9

0   25 miles

Ailsa Craig**   OS76

A precipitous hump in the Firth of Clyde some 17km (10½m) west of Girvan and best known as a major gannetry with up to 16,000 pairs. Almost without exception the birds nest on the exposed western cliffs, and the best views are obtained without actually landing on the island. Take a boat trip beneath the cliffs for really impressive views of all the birds.

Summer   Fulmar, Gannet, Guillemot, Razorbill, Puffin, Kittiwake

Boats leave regularly during the early summer from Girvan Harbour. Contact Publicity Department, Town Clerk's Office, Girvan, Ayrshire.

Clyde Estuary***   OS63/70

Though the Firth of Clyde holds interesting birds throughout its length, one of the best parts is surprisingly close to Glasgow just downstream from Clydebank beyond the Erskine Ferry. Here, surrounded by industry, wide mud banks offer feeding and roosting areas to large numbers of waders including over 8000 Redshank (over 8 per cent of the UK total). Large numbers of Eider, Shelduck, Goldeneye and Merganser occur, and there are good concentrations of Pintail, Dunlin, Curlew and Turnstone, plus a few regular wintering Greenshank. The best areas are the southern shores between Erskine and Woodhall and on the north bank between Milton Island and Cardross.

Further out the Hunterston Sands have good numbers of waders, including Bar-tailed Godwit, while at Ardrossan there are important concentrations of Ringed Plover, Turnstone, Purple Sandpipers and other waders along with divers, Eider and Merganser. Many of these birds roost among the docks, but some fly to Horse Island, which is an RSPB reserve. This island is best in summer when colonies of Common and Arctic Terns breed along with variable numbers of Roseate and Sandwich. Lesser Black-backed, Herring and Black-headed Gulls also breed along with 50 pairs of Eider. Offshore are Guillemot, Razorbill and Gannet.

The estuary of the Irvine and Garnock combined offers a muddy shoreline which attracts several waders, while the adjacent marshes hold 40 Whooper Swans and a couple of hundred Wigeon. Golden Plover may be numerous. The Troon area to the south has two bays, one to the north the other to the south. Though both can be good, the South Bay is best with good numbers of sea-duck plus Curlew and Purple Sandpiper. The gull roost (25,000) regularly holds Glaucous, Iceland or both. Doonfoot Bay south of Ayr also has three gulls as well as a wide variety of wildfowl and waders.

Winter   Divers, Whooper Swan, Shelduck, Wigeon, Mallard, Teal, Pintail, Goldeneye, Red-breasted Merganser, Scoter, Eider, Oystercatcher, Curlew, Ringed Plover, Dunlin, Knot, Turnstone, Purple Sandpiper, Redshank, Greenshank, Glaucous Gull, Iceland Gull

Summer Gannet, Eider, Oystercatcher, Ringed Plover, Common Tern, Arctic Tern, Sandwich Tern, Roseate Tern, Lesser Black-backed Gull, Herring Gull, Guillemot, Razorbill

Inner Clyde Access via the A8 which runs along the south bank 7km (4¼m) east of Port Glasgow at Langbank. At West Ferry access eastwards on foot along the seawall. On the northern shore a railway line makes access awkward, but there are vantage ponts at Dumbarton on the east and west banks of the Leven, and at Cardross.

Horse Island Leave Glasgow south-westwards on the A737 to Kilwinning, turn right to Ardrossan on the A738. Explore here and continue northwards on the A78 to view Horse Island and in 10km (6¼m) the Hunterston area, after frequent stops south of West Kilbride. Summer visits to Horse Island may be arranged locally – details from RSPB Scottish Office, 17 Regent Terrace, Edinburgh EH7 5BN. *Tel:* (031556) 5624.

Troon Leave Ardrossan southwards on the A78 to Irvine and explore the estuary on the south side. Continue southwards, turning right on the B746 to Troon and watch over North and South Bays.

Ayr Continue southwards on the A78 and A79 to Ayr and leave on the A719 to Doonfoot.

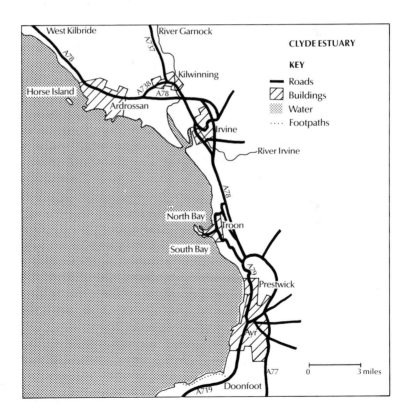

Dee Valley****   OS84

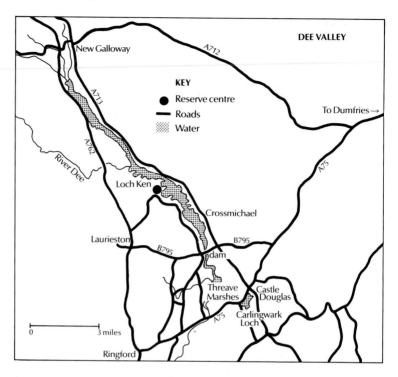

DEE VALLEY

New Galloway

A712

KEY
● Reserve centre
▬ Roads
▓ Water

To Dumfries →

A713

A762

River Dee

A75

Loch Ken

Crossmichael

Laurieston

B795

B795

dam

Threave
Marshes

Castle
Douglas

A75

Carlingwark
Loch

0   3 miles

Ringford

The whole of the Dee Valley has been flooded by the building of a dam to the north of Castle Douglas. This has created not a deep open water, but a shallow lagoon flanked by extensive marshes that is a major haunt of wildfowl and waders. There are always Greylags here and the flock of up to 400 Greenland Whitefronts is the only one in the area. A few Pinkfeet can usually be seen, and there is still a flock of Bean Geese, the only other flock is in East Anglia. These birds can often be seen in the Castle Douglas–Threave area, and there is a hide. Additionally, the RSPB has established a reserve aimed at providing a safe refuge for the Whitefronts, and breeding islands for ducks and waders. Whooper Swans, Wigeon and Teal can be seen, and there is always a variety of waders. Hen Harrier and Peregrine are usually present as are resident Buzzards. This is one of the most reliable sites in the country for the increasingly rare Barn Owl.

The RSPB reserve is well worth visiting in summer for Goosander, Kingfisher, Sedge and Grasshopper Warblers, Great Crested Grebe and duck. The woods hold Woodcock, Willow Tit, Pied Flycatcher and warblers and passage brings a variety of waders.

Winter   Whooper Swan, Greenland White-fronted Goose, Greylag Goose, Pink-footed Goose, Bean Goose, Wigeon, Teal, Goosander, Golden-eye, Hen Harrier, Peregrine, Barn Owl

Summer   Great Crested Grebe, Goosander, Buzzard, Snipe, Redshank, Oyster-catcher, Common Sandpiper, Woodcock, Kingfisher, Willow Warbler,

Wood Warbler, Sedge Warbler, Grasshopper Warbler, Redstart, Pied Flycatcher, Tree Pipit, Willow Tit

Castle Douglas–Threave Explore Carlingwark Loch for diving duck then move northwards to the Threave Marshes off the A713.

River Dee From the dam to 2km (1¼m) north of Crossmichael explore from the west bank for Greylags and Whitefronts.

Loch Ken Explore from the A762 on the western side and the A713 on the eastern side. Views may be obtained at several points. The RSPB reserve is at OS Refs: NX638765 and NX695694.

Islay*** OS60

One of the most beautiful and varied of the Scottish islands and, at 32km (20m) across, large enough for a full holiday of exploration. Its varied habitats include woods, moors, dunes, cliffs, lochs and sea lochs. Though best known as a winter haunt of up to 20,000 Barnacle Geese there are birds at all seasons with over 100 species breeding. These include Golden Eagle, Black Guillemot (at port Askaig and elsewhere), the occasional Scoter, Arctic Skua and one of Scotland's two colonies of Choughs on Oa in the south. Barnacles arrive in October and are impossible to miss until they depart in mid-April. Most roost on the tidal flats of Loch Gruinart, and the surrounding fields hold the largest concentrations. There are also up to 5000 Greenland White-fronts as well as large numbers of Scaup and Eider, Whooper Swan, Glaucous Gull, Great Northern Diver, together with decent flocks of waders in winter.

The RSPB has a large reserve at the head of Loch Gruinart that includes marshy saltings as well as farmland. This is prime goose country, but gulls and terns already nest and the Society plans to create lagoons for these and waders. The moorland areas hold Hen Harrier and Black Grouse.

Winter Great Northern Diver, Whooper Swan, Barnacle Goose, White-fronted Goose, Greylag Goose, Scaup, Eider, Curlew, Bar-tailed Godwit, Glaucous Gull, Chough, Twite

Summer Golden Eagle, Hen Harrier, Red-breasted Merganser, Red Grouse, Black Grouse, Black Guillemot, Guillemot, Razorbill, Kittiwake, Arctic Tern, Chough, Stonechat, Twite

Islay is served by ferries from West Loch Tarbert and by air from Glasgow. Accommodation is plentiful: contact the Tourist Association, Bowmore, Islay. Contact the RSPB warden on arrival at Grainel, Gruinart, Islay: he can be very helpful.

Rinns of Galloway*** OS82

The 'Hammerhead' of land at the western end of Galloway is a fine area of wild country offering a variety of habitats and birds. It is, however, off the beaten track with most visitors passing straight through to Stranraer on their way to Ireland – a pity. At the extreme south the Mull of Galloway is a RSPB reserve for cliff-nesting seabirds including Guillemot, Razorbill and Black Guillemot. Offshore lie Scar Rocks, a gannetry fast approaching 500 pairs. Though inaccessible, the birds are frequently seen from the Mull.

On the south side of the 'Hammerhead' lies Luce Bay with wildfowl and waders, especially around the river mouths on the eastern shore. Scoter, Merganser and Pintail are important, and large numbers of waders occur on passage. To the north is Loch Ryan with larger numbers of duck mainly on the southern shore between Stranraer and Leffnoll Point. Wigeon, Scaup, Goldeneye and especially Eider and Merganser form good flocks. Waders also gather along the southern shore, but also at a bay called The Wig on the western shore.

Slavonian and Black-necked Grebes occur here as well as at the Scottish WT reserve at Ballantrae at the mouth of the Stinchar to the north. Greylags are also found here as well as some waders and some good breeding birds. Geese and duck can be found at Black Loch and White Loch.

Summer Fulmar, Gannet, Shag, Cormorant, Kittiwake, Guillemot, Razorbill, Black Guillemot, Arctic Tern

Winter Black-necked Grebe, Slavonian Grebe, Greylag Goose, Wigeon, Scaup, Goldeneye, Eider, Red-breasted Merganser, Oystercatcher, Golden Plover

Mull of Galloway Leave Stranraer southwards on the A77, turning left on to the A716 to Drummore. Continue via Kirkmaiden on the B7041 to the Mull. Easy viewing from the cliff top near the lighthouse.

Loch Ryan The A77 runs eastwards along the shoreline from Stranraer. Westwards the A718 passes The Wig just south of Kirkcolm.

Black Loch and White Loch Leave Stranraer on the A75, and turn left at Castle Kennedy just before the disused airfield. To the south Loch Magillie and Soulseat Loch are also worth a look.

Luce Bay The A747 passes all the interesting areas southwards from Glenluce.

Ballantrae Leave Stranraer northwards on the A77. The mouth of the river can be explored southwards from the town. The Scottish WT reserve may be visited at the end of the shingle spit – some areas are marked off for nesting birds.

Glentrool** OS76/77

Forming part of the Galloway Forest Park, Glentrool lies 16km (10m) north of Newton Stewart, east of the A714. The area is owned by the Forestry Commission and apart from plantations of various ages, there is also an old oak forest to add to the bird diversity. The area offers a good selection of the birds of the region.

Summer Buzzard, Sparrowhawk, Hen Harrier, Peregrine, Black Grouse, Common Sandpiper, Woodcock, Short-eared Owl, Dipper, Ring Ouzel, Grey Wagtail, Stonechat, Whinchat, Pied Flycatcher, Redstart, Willow Tit, Tree Pipit, Grasshopper Warbler, Raven, Crossbill

Leave Newton Stewart northwards on the A714 and turn right at Bargrenan. After 3km (2m) turn right again and continue for 1km (½m) taking the second on the right to Caldon's Campsite. The Loch Trool Trail leads around the loch, through the sessile oakwoods and plantations.

Loch Lomond** OS56/57

Loch Lomond lies north-west of Glasgow and is a wonderful, open playground for the people of the industrial lowlands. It is an extremely beautiful area, and the lochside and many islands are well wooded with semi-natural oaks and recent conifers. Though Mergansers and Capercaillie breed, and the woodlands hold the usual Highland summer species, the main attraction is wildfowl in winter. These concentrate around the mouth of the Endrick in the south-east which is part of an NNR. Duck are numerous and Greylag number 1000. Whitefronts and Pinkfeet are occasional. Waders are regular on passage.

Winter Wigeon, Shoveler, Pochard, Tufted Duck, Red-breasted Merganser, Goldeneye, Greylag Goose, White-fronted Goose, Whooper Swan
Summer Red-breasted Merganser, Redstart, Grey Wagtail, Grasshopper and other warblers
Autumn Black-tailed Godwit, waders

Leave Glasgow northwards on the A809. Turn left on to the B837 at Drymen and continue to Balmaha. Access is restricted in parts of the reserve, and permission is required to visit these and to camp: contact the Warden, 22 Muirport Way, Drymen. Nature trail leaflets from shop or boatyard. Arrangements to visit the islands can be made at The Boat House, Balmaha.

Lochmaben* OS78

For those scurrying northwards, or southwards come to that, on non-birdy business, Lochmaben offers geese and other wildfowl only a short detour from the main A74. Although the meandering River Annan is worth exploring, Castle Loch has up to a 1000 Greylags along with Wigeon and Goosander. Whooper Swan, Shoveler and Pochard are often here on the adjacent floods. In summer Great Crested Grebe and Shelduck breed.

Winter Whooper Swan, Greylag Goose, Wigeon, Shoveler, Pochard, Goosander

Summer   Great Crested Grebe, Shelduck, Sedge Warbler

Leave the A74 westwards on the A709 at Lockerbie. This leads past Castle Loch in 5km (3m). Kirk Loch and Hightae Loch are also worthy of more than a cursory glance.

Lochwinnoch*   OS63

Lochwinnoch lies 30km (18½m) south-west of Glasgow and is a haunt of winter wildfowl. Barr Loch and Aird Meadow have been an RSPB reserve since 1974, and the shallow Castle Semple Loch to the north forms part of the Clyde Muirshiel Regional Park. The whole area is good for Whooper Swan and Greylag Goose, with up to 100 of the former and 500 of the latter using the area. Duck are numerous with Pochard and Tufted regularly breaking 1000.

In summer up to 11 pairs of Great Crested Grebe makes the area a Scottish stronghold of the species, and Teal and Shoveler both breed.

Winter   Cormorant, Whooper Swan, Greylag Goose, Teal, Wigeon, Pochard, Tufted Duck, Goldeneye, Short-eared Owl
Summer   Great Crested Grebe, Teal, Mallard, Shoveler, Tufted Duck, Curlew, Snipe, Sedge Warbler

Leave Glasgow via Paisley on the A737. Turn right on to the A760 following the signpost to Lochwinnoch, and the reserve centre is on the right-hand side of the road. The shop, educational displays and tower

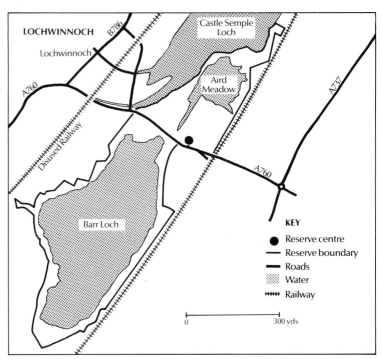

hide is open Thursday, Friday, Saturday and Sunday. For Castle Semple Loch take the B786 into Lochwinnoch. View the southern end of the loch and continue, passing under the railway and immediately turn right parallel to it. In 1km (½m) fork right over the railway back to the loch shore.

Scottish Solway***** OS83/84

The northern shores of the Solway Firth form one of the most important as well as the most exciting areas for birds in these islands. This is a winter place, but one that regularly attracts geese-starved southerners to make the long pilgrimage to this goose-mecca. Huge inter-tidal banks of mud and sand are backed by extensive areas of saltings and low-lying grassy fields – ideal conditions for geese. Mainly these are Pinkfeet and Greylags, but at Caerlaverock the marsh holds the entire population of Spitzbergen Barnacles. Some 5000 birds can be seen here – a magnificent sight. There are often larger numbers of Pinkfeet in the area, but they are most often seen flighting out over the Solway or feeding on Kirkconnell Merse on the west bank of the River Nith. This is also the best spot for Whooper Swan.

Duck are also present, often in large numbers, and the flock of over 2000 Pintail is one of the most important in the country. Numbers of all wildfowl are dwarfed by the 175,000 waders that include over 15,000 each of Oystercatcher, Knot and Dunlin. Indeed the Oystercatcher total of nearly 40,000 represents one-fifth of the UK total. Almost as important is the flock of 5000 Bar-tailed Godwit and 1400 Ringed Plover. The diversity of species indicates the richness of this splendid area.

Inevitably the area also attracts a wealth of other species including Peregrine, Merlin and Hen Harrier. There are Short-eared and Barn Owls and, as if all this were not enough, the Loch Ken area to the north is a refuge for more geese and different species. It merits (and receives) separate treatment.

At the outer edge of the estuary proper lies Southerness Point, a rocky area where Purple Sandpiper and other rocky-shore waders vie for attention with divers, grebes and a variety of seaduck. Further west still is a series of wide sandy estuaries that most visitors to the area include in their itinerary. Auchencairn Bay and Rough Firth, Kirkcudbright Bay, Fleet Bay and Wigtown Bay all hold interesting birds and are well worth exploring. The last has been treated separately.

Winter Red-throated Diver, Great Northern Diver, Great Crested Grebe, Whooper Swan, Pink-footed Goose, Greylag Goose, Barnacle Goose, Shelduck, Wigeon, Pintail, Shoveler, Scaup, Goldeneye, Red-breasted Merganser, Scoter, Velvet Scoter, Hen Harrier, Peregrine, Merlin, Oystercatcher, Ringed Plover, Golden Plover, Grey Plover, Knot, Sanderling, Dunlin, Bar-tailed Godwit, Curlew, Black-tailed Godwit, Redshank, Purple Sandpiper, Turnstone, Barn Owl
Passage Greenshank, Black-tailed Godwit

Caerlaverock Leave Dumfries southwards on the B725 alongside the Nith. At Glencaple look across the river for possible Pinkfeet and Whoopers. Continue to Shearington and soon after turn right on an unclassified road at a T-junction signposted Eastpark. Continue to the end of the road. The Wildfowl Trust have established their Caerlaverock Refuge here, and their grounds and escorted tours offer the best views of the mass of Barnacles. The Refuge is open daily from September to mid-May except Tuesday and Wednesday. Parties should make arrangements with the Refuge Manager. *Tel:* (038777) 200. The road to Eastpark often has Greylags and Pinkfeet and invariably Golden Plover. The NNR is also open daily: contact the warden. *Tel:* (038777) 275.

Nith The east side can be viewed from the B725 south of Dumfries. The west bank is more awkward. Leave Dumfries southwards on the west side of the Nith on the A710. Take a left turn after 5km (3m) to Kirkconnell. Park near the church and walk northwards towards Maxwellbank. Views of Whoopers and geese. Continue southwards on the A710 to Kirkbean and turn left to Carsethorn. Walk north and south along the shore.

Southerness Continue southwards on the A710 and take one of several roads to the left to Southerness Point.

Mersehead Sands Continue further westwards on the A710 to Caulkerbush. After 2km (1¼m) views may be had over an area of sand much frequented by sea-duck and waders from Lot's Wife Pinnacle. Greylag and Pinkfeet are regular, often in good numbers.

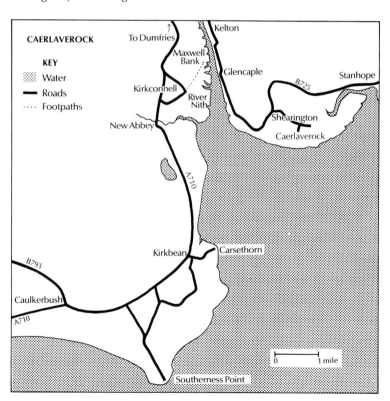

Tiree**   OS46

Unlike most of the Inner Hebrides, and certainly in contrast to its easterly neighbour Coll, Tiree catches the full effect of the Atlantic, as a result of which it has extensive shell-sand beaches in the west. It is thus more akin to the Outer Isles than the other Inner Isles. Wildfowl haunt the beautiful and shallow Loch a' Phuill and Loch Bhasapoll, although Whitefronts favour a marshy area in the centre of the island called The Reef. Gunna, to the north, holds a decent flock of Barnacle Geese.

In the summer there are good numbers of Arctic and Common Terns, Arctic Skua and Red-throated Diver. At Ceann a' Mhara the cliffs hold auks, and there is also the occasional pair of Red-necked Phalarope on the island. Spring passage brings Sanderling and Whimbrel.

Summer Red-throated Diver, Ringed Plover, Red-necked Phalarope, Arctic Tern, Common Tern, Guillemot, Razorbill, Black Guillemot
Spring Sanderling, Whimbrel, Turnstone
Winter Barnacle Goose, White-fronted Goose, Wigeon, Gadwall, Goldeneye, Eider, Red-breasted Merganser, Snipe, Jack Snipe

There are frequent flights from Glagow and regular sailings from Oban. There is a hotel at Scarinish as well as guest houses and cottages.

Treshnish Isles**   OS48

Composed of basalt and mainly steep sided and flat topped, these islands lie within the arms of Mull, south-west of Treshnish Point. There are large colonies of seabirds particularly on the Harp Rock off Lunga. Storm Petrels and Puffins nest here with Manx Shearwaters on Dutchmans Cap to the south. Barnacles winter on Cairn na Burgh Mor.

Winter Barnacle Goose
Summer Storm Petrel, Manx Shearwater, Fulmar, Razorbill, Guillemot, Puffin, Common Tern, Arctic Skua, Eider

At present the isles are used as seasonal grazing. There is no permanent settlement and visitors should be prepared to camp, and make local arrangements for transport. The Treshnish Isles seem, however, to be well worth the effort involved in getting there.

West Loch Tarbert***   OS62/68

This 18km (11m) long sea loch all but separates Kintyre from the Scottish mainland. It is also a major departure point for ferries to Islay and is worthy of attention at all times of the year. In winter it shelters good numbers of sea-duck, grebes and divers: it is a regular haunt of Great Northern. Barnacles are frequent in spring and a flock of up to 400 Greenland Whitefronts winters just south opposite Gigha where the Scottish WT has a reserve near Rhu. Among the Slavonian Grebes,

Long-tailed Duck and Scoter there are Velvet and the occasional King Eider (try Clachan at the mouth).

In summer there are Golden Eagle, Hen Harrier, Peregrine, Black Grouse and a good selection of woodland birds.

Winter	Great Northern Diver, Slavonian Grebe, White-fronted Goose, Greylag Goose, Eider, Velvet Scoter, Long-tailed Duck
Spring	Barnacle Goose
Summer	Golden Eagle, Hen Harrier, Peregrine, Merlin, Black Grouse, Redstart, Tree Pipit, Wheatear, Whinchat

Tarbert is easily reached via the A83 which continues along the southern shore to Rhu with the Scottish WT reserve. Knapdale, a high moor to the north of the loch, is good for upland birds in summer and, having come this far, it seems a pity not to go all the way south to Campbeltown and Southend. Sanda Island offshore has Black Guillemot, Puffin and passing Gannets.

North Wales

Clwyd, Gwynedd

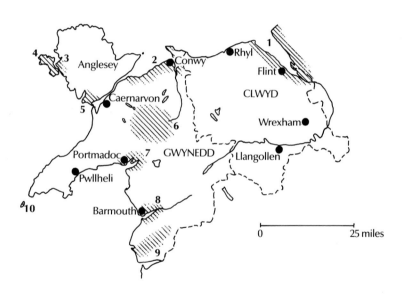

1 Dee Estuary
2 Conwy Bay
3 Inland Sea
4 Holy Island
5 Newborough Warren
6 Snowdonia
7 Traeth Bach
8 Mawddach Estuary
9 Dysynni Valley
10 Bardsey Bird Observatory

Bardsey Bird Observatory**   OS123

Bardsey lies at the north-western tip of Wales and is a privately owned bird reserve. The well-established observatory is based at a large stone-built farmhouse and can accommodate 12 visitors on a self-catering weekly basis from Saturday to Saturday. The island has good seabird colonies, including Manx Shearwater, about sixty pairs of Choughs, and migrants include good numbers attracted to the light-house, plus a sprinkling of rarities. There is a resident warden. Just about the right size and right amount of cover for a day's thorough scouring.

Summer   Manx Shearwater, Razorbill, Guillemot, Chough, Raven
Passage   Chats, warblers, flycatchers, rarities

Access is by boat from Pwllheli and the 30km (19m) crossing takes 3 hours. Observatory bookings via Mrs Helen Bond, 21A Gestridge Road, Kingsteignton, Newton Abbot, Devon. Cottages are available from Bardsey Trust, Tyddyn Du Farm, Criccieth, Gwynedd. *Tel:* 076 671 2239.

Conwy Bay***   OS115

The coastline of North Wales between Bangor and Llandudno is one of the very best birding areas in the principality, despite its reputation as a holiday resort. Birds are best at the western end around the outlet of the Afon Ogwen, the Traeth Lavan LNR, and along the coast as far as Aber. This is good inter-tidal birding with wildfowl and waders present in both number and variety. Duck tend to concentrate around the Ogwen outlet, while waders roost to the east towards Llanfairfechan as well as at the Ogwen. Mallard and Wigeon are the dominant duck, but up to 250 Mergansers moult here in late summer together with nearly 500 Great Crested Grebes. In both respects the area is of prime importance. They can be seen from either Aber or Llanfairfechan. Many remain in winter and are often joined by Black-necked and Slavonian Grebes and divers.

Among the waders Oystercatcher and Dunlin are by far the most abundant, but there are good numbers of Curlew, Redshank and Knot, and some 20 or so Greenshank are also here in winter. Passage periods bring a wider variety.

To the east lies Conwy Estuary, a fine site with excellent viewing both above and below the Llandudno Junction bridge. Many waders gather at the Deganwy golf course, but they are present throughout the area. Further east still is Great Orme's Head, a tourist spot for breeding auks, gulls and Fulmar. In winter Turnstone and Purple Sandpiper may be seen, especially at Little Orme.

Winter   Red-throated Diver, Slavonian Grebe, Black-necked Grebe, Great Crested Grebe, Shelduck, Wigeon, Goldeneye, Red-breasted Merganser, Knot, Dunlin, Purple Sandpiper, Turnstone, Curlew, Greenshank

Summer	Fulmar, Kittiwake, Guillemot, Razorbill, Puffin, Common Tern
Passage	Greenshank, Curlew Sandpiper, terns
Traeth Lavan	This is an LNR on the Ogwen estuary with a variety of species and planned hides. There are footpaths reached via a minor road off the A55 close to Tal-y-bont just outside Bangor, at OS Ref: SH609710, that lead to the shore near Aber Ogwen Farm.
Bangor	View from the promenade near the pier.
Lavan Sands	Leave Bangor eastwards on the A55 and turn left just beyond Crymlyn to the shore.
Llanfairfechan	Easy access near the station.
Conwy Estuary	Viewable from the east via the A546.
Great Orme's Head	Drive right up via Llandudno.

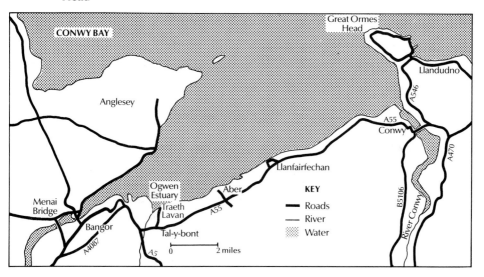

Dee Estuary***** OS108/116/117

The Cheshire Dee has long been famous as a major haunt of waders, with large numbers both in winter and on passage. Traditionally a substantial proportion of these birds roost at high tide at the famous Hilbre Islands where they are crowded tightly together while their feeding grounds are covered by the sea. Most of the great photographs of roosting waders have been taken at Hilbre, particularly at Little Eye. Over the past 15 years or so the islands have suffered severe disturbance, especially from anglers, and this spectacular sight is less frequent than formerly. Nevertheless the Dee still supports large numbers of birds. The gathering of up to 1000 Little Terns in autumn is significant.

The main channel runs close to the western shore, and as a result most birds concentrate on the huge flats on the east side. At the mouth, the Point of Air is a dune area, while on the eastern side near West Kirby there are large productive inter-tidal sand banks as well as Hilbre and the Red Rocks. All of these areas are important roosts.

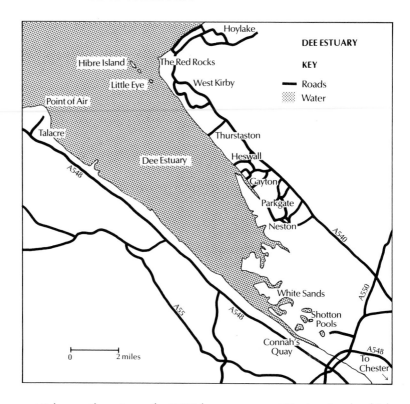

Higher up the estuary the RSPB has a reserve at Gayton Sands which now holds the most important wildfowl concentrations (up to 6000 Pintail) as well as many waders. Winter raptors include Peregrine and Hen Harrier as well as Short-eared Owl. The marshes near White Sands are also a wader roost. At the head of the estuary lies Shotton Steelworks with their famous, if unsalubrious, pools. This is probably the best place on the estuary for passage waders and regularly produces Bearded Tit. Connah's Quay Power Station, just across the river from Shotton, is another hot spot. The pools and scrape here regularly produce an excellent collection of waders as well as Barn Owl and winter Peregrine and Merlin. In autumn large numbers of terns gather near the mouth and sea-watching in stormy weather regularly produces shearwaters.

The estuary is particularly important for Pintail, 5000; Knot 30,000; Dunlin 28,000; Bar-tailed Godwit 5000; and Sanderling 6500 on passage. There are good numbers of raptors in winter.

Winter   Hen Harrier, Merlin, Peregrine, Shelduck, Mallard, Teal, Wigeon, Pintail, Shoveler, Goldeneye, Scaup, Scoter, Red-breasted Merganser, Oystercatcher, Ringed Plover, Grey Plover, Turnstone, Purple Sandpiper, Dunlin, Knot, Sanderling, Black-tailed Godwit, Bar-tailed Godwit, Curlew, Short-eared Owl, Brambling, Twite

Passage   Manx Shearwater, auks, Sanderling, Curlew Sandpiper, Spotted Redshank, Greenshank, Common Tern, Little Tern, Arctic Skua

Summer   Redshank, Reed Warbler, Grasshopper Warbler

202

Hilbre These islands are an LNR and permission must be obtained from Wirral Council Leisure Dept., Riversdale Road, West Kirby, Merseyside, to visit. Most can be seen from the adjacent coast and there are plenty of waders off the Hoylake Promenade and eastwards to Leasowe. There is a bird observatory here.

Eastern Shore View from West Kirby and at several places off the A540 via Thurstaston, Heswall, Gayton and Parkgate.

Gayton Sands Situated at OS Ref: SJ274786 near Neston off the A540. The RSPB hides and scrapes make this one of the best spots on the whole of the Dee.

Shotton Pools Strictly private, but permits may be obtained from Personnel Services, British Steel, Shotton Steelworks, Deeside. Leave Chester westwards on the A548 and continue until it joins the A550. Turn right, and the works road is the second on the left. Hides overlook the lagoon.

Connah's Quay Lies directly off the A548 and may be visited by members of the Deeside Naturalists' Society and by non-members at weekends. Contact The Station Manager, Connah's Quay Power Station, Connah's Quay, Deeside.

Point of Air Walk from Talacre on the A548.

Dysynni Valley** OS124/135

The River Dysynni starts high among the forbidding fastnesses of Cader Idris (breeding Raven and Ring Ouzel) and runs through a beautiful and rather unfrequented valley to the sea. There it forms a tiny estuary called Broad Water that holds small numbers of the more common duck and waders, with divers offshore. Inland the valley floor is flat and fertile with Buzzard and possible Peregrine in evidence. Some 9km (5½m) up the valley a rocky outcrop called Bird Rock Towyn has a colony of Cormorant. Higher still the road curves away to the right leaving only a no-through-road penetrating the upper valley. Here the old oak woods support a population of Buzzard, Sparrowhawk, Pied Flycatcher, Redstart and Wood Warbler in the most delightful surroundings. Whinchats abound on the bracken covered hills.

Summer Cormorant, Buzzard, Sparrowhawk, Peregrine, Wheatear, Whinchat, Redstart, Tree Pipit, Pied Flycatcher, Wood Warbler

Winter Divers, grebes, Wigeon, Goldeneye, Teal, Red-breasted Merganser, Buzzard, Peregrine, Dunlin, Turnstone, Curlew

Leave Towyn northwards on the A493 and turn right up the valley by taking the next turning past the B4405. Drive along, keeping left on to the no-through-road, and park at the end where riverside woods may be explored.

Broad Water should be explored from the south via a no-through-road along the seaward side for winter divers, wildfowl and waders.

Holy Island**

Holy Island is the small island off the west coast of Anglesey dominated by Holyhead, the port and car ferry terminal for Ireland. In the north and west the RSPB has established the South Stack Cliffs Reserve. This is divided into two parts, with the stretch from North Stack to Ellen's Tower being the better for birds. This is a beautiful area with nine breeding sea-birds including 2000 pairs of Guillemot, 600 Razorbill, 500 of Puffin as well as Fulmar, Shag and Kittiwake.

Of great interest are the breeding Choughs, and Peregrines formerly bred and may well return now that summer climbing is banned.

Summer Fulmar, Shag, Kittiwake, Guillemot, Razorbill, Puffin, Chough, Raven, Stock Dove, Rock Pipit, Stonechat

Leave Holyhead westward on minor roads to South Stack Steps and explore along the cliff-top paths.

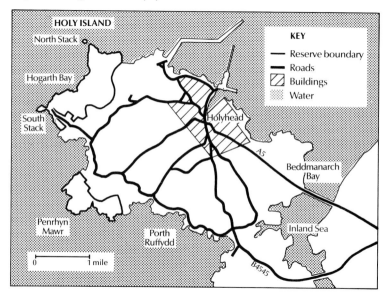

Inland Sea**

There are two bridges that connect Holyhead Island with Anglesey, between the two is an inter-tidal area called Inland Sea. Both it and the two 'unenclosed' parts of the channel are excellent wildfowl and wader areas. Many gather at the Alaw estuary and in Beddmanarch Bay. Though a wide variety of species occurs here, most are present in relatively small numbers, though up to 1000 Wigeon and 250 Bar-tailed Godwit occur regularly. Grebes are often present and Ringed Plover are important. Not far away lies Llyn Llywenan, the best inland water on Anglesey. Whooper Swans are regular and there are good numbers of duck in winter.

Winter Whooper Swan, Shoveler, Pintail, Wigeon, Teal, Goldeneye, Dunlin, Bar-tailed Godwit, Curlew, Redshank, Turnstone

Inland Sea View from both Holyhead bridges and by walking north and south along the shore.

Llyn Llywenan Take the B5109 off the A5025 to Bodedern and then the next left on to a road that runs along the west and north sides of the lake.

Mawddach Estuary*   OS124

The inter-tidal area extends inland for 9km (5½m) to the toll bridge at Penmaenpool. The resort at Barmouth lies on the northern shore opposite the narrow exit. For quite a large estuary it holds comparatively few birds with Wigeon and Dunlin dominant in winter, a good passage of Ringed Plover and occasional Whooper Swan. The woods along the shore-line are, however, beautiful and rich in species. Typical is Coed Garth Gell, an RSPB reserve on the northern shore, that was formerly worked by goldminers. Buzzard, Raven plus hosts of Wood Warblers and Pied Flycatchers breed, along with Redstart, Dipper and Lesser Spotted Woodpecker.

Winter Whooper Swan, Shelduck, Buzzard, Dunlin, Oystercatcher
Summer Buzzard, Raven, Dipper, Grey Wagtail, Lesser Spotted Woodpecker, Pied Flycatcher, Redstart, Wood Warbler

Leave Barmouth eastwards on the A496 and view southwards. The RSPB reserve can be explored by a footpath starting just west of the north side of the toll bridge OS Ref: SH687 191. The RSPB has an information centre at Penmaenpool just 2km (1¼m) to the south.

Newborough Warren***   OS114

An NNR with adjacent estuary and pools, famous as the home of bird artist, the late Charles Tunnicliffe, and the scene of many of his paintings. This beautiful area offers a variety of habitats in a relatively small area and is consequently rich in species. The warren itself is a huge area of dunes now largely planted with conifers, but still with open areas with slacks and scrub. The estuary of the Cefni, known as Malltraeth Sands, is full of wildfowl and waders, while at its head lies The Cob, a wall that separates the estuary from an excellent wader pool. Between them a fine collection of waders can be seen virtually throughout the year. Pintail are important, but Wigeon, Whooper Swan, Shelduck, Teal and others occur along with good numbers of the more common winter waders. A Peregrine is often present. On passage Whimbrel, Spotted Redshank, Little Stint and others occur, often on The Cob pool.

Winter Whooper Swan, Shelduck, Pintail, Wigeon, Teal, Oystercatcher, Curlew, Dunlin, Turnstone, Sanderling

Passage   Whimbrel, Spotted Redshank, Bar-tailed Godwit, Little Stint

The Cob is an excellent vantage point – the A4080 passes across it. The NNR can be explored along well-marked paths and tracks, notice boards show details along the A4080 south of The Cob. A guide to the NNR also shows paths and tracks that may be used on a practical map of the area. By turning left to the church in the village it is possible to drive through the forest to the shore at Llanddwyn Bay.

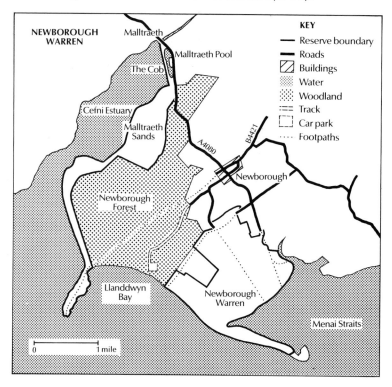

Snowdonia* OS115

Snowdonia is contained within a rectangle joining Conway, Betws-y-Coed, Portmadoc and Caernarvon, yet to the climber and fell walker there is almost no need to look any further than the Llanberis pass and Ogwen Valley. It is a beautiful rugged landscape with bare grass and heather moors in the north, the peaks and mountain passes in the centre, and beautiful wooded valleys to the south. Over such a vast area there are many bird-watching places, and the visitor is urged to make his own explorations.

The heather moor north of the Llyn-y-mynydd Reservoir west of Bethesda is worth a try for waders and grouse, and the Glaslyn valley south of Beddgelert is good for woodland species.

206

Choughs breed in some of the slate quarries, Ring Ouzels are found on the high screes, and a Peregrine might be seen anywhere. Whooper Swans are the only wildfowl of interest and almost the only inhabitants of the large lakes.

Winter   Whooper Swan, Buzzard, Raven, Peregrine, Dipper

Summer Buzzard, Raven, Dipper, Grey Wagtail, Pied Flycatcher, Chough, Redstart, Wood Warbler, Wheatear

Walking over the area is generally permitted, though the usual court-esies are as important here as anywhere. There are numerous paths which should be used wherever possible. The list of areas which follows is only intended as an outline guide:

1 Llyn Dinas, Llynan Mymbr, Cwm-y-Glo often hold Whooper Swans.
2 The oak woods at Capel Curig, with their entrance across the bridged stream opposite the Corwen Hotel, are both beautiful and full of birds.
3 The A498 north of Beddgelert is good for Buzzards.
4 The moors north of Lln-y-mynydd Reservoir and west of Bethesda for possible Red Grouse, Golden Plover, etc.
5 The first bridge north of Bethesda on the Nant Ffrancon for Dipper and Grey Wagtail.
6 Cwm Idwal in the Ogwen Valley for Wheatear, Ring Ouzel, beautiful scenery, and alpine flowers.
7 The woods around Betws-y-Coed for woodland species.
8 Vale of Ffestiniog for delicious and extensive oakwoods for Pied Flycatchers, etc.

There are several hotels to choose from at Llanberis, Capel Curig, and Beddgelert, all are splendidly central. Climbers and walkers camp all over the place and there are many cheap 'barns' for those who rough it.

Traeth Bach**   OS124

This area is actually the estuaries of the River Glaslyn and Dwyryd. Though relatively small rivers, the south of the estuary is partially blocked by the huge dune system of Morfa Harlech creating a substantial inter-tidal zone. Decent numbers of waders and wildfowl occur in winter with a greater variety during passage periods. The fact that none occur in nationally important numbers does not reduce the attraction, for there are always several hundred Dunlin, Redshank and Curlew along with Knot and Bar-tailed Godwit, plus 1000 or so Oystercatcher. Wildfowl include good numbers of Wigeon and Pintail, plus Goldeneye, Merganser and a few Whooper Swans on Glaslyn Pool which lies north of the ballast bank east of Portmadoc.

On passage a variety of waders and terns occurs.

Winter   Whooper Swan, Pintail, Wigeon, Teal, Shelduck, Shoveler, Golden-eye, Red-breasted Merganser, Scaup, Eider, Dunlin, Redshank, Cur-lew, Knot, Bar-tailed Godwit

Passage Greenshank, Green Sandpiper, Common Sandpiper, Common Tern

Take the A497 eastwards from Portmadoc and view to north over the Glaslyn Pool and south over the estuary. Continue eastwards and take the minor road on the right across the Llandecwyn Bridge to join the A496. Turn right and then right again 1.5km (1m) past Tolsarnau on the B4573. This leads to the shoreline. Many duck gather near Harlech Point.

South and Central Wales

Dyfed, Glamorgan, Gwent, Powys

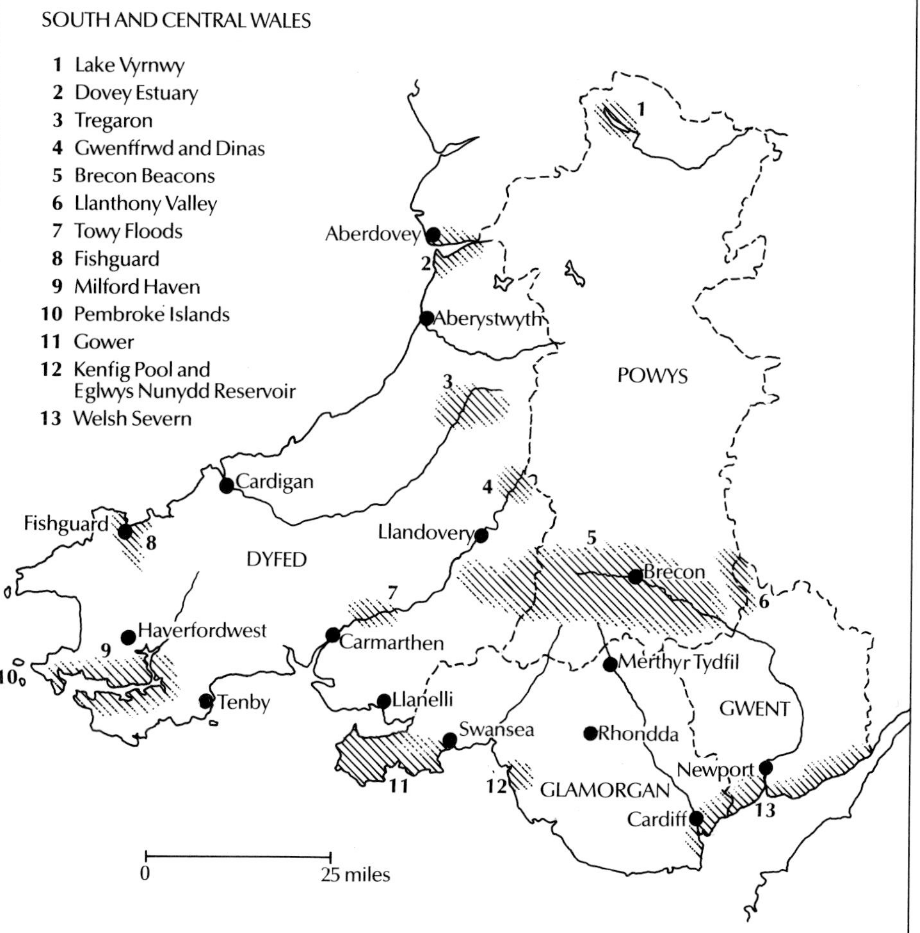

SOUTH AND CENTRAL WALES

1 Lake Vyrnwy
2 Dovey Estuary
3 Tregaron
4 Gwenffrwd and Dinas
5 Brecon Beacons
6 Llanthony Valley
7 Towy Floods
8 Fishguard
9 Milford Haven
10 Pembroke Islands
11 Gower
12 Kenfig Pool and
   Eglwys Nunydd Reservoir
13 Welsh Severn

POWYS

Aberdovey

Aberystwyth

Cardigan

Fishguard

DYFED

Llandovery

Brecon

Haverfordwest

Carmarthen

Merthyr Tydfil

Tenby

Llanelli

Swansea

Rhondda

GWENT

Newport

GLAMORGAN

Cardiff

0   25 miles

Brecon Beacons* OS160/161

Though the famous Becon Beacons lie north of Merthyr Tydfil east of the A470, the name is used somewhat liberally here to include the whole upland area that extends from Crickhowell westwards to Llandeilo. It thus includes Fforest Fawr, the Black Mountains and Llangorse Lake. The latter apart, this huge area has many common characteristics and the birds are more or less the same all over. High grassy moors with patches of heather are cut by steep-sided valleys, often still clad in hanging oak woods. There is considerable reafforestation and several high-level reservoirs. This is good walking country that can be explored throughout, though by sampling the habitats of one area one sees the birds of the whole.

Llangorse Lake lies some 10km (6¼m) east of Brecon near the Usk Valley. It is a natural lake and is surrounded by extensive reed beds that shelter a variety of species, including both Sedge and Reed Warblers. In winter the occasional wild swan may join the Goosander and other duck.

Summer	Great Crested Grebe, Buzzard, Red Kite, Sparrowhawk, Merlin, Red Grouse, Dunlin, Curlew, Raven, Grey Wagtail, Dipper, Ring Ouzel, Pied Flycatcher, Redstart, Wood Warbler, Reed Warbler, Sedge Warbler
Autumn	Greenshank, Green Sandpiper, Common Tern, Black Tern
Winter	Pintail, Teal, Goosander

Black Mountains	The A4069 crosses the range and gives access to several good valleys on the northern side.
Fforest Fawr	Several roads cross the range southwards from the Usk Valley, though Sennybridge is the best starting point and the minor road along the Afon Senni is probably the best route.
Brecon Beacons	Accessible from the A470 near the Storey Arms and southwards from Tal-y-bont and Brecon. Much of the area is now reasonably free of access.
Llangorse Lake	Leave Brecon south-eastwards on the A40 and turn left on the B4560 at Bwlch to Llangorse. Access from here and Llangasty church.

Dovey Estuary*** OS135

The Dovey is the largest estuary in central west Wales and one of the best birding spots in the principality. The inter-tidal area is quite extensive in the south with saltings backed by extensive wet grazing meadows. Near the mouth is a large dune area, while at the head of the estuary lies the RSPB reserve of Ynys-hir. The latter, with its well-sited hides, is one of the best places to see estuarine birds including the small flock of about 25 Greenland Whitefronts, the most southerly in Britain, though these birds are often found a little to the west of the reserve. Other wildfowl include up to 2000 Wigeon and good numbers of Pintail. Winter waders are often disappointing, but on passage Sanderling, Dunlin and Ringed Plover are all important. One of the joys of the area is the variety of habitat available within such a small space. Thus the fine old woods that abut the estuary are alive with Pied Flycatcher and Wood Warbler, and Buzzard and Sparrowhawk both breed. The heaths hold Whinchat and Tree Pipit, and Red Kite is a regular. The streams have Grey Wagtail, Dipper and Common Sandpiper, and Kingfisher is regular.

Winter   Little Grebe, White-fronted Goose, Mallard, Teal, Wigeon, Pintail, Shoveler, Goldeneye, Red-breasted Merganser, Shelduck, Buzzard, Sparrowhawk, Bar-tailed Godwit, Redshank, Dunlin, Raven, Rock Pipit

Summer   Red-breasted Merganser, Buzzard, Sparrowhawk, Common Sandpiper, Grey Wagtail, Dipper, Kingfisher, Nightjar, Redstart, Wood Warbler, Pied Flycatcher, Grasshopper Warbler, Raven, Redpoll

Passage   Ringed Plover, Sanderling, Greenshank, Whimbrel, Knot, Arctic Tern, Common Tern

Ynys-hir   Leave Machynlleth westwards on the A487 to the village of Furnace. The entrance is on the right opposite a large water mill. The reserve is open Saturday, Sunday, Wednesday and Thursday from April to September and on Sunday and Wednesday during the winter.

North Shore   Can be seen from the A493, but is not brilliant for birds.

South Shore   Leave the A487 at Trer-ddol on to the B4353 for views northwards over the sand dunes and backing grazing marshes. There is a car park off the B4353 at Ynyslas, giving access to part of an NNR.

Fishguard*   OS157

The small estuary of the River Gwaun holds a few Oystercatchers and not much more, but higher up, its banks are lined with oakwoods and are alive with summer birds. Dipper and Grey Wagtail, Wood Warbler and Pied Flycatcher can all be seen. Follow the river higher still and the Prescelly Mountains have Ring Ouzel and Raven. Indeed, along this single valley most of Wales' best birds can be seen. To east and west of Fishgard lie Dinas Head and Strumble Head offering spectacular seabird cliffs for very little effort. Of the two Strumble is the better with Chough among the auks and gulls.

Summer   Fulmar, Cormorant, Buzzard, Sparrowhawk, Guillemot, Razorbill, Kittiwake, Raven, Chough, Dipper, Grey Wagtail, Ring Ouzel, Tree Pipit, Pied Flycatcher, Wood Warbler

Gwaun Valley   Leave Fishguard south-eastwards on the B4313. Turn left after 5km (3m) to Cilrhedyn and follow the valley. To the south the B4329 crosses the high Prescelly Mountains.

Dinas Head   Leave Fishguard eastwards on the A487. At Dinas turn left to Brynhellan, pass through the village and continue to a small cove on the west of the headland. From here take the cliff-top path.

Strumble Head   Follow a maze of roads westwards to the Head with the aid of an OS map.

Gower****   OS159

The beautiful Gower peninsula lies immediately west of Swansea and offers some of the best birding in Wales in the most idyllic surroundings. To the north lies the Burry Inlet, actually the over-large estuary of the River Loughor. Best known for its huge concentrations of Oyster-catcher, over 10,000 at times, it also attracts a wide variety of other species both in winter and on passage. Dunlin and Knot also reach five figures while Redshank, Turnstone and Curlew also top the 1000 mark. Both godwits winter along with the occasional Greenshank. On passage there are Spotted Redshank and Whimbrel as well as a scattering of Little Stint and Curlew Sandpiper.

Brent Geese winter and are increasing, and Pintail and Wigeon reach good numbers. Divers can often be seen at the mouth of Whiteford Burrows and Black-necked and Slavonian Grebes are regular. Peregrine and Hen Harrier usually appear in winter.

In the south of Gower lies Oxwich Bay, a little gem that is an NNR. Hemmed in by limestone hills this 3km (2m) bay has a dune-lined beach backed by marshes and reeds. It is the most westerly point in Britain for Reed Warbler and has a good reputation for producing the unusual. Waders and terns are good on passage and wildfowl are worthy of a look in winter. This season often brings a few divers close inshore.

At the south-west corner of Gower lies Worm's Head, a 1½km (1m) long, rocky promontory that is separated from the mainland at high tide. The Head is an NNR and breeding birds include auks. Sea-watching may be productive of shearwaters and skuas in autumn. As if all this were not enough, the area of Swansea Bay, despite being developed by industry, is good for waders with Ringed Plover and Sanderling present in decent numbers, and Bar-tailed Godwit, Grey Plover and Knot numerous. Most of these birds gather at high tide at Black Pill where there is also a small (10,000) gull roost. In this somewhat uninspiring setting Ring-billed Gulls have made a habit of appearing regularly along with Mediterranean Gulls.

Winter Red-throated Diver, Slavonian Grebe, Black-necked Grebe, Brent Goose, Shelduck, Wigeon, Pintail, Scaup, Eider, Red-breasted Merganser, Peregrine, Hen Harier, Oystercatcher, Grey Plover, Turnstone, Purple Sandpiper, Dunlin, Knot, Sanderling, Redshank, Bar-tailed Godwit, Black-tailed Godwit, Curlew

Summer Guillemot, Razorbill, Puffin, Sedge Warbler, Reed Warbler

Passage Manx Shearwater, Whimbrel, Spotted Redshank, Greenshank, Little Stint, Curlew Sandpiper, Common Tern, Black Tern, Arctic Skua

Oxwich Bay Leave Swansea westwards on the A4118 which passes along the bay and turn left to Oxwich village. The whole of this road is worth exploring on foot. Access to the salt marsh is by a footpath on the left of the marsh road from Oxwich Towers. There is a reserve centre with information to explore the reserve and a nature trail. Access to the beach is unrestricted.

Worm's Head Continue westwards on the A4118 and turn right on to the B4247 to Rhosili. A footpath leads along the cliff top to the coastguards and continues down to the rocky causeway which is uncovered for about 5½ hours at low tide. Consult the tide tables at the coastguards before crossing. While crossing keep to the northern side on approach, work across to the middle and veer again to the northern side near Inner Head. Do not get marooned and do not pick flowers, light fires, or disturb breeding birds.

Burry Inlet Return to the A4118 and find the way via Reynoldston to Cheriton. In ½km (¼m) this road merges with another. Stop and take Frog Lane on the right-hand side down toward Burry Pill, past an old quarry, along the footpath to Pill House, across the seawall, turn north and, skirting the sand dunes, continue to the end of the Burrows. Returning to Swansea take the B4293 to Pen-clawdd for views of the inner estuary.

Gwenffrwd and Dinas** OS147

These two areas lie 18km (10½m) north of Llandovery and have been an RSPB reserve since 1967. They are typical Welsh valleys, with oakwoods clinging to the valley sides, moors above and lush grassy fields on the valley floor. Buzzards are common and Sparrowhawks are regular. In summer the woods are alive with Wood Warbler, Pied Flycatcher and Redstart, while Grey Wagtail and Dipper haunt the streams. Red Kites are often seen, especially in winter when they tend to hunt lower, but they are far from certain at this reserve.

Summer Buzzard, Sparrowhawk, Red Kite, Red Grouse, Woodcock, Common Sandpiper, Dipper, Grey Wagtail, Tree Pipit, Redstart, Pied Flycatcher, Wood Warbler, Garden Warbler, Blackcap
Winter Buzzard, Sparrowhawk, Red Kite

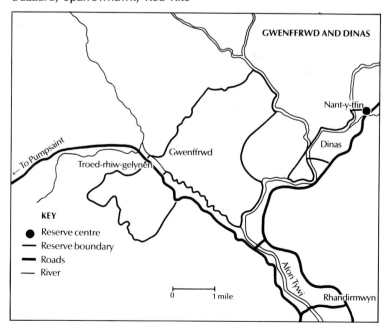

Leave Llandovery northwards on minor roads up the Tywi valley to Rhandirmwyn. Further north the Gwenffrwd lies to the west of the river, but continue up the east bank to the Dinas Reception at Nant-y-ffin. There is a nature trail with free access at all times. Permits are available to visit Gwenffrwd during the summer from RSPB headquarters. The Warden can be contacted at Troedrhiwgelynen, Rhandirmwyn, Llandovery SA20 0PN.

Kenfig Pool and
Eglwys Nunydd Reservoir*   OS170

These two waters lie within a short distance of each other near British Steel's Margam Works; indeed the reservoir is part of the works. Their position close to the sea accounts for their attraction, for both are regular winter haunts of sea-duck, and birds fly regularly from one to the other. Both hold winter wildfowl, including wild swans, and passage waders may prove interesting. Rarities can and do turn up here.

Winter Red-throated Diver, Great Crested Grebe, Whooper Swan, Bewick's Swan, Wigeon, Goldeneye, Long-tailed Duck, Red-breasted Merganser, Goosander, Merlin, Short-eared Owl

Passage Common Sandpiper, Greenshank, Spotted Redshank, Little Stint, Black Tern

Kenfig Pool is an LNR with a reserve centre and hide at OS Ref: SS802811 between North Connelly and Porthcawl. For advice and information contact the Warden. *Tel:* (0656) 743386. Eglwys Nunydd is a reserve of the Glamorgan NT and access is to members only.

Llanthony Valley*   OS161

Lies 10km (6¼m) north of Abergavenny and cuts deep into the heart of the Black Mountain – the eastern Black Mountain tight against the Hereford Border. The beautiful Honddu Stream runs between steep hillsides and old oakwoods, and the whole harbours the usual upland species. Beyond, the Sugar Loaf and Blorenge are worth climbing for moorland birds.

Summer Buzzard, Sparrowhawk, Merlin, Red Grouse, Dunlin, Raven, Dipper, Grey Wagtail, Ring Ouzel, Pied Flycatcher, Redstart, Wood Warbler

Leave Abergavenny northwards on the A465 to Llanvihangel Crucorney and turn left up the valley on the B4423.

Milford Haven** OS157

Despite the development of this huge natural harbour as a major oil port, Milford Haven still has important birding attractions. Six distinct estuaries flow into the haven with the Pembroke River and the Western Cleddau being the most important both for waders and wildfowl. Wigeon are often numerous and some of the wader flocks reach decent proportions. Among the winter visitors are Greenshank, Black-tailed Godwit and Common Sandpiper, and grebes and divers often take refuge in the haven. On passage a variety of waders may occur, and the tiny Bicton Irrigation Reservoir may hold the odd rarity.

Winter Red-throated Diver, Slavonian Grebe, Wigeon, Teal, Ringed Plover, Curlew, Dunlin, Knot, Black-tailed Godwit, Greenshank, Common Sandpiper

Passage Whimbrel, Spotted Redshank, Ruff, Greenshank, Common Sandpiper

Pembroke River View from Lambeeth where a footpath leads east and west. Leave the B4320 northwards to Pwllcrochan and turn right at Wallaston Cross.

Western Cleddau View from Dungeon Hill. Leave Haverfordwest on the A4076 southwards and turn left at Merlin's Bridge to Freystrop Cross. Turn left to Hook and left again to Dungeon Hill. A footpath follows the estuary bank.

Bicton Reservoir Can be seen from the road east of St Ishmaels, west of Milford Haven.

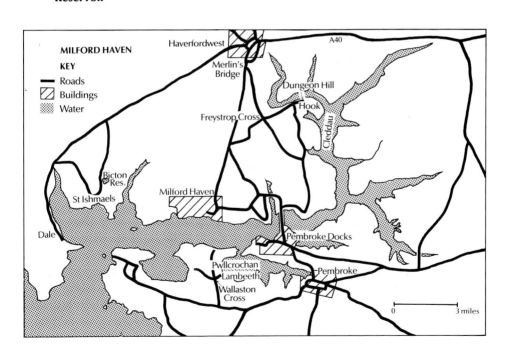

215

Pembroke Islands*****   OS157

The islands of Skokholm, Skomer and Grassholm offer one of the great
seabird spectaculars, yet they are far from being three of a kind.
Skokholm is the site for serious bird study by members of the West
Wales NT prepared to stay a week or more. It has 35,000 pairs of Manx
Shearwaters, 7000 pairs of Storm Petrels and the usual auks. Grassholm
is dominated by Gannets, over 20,000 pairs of them. It is a reserve of
the RSPB, and landing is decidedly difficult as well as unnecessary.
Skomer is for everyone and splendid it is too. The cliffs hold all the usual
auks and offer superb opportunities for photography especially at a
deep cleft called 'The Wick'. Manx Shearwater (100,000 pairs), Storm
Petrel, Puffin (10,000 pairs) and Buzzard all breed, while Choughs are
regular visitors.

Summer   Manx Shearwater, Storm Petrel, Fulmar, Gannet, Shag, Cormorant,
Buzzard, Kestrel, Guillemot, Razorbill, Puffin, Kittiwake, Short-eared
Owl, Raven, Chough

Skomer   Daily boats from Martin's Haven at 10.30 am at Easter and from the
spring Bank Holiday to September. It may be possible to charter a boat
here to circumnavigate Grassholm, but do not approach so close that
the birds are put to flight.

Skokholm   Welcomes visitors to the bird observatory who are prepared to help
with its scientific work and stay a week or more. All visitors must be
members of the West Wales Naturalists' Trust (WWNT). Migrants and
rarities turn up every year. Details: Hon. Gen. Sec., 4 Victoria Place,
Haverfordwest.

Welsh Severn**   OS171

The inter-tidal areas extending westwards from the mouth of the Wye to
Cardiff and beyond are a favourite haunt of birders in this part of Wales.
Mostly the attraction is waders with significant numbers of Dunlin and
Knot and good gatherings of Ringed and Grey Plovers. Whimbrel are
important in spring and often top 100. The shoreline is backed by
grazing meadows, and passage and roosting birds often gather here
when they are flooded. Wildfowl are not particularly numerous, though
Shelduck, Shoveler and the occasional party of Whitefronts do occur.

Though completely surrounded by industrial developments the
Penarth Flats (Taff estuary) is a wader haunt and gull roost, while
Lavernock Point is a noted sea-watch and migration station. Weather is
very important here, but with favourable winds shearwaters and skuas
may appear. Autumn brings the normal warblers, chats and flycatchers,
but with a decent sprinkling of rarities.

East of Cardiff the Rhymney outlet is good, as are the flats off Rumney
Great Wharf. Further east there are wader concentrations at Collister Pill
and Magor Pill and at the lagoons of the Uskmouth Power Station.

This is one of those areas that is good once you know your way
around, but is generally disappointing to the casual visitor. Similarly the

two stone-banked reservoirs of Llanishen and Lisvane in the Cardiff suburbs are best left to local watchers.

Winter   White-fronted Goose, Shelduck, Shoveler, Dunlin, Knot, Grey Plover, Golden Plover
Spring   Whimbrel
Autumn   Ringed Plover, Dunlin, Knot

Penarth   Freely accessible, including the docks.
Rhymney   Leave Cardiff north-westwards on the A48. Immediately after crossing
Outlet   the Rhymney River turn right and after 1 km (½m) turn right again over a narrow bridge. This heads to the sea wall. Continue to Rumney Great Wharf.
Magor   Leave the M4 at Exit 23 and head south to Magor. Take the gate at Magor Pill Farm, south of Whitewall Common, to enter Gwent TNC reserve with hide overlooking marsh and footpath. Non-members write in advance to Gwent TNC, 14 Westfield, Caldicot, Gwent.
Usk   Leave Newport south-eastwards through Somerton to Goldcliff and view from the sea wall. Permission should be obtained at the farmhouse.

Towy Floods** OS159

Between Carmarthen and Llandeilo the River Towy meanders over a flat plain that frequently floods in winter. At such times it holds a flock of up to 1000 Whitefronts and often as many Wigeon. Mallard and Teal are also numerous and the flock of Golden Plover is among the largest in the country.

Winter   White-fronted Goose, Wigeon, Teal, Golden Plover

Leave Carmarthen eastwards on the A48 and fork left on to the B4300 to Llandeilo. Several roads to the left cross the valley and the geese usually concentrate at the eastern end between Dryslwyn Castle and Golden Grove and can be seen from the B4300.

Tregaron*** OS147

Cors Tregaron, or Tregaron Bog as it is generally known, is an NNR and probably the finest example of a raised bog in England and Wales. Not so long ago it was the haunt of a flock of Greenland Whitefronts, but these birds have moved away and the winter birder will have to be content with raptors. Taking in the surrounding hills, up to seven species can be seen in a day with Kestrel, Buzzard, Hen Harrier, Red Kite, Sparrowhawk and Merlin being regular, and Peregrine occasional.

Above all, this is the Red Kite spot and for the best chance of seeing this bird in the whole of the country, one needs do no more than walk the B4343 watching eastwards over the crags and forests. The car park where the old railway track hits the B4343 is as good a place as any.

This track is the main access to the Bog itself and has a good (if cold) tower hide.

From the small town of Tregaron a minor road leads eastwards up into the hills to Llanwrtyd Wells. This so-called Tregaron Mountain Road explores really wild country, passing through conifer plantations and stream-filled valleys, and is another hot Red Kite area. Dipper, Grey Wagtail, Common Sandpiper and Hen Harrier are all likely. Here and there an old oak wood holds Pied Flycatcher and Wood Warbler in summer.

Winter	Red Kite, Hen Harrier, Sparrowhawk, Buzzard, Merlin, Peregrine, Wigeon, Teal, Goldeneye
Summer	Red Kite, Sparrowhawk, Buzzard, Common Sandpiper, Dipper, Grey Wagtail, Pied Flycatcher, Wood Warbler
Bog	Leave Tregaron northwards on the B4343 and stop after 3km (2m) at a lay-by on the left where the old railway track leads northwards (NNR signs). Walk the track to a tower hide in 2km (1¼m).
Mountain	Leave Tregaron eastwards on a minor road to Llanwrtyd Wells. Stop frequently.

Lake Vyrnwy*   OS125

This reservoir 9km (5½m) long was constructed to serve Liverpool. The shores and surrounding hillsides have been afforested and now offer woodlands of varying age, though all at considerable altitudes. The RSPB has a reserve covering most of the available habitats, including

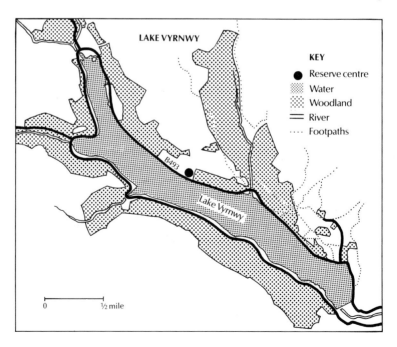

LAKE VYRNWY

KEY
● Reserve centre
Water
Woodland
River
Footpaths

0   ½ mile

open moorland where Red Grouse and Curlew breed. There are Merlin and Hen Harrier here. Areas of sessile oak support Pied Flycatcher, Redstart and Wood Warbler as well as Willow Tit, Tree Pipit, Siskin and Crossbill. In some areas Black Grouse can still be found.

Summer   Great Crested Grebe, Goosander, Hen Harrier, Buzzard, Sparrow-hawk, Merlin, Black Grouse, Common Sandpiper, Curlew, Golden Plover, Raven, Great Spotted Woodpecker, Nuthatch, Treecreeper, Dipper, Grey Wagtail, Tree Pipit, Pied Flycatcher, Redstart, Wood Warbler, Goldcrest, Willow Tit, Siskin, Crossbill

The B4393 runs around all sides of the lake with the RSPB reserve at OS Ref: SH985215. There is an information centre and a public hide is situated at the north-east corner of the lake.

Useful Contact Addresses

Though addresses and telephone numbers are given under the access details of many areas the major national bodies are listed below.

Countryside Commission, John Dower House, Crescent Place, Cheltenham, Glos GL50 3RA. *Tel:* (0242) 21381

Countryside Commission for Scotland, Battleby, Redgorton, Perth PH1 3EW. *Tel:* (0738) 27921

Field Studies Council, Preston Montford, Montford Bridge, Shrewsbury SY4 1HW. *Tel:* (0743) 850674

Forestry Commission, 231 Corstorphine Road, Edinburgh EH12 7AT. *Tel:* (031) 334 0303

National Trust, 42 Queen Anne's Gate, London SW1H 9AS. *Tel:* (01) 222 9251

National Trust for Scotland, 5 Charlotte Square, Edinburgh EG2 4DU. *Tel:* (031) 226 5922

Nature Conservancy Council, Northminster House, Peterborough PE1 1UA. *Tel:* (0733) 40345

Royal Society for Nature Conservation, The Green, Nettleham, Lincoln, LN2 2NR. *Tel:* (0522) 752326

Royal Society for the Protection of Birds, The Lodge, Sandy, Beds SG19 2DL. *Tel:* (0767) 80551

Scottish Ornithologists' Club, 21 Regent Terrace, Edinburgh EH7 5BT.

Scottish Wildlife Trust, 25 Johnston Terrace, Edinburgh EH1 2NH. *Tel:* (031) 226 4602

Wildfowl Trust, Slimbridge, Gloucester GL2 7BT. *Tel:* (045 389) 333.

Index Bold type denotes a main entry